EDUCATING CHINESE–HERITAGE STUDENTS IN THE GLOBAL–LOCAL NEXUS

"This book fills [a] void by looking at Chinese diaspora in multiple geographic regions and countries . . . with regard to the learning of the host language and English, as a lingua franca, while also learning and maintaining Chinese language and culture as a heritage language. . . . [It] gives readers an opportunity to compare and contrast the varied, data-driven studies and ethnographic accounts that represent the rich, yet complex intersection of sociocultural, multilingual and psycho-emotional perspectives."

Jun Liu, Vice Provost for Global Affairs and
Professor of Linguistics, Stony Brook University,
USA, from the Foreword

"This volume present[s] a great variety of contexts and different challenges, issues and experiences of different kinds of CHLs in different parts of the world. . . . [and] provide[s] us with some important pointers about what future work needs to be done."

Angel M. Y. Lin, Professor of English Language and Literacy Education,
University of Hong Kong, from the Afterword

Weaving together a richly diverse range of student voices, perspectives, and insights, this collection of studies from around the world offers the educational community a better understanding of K–12 and adult Chinese–heritage students' languages, cultures, identities, motivations, achievements, and challenges in various cross-cultural settings outside North America. Specifically, it addresses these overarching questions:

- What are Chinese–heritage students' experiences in language and education in and outside schools? How do they make sense of their multiple ethnic and sociocultural identities?
- What unique educational challenges and difficulties do they encounter as they acculturate, socialize, and integrate in their host country? What are their common struggles and coping strategies?
- What are the instructional practices that work for these learners in their specific contexts? What educational implications can be drawn to inform their teachers, fellow students, parents, and their educational communities in a global context?

Individual chapters employ different theoretical frameworks and methodological instruments to wrestle with these questions and critical issues faced by Chinese–heritage learners.

Guofang Li is a Professor and Tier 1 Canada Research Chair in the Department of Language and Literacy Education at the University of British Columbia, Canada.

Wen Ma is an Associate Professor of Education at Le Moyne College, USA.

EDUCATING CHINESE–HERITAGE STUDENTS IN THE GLOBAL–LOCAL NEXUS

Identities, Challenges, and Opportunities

Edited by Guofang Li and Wen Ma

NEW YORK AND LONDON

First published 2018
by Routledge
711 Third Avenue, New York, NY 10017

and by Routledge
2 Park Square, Milton Park, Abingdon, Oxon, OX14 4RN

Routledge is an imprint of the Taylor & Francis Group, an informa business

© 2018 Taylor & Francis

The right of Guofang Li and Wen Ma to be identified as the authors
of the editorial material, and of the authors for their individual chapters,
has been asserted in accordance with sections 77 and 78 of the
Copyright, Designs and Patents Act 1988.

All rights reserved. No part of this book may be reprinted or
reproduced or utilised in any form or by any electronic, mechanical,
or other means, now known or hereafter invented, including photocopying
and recording, or in any information storage or retrieval system,
without permission in writing from the publishers.

Trademark notice: Product or corporate names may be trademarks
or registered trademarks, and are used only for identification
and explanation without intent to infringe.

Library of Congress Cataloging-in-Publication Data
Names: Li, Guofang, 1972– editor. | Ma, Wen, editor.
Title: Educating Chinese-heritage students in the global-local nexus :
identities, challenges, and opportunities / edited by Guofang Li and Wen Ma.
Description: New York : Routledge, 2018. | Includes bibliographical
references and index.
Identifiers: LCCN 2017007970| ISBN 9781138227842 (hardback) |
ISBN 9781138227859 (paperback) | ISBN 9781315394541 (ebook)
Subjects: LCSH: Chinese—Education—Foreign countries. | Heritage language
speakers—Education—Cross-cultural studies. | Chinese language—Study and
teaching—Foreign countries.
Classification: LCC LC3057 .E38 2018 | DDC 371.829/951—dc23
LC record available at https://lccn.loc.gov/2017007970

ISBN: 978-1-138-22784-2 (hbk)
ISBN: 978-1-138-22785-9 (pbk)
ISBN: 978-1-315-39454-1 (ebk)

Typeset in Bembo and Stone Sans
by Florence Production Ltd, Stoodleigh, Devon, UK

To Francis, Patrick, and Amanda, who continue to teach me about the importance of language, identity, and culture in their transnational journeys.

To Rose, whose educational journey reminds me that achieving academic excellence is not only a teacher's responsibility, but also a learner's choice.

CONTENTS

Acknowledgments	x
Foreword by Jun Liu	xi

Introduction: Understanding Chinese–Heritage Learners'
Lived Educational Experiences in the Global–Local Nexus:
Languages, Cultures, and Identities   1
Wen Ma and Guofang Li

Part I
Languages, Cultures, and Identities of Chinese–Heritage Learners in Glocalized Realities   11

1. "Local-Born" Chinese-Heritage Language Learners in
   Hong Kong: Identity and Positioning   13
   Zhen Li

2. Chinese International Students in English-Medium
   Programs in Japan: Experiences and Life Strategies   31
   Hanae Tsukada

3. Learning Chinese as a Heritage Language by Two
   Multilingual Youths in Indonesia   47
   Anita Lie

4. Speaking or Being Chinese: The Case of South African-
   born Chinese   67
   Ke Yu and Elmé Vivier

viii Contents

5. Impact of the "Hidden Curriculum" on the Understanding of Chinese International Students in New Zealand 85
Xiudi Zhang

Part II
Motivation, Challenges, and Adaptation of Chinese–Heritage Learners in and across Globalized Contexts 103

6. Mainland Chinese Undergraduates' Challenges and Strategic Responses in Adapting to Hong Kong 105
Jian (Tracy) Tao and Xuesong Gao

7. A Second-Generation Chinese Student's Education in Spain: Challenges and Opportunities 123
Iulia Mancila

8. Chinese-Background Australian Students' Academic Self-Concept, Motivational Goals, and Achievements in Math and English 141
Alexander Seeshing Yeung and Feifei Han

9. Understanding Undergraduates of Chinese Heritage in the UK: Motivations and Challenges 161
Jiayi Wang

10. Training for Transnationalism: Chinese Children in Hungary 177
Pál Nyíri

Part III
Teaching, Schooling, and Pedagogical Possibilities for Chinese–Heritage Learners 189

11. A Multi-Case Study of the Language Experiences of Chinese Children in Australian Early Childhood Centers 191
Jiangbo Hu

12. Chinese Language Instruction in Singapore: Voices of Children and Views of Teachers 209
Baoqi Sun and Xiao Lan Curdt-Christiansen

13. Overseas Chinese-Heritage Students Learning to Be
Chinese Language Teachers in Taiwan: A Journey
of Comparisons and Affirmations 227
Ya-Hsun Tsai and Jason D. Hendryx

Part IV
Summary and Closing Thoughts 247

14. Chinese-Heritage Learners De/Re-Territorializing
Transnational Social Field: Identities, Conflicts,
and Possibilities 249
Guofang Li and Wen Ma

Afterword: Towards *Worlding Practice* 257
Angel M. Y. Lin

Notes on Contributors 261
Index 264

ACKNOWLEDGMENTS

There are so many individuals to whom we are indebted as we complete this edited volume. First of all, we would like to thank the chapter authors who have shared their research on the educational experiences and life journeys of numerous Chinese-heritage students around the world. Their scholarly insights and implications, which fill the pages of this volume, will contribute to the wellbeing and lives of Chinese and other minority learners in global contexts. We are grateful to the invaluable contributions of Jun Liu and Angel Lin, who wrote the Foreword and Afterword respectively. We are especially indebted to Alan Luke who pushed us to think deeper about the collective issues confronting Chinese-heritage learners in the global-local contexts. As editors, we have genuinely enjoyed working with Naomi Silverman, Emma Ortega, and other Routledge staff. We could not have asked for a better editor than Naomi to guide us throughout the review and publication process! We are also grateful to the two doctoral students from UBC and Zhuo Sun, who provided helpful editorial assistance to this volume. Finally, we of course thank our families. To our spouses and children, words cannot express the depth of our feelings! Your unceasing love and support not only energize us in all our professional pursuits, but also make our own work and lives worthwhile.

FOREWORD

I moved to New York not long ago and have been working in one of the SUNY flagship research universities on Long Island. During the first few months I was surprised and delighted to see so many Asian faces as I walked around campus, many of them Chinese. However, after talking with colleagues in the Asian and Asian American Studies Department, I learned that many of these Chinese faces were not traditional Chinese international students. They were either born in the United States or immigrated here with their parents during their middle school or high school years. Some maintain good English speaking skills from living in the United States for a few years, but are not yet solid in English literacy. Others are rusty or completely lacking in their Chinese literacy skills, and seldom practice speaking it outside their home or local community. Both groups are identified as Chinese-heritage learners. The question that has always been on my mind is: How do we characterize these learners? Or if indeed, are we able to capture the multitude of this group at all, given their diversity and complexity? At very least we should try to do so, as they need viable pedagogical strategies and interventions to help them succeed.

This book takes a step further in deciphering these issues by addressing three pertinent and related questions: Who are Chinese-heritage learners in the global context? How are they changing the landscape and dynamics of Chinese diaspora? How are they prepared to fare in multicultural settings and as global citizens?

For years, Chinese diaspora has been researched from multiple angles: historical, linguistic, sociological, psychological, political, and geographical. Given rapid technological advancement and ever-increasing globalization, this phenomenon is even more complicated and complex, requiring an interdisciplinary and comprehensive approach to capture the transmigration experiences and identities of Chinese-heritage learners in global-local contexts. This book fills that void by

xii Foreword

looking at Chinese diaspora in multiple geographic regions and countries, including Japan, Hungry, Australia, Indonesia, South Africa, Spain, the UK, Hong Kong, New Zealand, the Netherlands, Singapore, and Taiwan, as well as studying the issue with regard to the learning of the host language and English, as a lingua franca, while also learning and/or maintaining Chinese language and culture as a heritage language. Embedded in the multiple language learning experience is the constructing and reconstructing of multiple social identities through self-initiated or other-imposed processes of acculturation, accommodation, and adaptation. Professors Li and Ma, the editors of this volume, did an excellent job in assembling the chapters as a whole to give readers an opportunity to compare and contrast the varied, data-driven studies and ethnographic accounts that represent the rich, yet complex intersection of sociocultural, multilinguistic, and psycho-emotional perspectives.

This book is well situated in the educational setting on a continuum from K to 20, basically covering the whole spectrum of one's educational experience: Language acquisition and learning, cultural identities and social integration, learning adjustment and adaption. Anyone teaching in the global context will benefit from reading this book and anyone interested in understanding Chinese-heritage learners will find this book a valuable resource and a comprehensive introduction.

I applaud the effort and expertise of Professors Li and Ma and the chapter contributors to publish this volume through Routledge, one of the most reputable publishers of our time.

Jun Liu
Vice Provost for Global Affairs
Professor of Linguistics
Stony Brook University

INTRODUCTION

Understanding Chinese–Heritage Learners' Lived Educational Experiences in the Global–Local Nexus: Languages, Cultures, and Identities

Wen Ma and Guofang Li

In *Chinese-heritage students in North American schools: Understanding hearts and minds beyond test scores* (Ma and Li, 2016), we explored the academic, sociocultural, psycho-emotional, and multilingual issues confronting Chinese-heritage learners across K-12 schools in the United States and Canada. In light of the apparent complexity and multiplicity in their experiences and perspectives, the volume presents dynamic close-ups rather than a static group profile for these diverse cohorts of learners. In his foreword, Allan Luke challenged us to carefully consider "who and what are Chinese students" in global contexts. This new book, as a sequel to the previous volume, aims to examine the conditions of Chinese-heritage students in the global-local nexus outside North America. It is therefore fitting that we start off in this introduction with these critical questions: Who are the millions of individuals from diverse Chinese backgrounds who live outside of Greater China? To what extent do they constitute a Chinese diaspora? And who are Chinese-heritage students in the twenty-first-century globalized world?

Partly because few countries keep accurate population data based on ancestry, and partly because it is complex and difficult to define overseas Chinese since they migrated from China under very different circumstances and at different times, dating back to the early colonial days (Kuhn, 2008), it is impossible to know their exact number. Wikipedia's (2012) estimate is that there are more than 50 million overseas Chinese, scattered in smaller, localized communities in virtually every corner of the world, although most of them are concentrated in Southeast Asian countries, relatively closer to south China's Guangdong and Fujian provinces, such as Indonesia, Malaysia, the Philippines, Singapore, Thailand, and

Vietnam. Because of widespread discrimination, even violence, against ethnic Chinese in these countries, since the 1960s many of them made re-immigration or secondary migration to North America and Australia following the latter's abandonment of race-based immigration policies. Meanwhile, there are earlier generations of laborers from Guangdong and Fujian working in mines or railway construction who have already settled in the United States. Additionally, a large number of well-educated and skilled professionals emigrated to North America and Europe from Taiwan and Hong Kong due to economic opportunities or political uncertainties. After China adopted its open-door policies in late 1970, the world has seen more and more Chinese students and entrepreneurs as well. All of these variables add to the overseas Chinese population, with multidimensional differences in terms of places of origin (e.g., Guangdong, Fujian, and any other region), patterns of settlement (between ethnic-centered enclaves like Chinatowns and spread-out dwellings among locals), types of migration (e.g., settlers, sojourners, and re-migrants), dialects (e.g., Cantonese, Hokkien, and Mandarin), socioeconomic status and professions (e.g., unskilled workers, middle-class professionals, and wealthy entrepreneurs), political affiliations (e.g., between PRC in Mainland and Republic of China in Taiwan), generations (between descendants of settlers and newcomers), identities (between those who view themselves as Chinese and those who do not), etc. Therefore, it is very difficult to classify them using any rigid conceptual lenses and analytical categories.

Despite all the aforementioned attributes among the overseas Chinese communities and contexts, there are varying degrees of *Chineseness* functioning as commonality that somehow bonds them together from non-Chinese. This point is thus captured by Skeldon's (2003) remarks, "To the outsiders the immigrants, irrespective of background, are 'all Chinese;' to the insider, a common Chinese front is in the best interests of self-protection" (p. 62). While Skeldon recognized that "there has been a Chinese diaspora in the sense of a spreading of Chinese peoples around the world" (p. 63), he also cautioned us that it would be deceptive to assume homogeneity, uniformity or essentialized diasporic events across the numerous communities and contexts. In other words, yes, there exists a Chinese diaspora, but it is a diaspora of extremely complex mix of people with quite divergent backgrounds, experiences and identities.

In recent years, historians, anthropologists, sociologists, psychologists, geographers, political scientists, and linguists have all approached the Chinese diaspora from a multitude of disciplinary perspectives, and this is reflected by the growing Chinese diasporic studies (see Barrett, 2012; Benton and Gomez, 2014; Kuhn, 2008; Li, 2016; Ma and Cartier, 2003; Peterson, 2012; Tan, 2013). For example, Ma and Cartier (2003) discussed the Chinese diaspora from angle of geography and transnationalism. Arguing for studying the Chinese diaspora as an amalgam of human ecologies anchored in specific geographic places and settings, the chapters in the book examined the historical roots of the Chinese diaspora, Mainland China, Hong Kong, and Taiwan as diasporic homelands, and the ethnicity, identity, settlement, and migration in their new homelands abroad. It is apparent that while the places of origin for the Chinese diaspora matter, it is even more critical to understand the individuals' transmigration experiences and identities that have been shaped up in the global-local spaces, communities and contexts.

In a special issue of *Ethnic and Racial Studies* (2014), Benton, Gomez and an international team of researchers analyzed the ethnic and national identity formation mechanisms, processes, and outcomes by the Chinese immigrants and the harsh realities behind the racial bias, discrimination, even attacks against them. In addition to migration, transnationalism, hybrid identity, and racial relations, some of the articles also looked at the role of education for the second generations (i.e., those born or raised in the country of residence). For instance, Marsden's (2014) article depicted how so many children from lower-class Chinese immigrant families dropped out of secondary schools as they felt hopeless to gain acceptance by the mainstream Italian society, hence self-fulfilling the stereotype that they lacked Italian identity. On the other hand, Zhou's (2014) article showcased how Chinese American youth achieved upward social mobility through the means of education by organizing and utilizing community resources. This contrast underscores ways in which education may function as a double-edged sword: the outcome all depends on what the Chinese diasporans make out of it. Another theme explored in the issue is the intricate sense of self-identity and cultural alignment expressed by the situated choice of ethnic language (whether it is Mandarin Chinese, Cantonese, or another dialect), host language (whether it is Hungarian, Italian, Malay, or English as the national language of a host nation), and English as the de facto international lingua franca (in countries where English is not used as the national language). Collectively, these chapters depict a more hybrid and dynamic picture of Chinese diasporans' ethnic, national, and global experiences and identities across different sociocultural and geopolitical settings.

More recently, W. Li's edited book (2016) presented more systematic studies on the Chinese diasporans' linguistic practices and experiences in international settings. In a broad sense, W. Li argued that this vast and diverse population be viewed and interpreted as constituting a diaspora, with *Chineseness* (i.e. sharing Chinese ancestry, Chinese language, and Chinese culture) being a common background for self-identification and mutual bond in an imagined diasporic immigrant community. As such, the chapters in W. Li's edited volume examined the maintenance, loss, learning, and re-learning of Chinese as a heritage language, family language practices and experiences, and their interactions and relationships with the host language in a context of host-country language policy, and the ensuing results of multilingualism, acculturation, socialization, identity development, and linguistic attitudes and ideologies.

Nevertheless, the maintenance of Chinese language may also trigger a thorny set of inter-language relationships. For example, Gabriel (2014) contextualized how Malay Chinese clinging to the Chinese tongue are viewed as "outsiders" by other Malaysians, a sign of unwillingness to be nationalized as Malay citizens.

Similarly, Marsden (2014) revealed how the mainstream Italian society considers the Chinese descendants who persist in using Chinese language and maintaining Chinese cultural traditions as "social exclusion," self-marginalization, and un-Italian affinity. Meanwhile, Tsukada, Lie, and Nyíri (Chapters 2, 3, and 10 in this volume) described how diverse Chinese diasporans (e.g., Chinese international students in Japan, Chinese Indonesian teenagers, or Chinese students born and raised in Hungary) embraced English, over either the host language or Chinese, due in large part to English's unrivaled dominance as an international language. This linguistic pluralism seems to have underscored ethnic Chinese's desire to be optimally positioned linguistically. As a result, we see a budding linguistic typology of the Chinese diaspora: psycho-emotionally, they prefer to be anchored in Chinese as heritage language, locally, they choose to be grounded in the host language and society, but globally, they choose to be connected via English as the lingua franca. In this sense, the learning and use of English becomes an important aspect penetrating through the Chinese diasporic experience.

All of these studies took place within the broad context of China's rise as an emerging economic powerhouse and political player on the international stage. Recently, in a policy speech, Wang (2016) estimated that there are as many as 120 million people from Mainland China alone who travel abroad to study, work, or visit each year, making it the largest migratory population in human history. Just in terms of their size and China's continual rise as an emerging superpower, there is growing need to better understand these overseas ethnic Chinese. According to Pan (2012), during the first decade of the twenty-first century, China's rise dominated Western media coverage, overshadowing the September 11 terrorist attack that changed the international political and military landscape, and the financial crisis that set so many countries' national economies into deep turmoil, even the risk of bankruptcy. Arguably, such coverage typically employed a binary lens, exposing China either as threat to the existing international order (Sinophobia at one end) or as opportunity for new possibilities (China interest at the other). Behind such media fever is an unmistakable message: what the Chinese do is having some global impact.

China's education is one of the contentious areas to which the world is paying more attention. During the past few decades, over a million Chinese students have gone to study at Western colleges and universities, bringing with them Chinese education's strengths (e.g., having strong foundational knowledge and skills, especially in STEM areas), as well as shortcomings (e.g., relatively weaker critical thinking and problem-solving abilities). An example is reflected by Shanghai middle school students outperforming their counterparts from all other OECD countries in math, science, and reading tests, causing intense debates about the role of testing. Such impeccable test scores add fuel to "the-Chinese-are-a-model-minority" discourse (although this has been debunked as a stereotype in more recent literature) in North America, but less is known about how the Chinese diasporans are doing educationally across the international spectrum.

Just as heterogeneous as the Chinese diaspora itself, learners from the diaspora vary considerably in their ability levels, aspirations, needs, attainments, problems, and experiences. Also different are their proficiency in Chinese (as a heritage language), host language(s) (either the official or dominant language in the country of residence), English (as the international lingua franca), and so are the actual educational policies and practices in the host country (whether it is an Asian, Australian, European, or South African context). They may have divergent attitudes and behaviors towards Chinese culture and the culture of the host country as well. Additionally, there may be intergenerational, intragenerational, and regional variations among themselves. Recognizing all these differences, we view each of them not as a member of a homogeneous group, but as a product of their individual transnational journeys and circumstances as they simultaneously participate in co-producing the sociocultural environments in which they live. As such, we aim to present their lived educational experiences and journeys rooted in local communities and contexts and global sociocultural realities concurrently.

Finally, in this book we use the term *Chinese-heritage students* to refer to these learners from various Chinese diasporic communities and contexts. Such a focus on education sets the book apart from the other studies discussed earlier. Specifically, this volume features K-12 and adult Chinese-heritage students' languages, cultures, identities, motivations, achievements, and challenges in various sociocultural settings, as elaborated below.

Objectives of the Book

Why is such a book needed in the present sociocultural milieu? First of all, it is important to investigate the conditions of the millions of K-20 Chinese-heritage students in schools, homes, and communities nested in the global-local nexus, not only because of the rich experiences and perspectives to be gained from such exploration, but also because of the multitude of challenges and promises for their learning, career choices, and future lives. Just in terms of their formidable size (which continues to grow), they are learners that merit close attention by the international educational community. For example, who are the Chinese-heritage students in Australia, Britain, Hungary, Indonesia, Japan, Spain, South Africa, New Zealand, or any other country where they are fast growing in number? What are the specific geographic contexts and language policies in the host country/region? What are their psychological/emotional needs, linguistic and cultural challenges, and personal identities in different sociocultural settings? What unique experiences and perspectives do they have in their schooling and socialization processes? What are their "glocalized" educational achievements, challenges, and opportunities in relation to peers in the host culture? What are the implications for teaching? Inarguably, answers to such questions will add to the existing research literature, promote new thinking and culturally relevant teaching practices, as well as help to flesh out the larger sociocultural/theoretical/pedagogical/practical issues in the global-local nexus. Therefore, it is valuable to look comprehensively at their academic, sociocultural, and psycho-emotional development across the international educational spectrum.

What are the central themes of this text? This edited volume unravels the divergent issues related to Chinese-heritage K-20 students' languages, cultures, identities, challenges, and achievements through the global-local nexus lenses. Our goal is to continue to "capture difference within difference" (Luke and Luke, 1999, p. 240) among Chinese-heritage students, while acknowledging the historical, generational, cultural, social, geographical, and demographic complexities. Specifically, this book addresses the following overarching questions:

1. What are Chinese-heritage students' experiences in language and education in and outside schools? How do they make sense of their multiple linguistic, ethnic, and sociocultural identities?
2. What unique educational challenges and difficulties do they encounter as they acculturate, socialize, and integrate in their host country? What are the common struggles and coping strategies?
3. What are the instructional practices that work for these learners in their specific contexts? What educational implications can be drawn to inform their teachers, fellow students, parents, and the educational communities in a global context?

Focusing on these central questions, individual chapters in the book employ different theoretical frameworks and methodological instruments to wrestle with language and literacy challenges, learning across the curriculum, social, cultural, and personal identities, prices for academic pursuits, acculturation and socialization, emotional-psychological development, effective instructional practices, or other critical topics confronting them as Chinese-heritage learners.

As the chapters will demonstrate, three central themes emerge from the chapters:

1. Learning host language and English (following the globalization tide) (e.g. in Japan, Hungary, etc.).
2. Learning Chinese and maintaining Chinese language/culture (e.g. in Australia, Indonesia, South Africa, Spain, UK).
3. Acculturation, adaptation, and identity (e.g. in HK, New Zealand, Singapore, Taiwan).

We have addressed several thematic strands related to these Chinese-heritage learners, including languages, cultures, and identities (in the interface of Chinese and English, Japanese, Spanish, or Hungarian, between intergenerational and late arrivals, and between "local-born" and those "fresh off the boat"—FOBs), motivations, challenges, and adaptations (between entrepreneurial background and minority mindset, between sociocultural constraints and imagined possibilities, between acculturation and transnationalism, and between individuals who are ethnic Chinese and those from hybrid backgrounds), and contextualized schooling and socialization (between the overt curriculum and the hidden curriculum, between learning Chinese vocabulary and acquiring information-intensive English expressions, among home, community and school connections, and among conventional language-training programs, participatory video and social networks). By diving into such a multitude of sociocultural, multilinguistic, and psycho-emotional domains, we hope to arrive at a deeper understanding of their holistic educational experiences and lives as they navigate complex geography, race, ethnicity, and class landscapes in a global context. This in-depth understanding will in turn provide useful insights for their teachers to better teach them (hopefully other peer groups, too).

Organization of the Book

In addition to the Foreword, Afterword, Conclusion, and this Introduction, there are 13 chapters, divided into three sections. Part I addresses the language learning, cultural adaptation, and identity development issues faced by Chinese-heritage students in complex global-local settings. Specifically, Chapter 1 begins with Chinese-heritage learners' identity formation in Western-style international schools in Hong Kong, where "the East meets the West." Through describing their linguistic practices and educational experiences between home and school, the chapter presents concrete evidence about how their identity is constructed and negotiated as "local-born Chinese-heritage students." Chapter 2 continues with the challenges, opportunities, and dilemmas experienced by 27 Chinese-heritage students in the context of Japan's internationalization of its higher education. The chapter also showcases how English, Japanese, and Chinese interact with one another to jointly shape the students' current educational experiences and future possibilities. Chapter 3 wrestles with the issue of intergenerational literacy practices in Indonesia. The findings not only shed light on the relationship between learning Chinese-heritage language and maintaining Chinese cultural identity by multilingual Indonesian youth, but also provide evidence about how generations of families from Chinese descent cope with their psychological and emotional needs. Chapter 4 further explores the relationship between language and identity, this time moving to a South African context. Focusing on four South African-born students' identity and language shifts and the variables driving such shifts, the chapter argues that Chinese identity has multiple degrees and expressions, and specific social and historical contexts shape the needs and motivations of the individuals in their language choice. Therefore, the language-identity relation helps to explain "the weak and strong language-identity links that occur at the micro-level." Chapter 5 considers how the "hidden curriculum" impacts the identity of Chinese students in New Zealand universities. The chapter suggests more attention needs to be paid to Chinese students' idiosyncrasies.

Collectively, the chapters in this section not only offer conceptual lenses to untangle the multidimensional and multifaceted relationships across language, culture, and identity, but also provide concrete evidence about diverse Chinese-heritage learners' situated experiences and perspectives in various sociocultural settings. These insights help us better facilitate individual students learn Chinese as a heritage language or acquire other host languages, maintain Chinese culture and the host country's culture as asset, as well as enrich dynamic and balanced identity development in the global-local nexus.

Part II delves into the motivation, challenge, and adaptation aspects for Chinese-heritage students. Specifically, Chapter 6 discusses the challenges confronting 26 undergraduate students from Mainland China in Hong Kong. These challenges range from gaining and sustaining access to local social networks, to the strategic efforts they make to connect and align with their Hong Kong-born counterparts. These findings urge educators to look into this area to promote better understanding among newcomers and native-born students. Chapter 7 is a qualitative case study that features one second-generation Chinese-heritage adolescent in Spain. Through exploring the difficulties, problems, and tensions spanning kindergarten and high school, the chapter offers a multi-year study about home–school relations, peer pressure and relationship, teacher expectations, and pedagogical and extracurricular practices. Chapter 8 examines the notion of "competence beliefs" such as academic self-concept and motivational goals. Drawing from the survey results involving 461 Chinese-heritage students and 1,901 Anglo-background students in Australian secondary schools, this chapter reports the effects of culture and gender and interaction of the two. Of particular significance is the issue of how to boost Chinese-heritage students' competence beliefs. Chapter 9 digs into open-ended questionnaire and follow-up interview data to probe how and why Chinese-heritage students pursue a degree in Chinese in a British university setting. The findings not only identify the motivational factors for these students, but also identity unique challenges for them. Chapter 10 centers on the educational experiences and strategies of a unique cohort of Hungarian-born and raised children whose parents are Chinese entrepreneurs who migrated to Hungary in the 1990s. The chapter argues that these children's educational experiences are different from other minority students because they are being trained for sustained transnationalism. Combined together, the chapters in this section further highlight the multilayered difficulties and challenges to Chinese-heritage students across various sociocultural contexts, as well as under-scoring the unmistakable motivation and a variety of adaptation strategies they employ to cope with and fit in local circumstances.

Finally, Part III grapples with pedagogical practices for Chinese-heritage students. Chapter 11 uses a multi-case research method to investigate the language experiences of five Chinese-heritage children in Australian early childhood centers. The findings help early childhood professionals better understand Chinese-heritage children's language experiences, especially in terms of enriching their language use through daily communication with them. Chapter 12 presents both the voices of Chinese-heritage children in an elementary school on Chinese language learning and the views of teachers who promote a new morphological approach to Chinese instruction in a Singaporean context. The findings have implications for the language policies and ongoing curriculum reforms in Singapore. Chapter 13 shifts to a Taiwan-based Chinese program intended to train teachers from Southeast Asian countries for teaching Chinese language back in their home countries. A unique feature of the study is that it compares, contrasts, and then weaves together the Southeastern learners' and their Taiwanese professors' perspectives. In summary, these chapters help us recognize the breadth, depth, and diversity involved in teaching Chinese-heritage students across grade level, content areas, and sociocultural settings.

As underscored by these chapters, Chinese-heritage students are indeed a very diverse mix of learners who live and study in vastly different settings. Some of them are overachievers, some of them are underachievers, and many more are in the middle. As it is with their academic performance, other non-academic-related variables, such as practical constraints on their acculturation and socialization, peer relations within the host country, self-knowledge and coping strategies, psycho-emotional health, and cultural affiliations, also range widely. The implications of all these findings will be further discussed in the Conclusion, Chapter 14, where we highlight the impact of dual processes of glocalization on learners' formation of cultural and linguistic identities and how their efforts to distance from or reconnect with Chinese, local languages, and English might lead to different trajectories toward their future possibilities. We advocate more interdisciplinary research on the interaction between learner agency and their glocalized educational contexts and more nuanced distinctions among the different Chinese-heritage learners to address their particular linguistic and identity needs to ensure that they achieve the full potential of multilingualism. We hope these studies and the insights that emerge from them will help you better understand the experiences and lives of these learners found in the global-local nexus.

References

Barrett, T. (2012). *Chinese diaspora in South-East Asia: The overseas Chinese in Indochina*. London, UK: I. B. Tauris & Company, Limited.

Benton, G., and Gomez, E. T. (2014). Belong to the nation: Generational change, identity and the Chinese diaspora. *Ethnic and Racial Studies, 37*(7), 1157–1171.

Gabriel, S. P. (2014). "After the break": Reconceptualizaing ethnicity, national identity and "Malaysian-Chinese" identity. *Ethnic and Racial Studies, 37*(7), 1211–1224.

Kuhn, P. A. (2008). *Chinese among others: Immigration in modern times*. Lanham, MA: Rowman and Littlefield Publishers, Inc.

Li, W. (Ed.). (2016). *Multilingualism in the Chinese diaspora worldwide: Transnational connections and local realities*. New York, NY: Routledge.

Luke, C., and Luke, A. (1999). Theorizing interracial families and hybrid identity: An Australian perspective. *Educational Theory, 49*(2), 223–249.

Ma, L. J. C., and Cartier, C. (Eds.). (2003). *The Chinese diaspora: Space, place, mobility, and identity*. Lanham, MA: Rowman and Littlefield Publishers, Inc.

Ma, W., and Li, G. (Eds.). (2016). *Chinese-heritage students in North American schools: Understanding hearts and minds beyond test scores*. London, UK: Routledge.

Marsden, A. (2014). Chinese descendants in Italy: Emergence, role and uncertainty identity. *Ethnic and Racial Studies, 37*(7), 1239–1252.

Pan, C. (2012). *Knowledge, desire and power in global politics: Western representations of China's rise*. Cheltenham, UK: Edward Elgar Publishing Limited.

Peterson, G. (2012). *Overseas Chinese in the People's Republic of China*. New York, NY: Routledge.

Safran, W. (1991). Diasporas in modern societies: Myths of homeland and return. *Diaspora: A Journal of Transnational Studies, 1*(1), 83–99.

Skeldon, R. (2003). The Chinese diaspora or the migration of Chinese peoples? In L. J. C. Ma and C. Cartier (Eds.), *The Chinese diaspora: Space, place, mobility, and identity* (pp. 51–66). Lanham, MA: Rowman and Littlefield Publishers, Inc.

Tan, C. B. (Ed.). (2013). *Routledge handbook of the Chinese diaspora*. New York, NY: Routledge.

Wang, Y. (2016). Statesmen's forum: Wang Yi, Minister of Foreign Affairs, PRC. Retrieved from http://csis.org/event/statesmens-forum-wang-yi-minister-foreign-affairs-prc.

Wikipedia. (2012). *Overseas Chinese*. Retrieved from https://en.wikipedia.org/wiki/Overseas_Chinese.

Zhou, M. (2014). Segmented assimilation and socio-economic integration of Chinese children in the USA. *Ethnic and Racial Studies, 37*(7), 1172–1183.

PART I

Languages, Cultures, and Identities of Chinese–Heritage Learners in Glocalized Realities

1

"LOCAL-BORN" CHINESE–HERITAGE LANGUAGE LEARNERS IN HONG KONG

Identity and Positioning

Zhen Li

This chapter explores the identity of "local-born" Chinese-heritage language (CHL) learners who were raised and educated in the international school system in Hong Kong. In the literature, "CHL learners" refers predominantly to students who grew up in countries where the majority language is not Chinese. However, CHL learners could be raised in any society as long as schools did not provide them with adequate training in Chinese during their K-12 years (Rothman, 2009). In the case of Hong Kong, children who were born into native Chinese-speaking families but educated in international schools where English is the medium of instruction may be viewed as CHL learners, since those schools do not provide them with adequate academic support in Chinese. However, little research is available on this type of "local-born" CHL learners.

Previous studies show that for many CHL learners, learning the Chinese language is not merely associated with inheriting their background culture, but more importantly, with reconstructing new identities (Li and Zhu, 2013; Mu, 2014). Identity itself is a complex concept since its construction in heritage language (HL) learners often encompasses how they perceive themselves and how they are perceived by others (Hornberger and Wang, 2008). Furthermore, identity is highly context-specific because individual learners may construct their identities in various ways, depending on the context. However, the dynamic meanings attributed to CHL learner identity have not yet been explored to any extent concerning local contexts and practices. Following a discourse-based approach to identity analysis, the present chapter explores how identity can be understood in narrative discourses and how positioning analysis can provide insights into the dynamicity of identity construction. Specifically, this study focuses on five Hong Kong-Chinese students who were educated in Western-based international schools and were receiving their undergraduate education in a Hong Kong university during the data collection. Following Continua of Biliteracy

(Hornberger, 1989) and the concept of positioning (Davies and Harré, 1990) as theoretical lenses to analyze their narratives about their experience learning Chinese, the chapter explores how they construct their identities as CHL learners across a series of translingual spaces (Canagarajah, 2013).

"Local-Born" CHL Learners in Hong Kong

Most research on CHL learners so far has focused on North American or West European contexts, yet little attention has been given to CHL learners in Hong Kong, where there has been an increasing number of Hong Kong-Chinese students studying in English-medium international schools. Although international schools in Hong Kong were initially set up to provide education for children from expatriate families, they are currently populated by a large number of children from local Chinese families (Ng, 2011). With teaching staff who are mainly native English speakers, the international schools that adopt North American and Western European curricula or the International Baccalaureate (IB) programs enhance students' opportunities to enter top universities in the West. What is more, these schools provide an education with a less pressurized curriculum as compared with other local schools in Hong Kong (Bray and Yamato, 2003). Thus, many Hong Kong parents decide to send their children to international schools (Igarashi and Saito, 2014). In 2010, Chinese-background students occupied over 50% of the international school places in Hong Kong. Of the Chinese-background students, 10% are local Chinese who have never lived abroad before, 30% are Chinese with foreign passports, and 10% are from mixed families with one parent of Chinese origin (Forse, 2010, p. 59).

The increasing enrollment of Hong Kong-Chinese children in international schools has received attention from some educators and researchers (e.g., Forse, 2010; Jabal, 2010; Schmidt, 2010). Most Hong Kong-Chinese children speak Cantonese at home and English at school, using both languages daily. Although these students do not need to cross national borders, they still need to negotiate transitions among multiple contexts that are linguistically, culturally, and ideo-logically different from one another (Jabal, 2010). What is more, since most international schools offer Chinese as a foreign language (CFL) as a compulsory module to students from non-Chinese speaking families (Li, 2014), the Hong Kong-Chinese children have to take the CFL classes with mixed-background students who are from non-Chinese-speaking families. Although they are bilingual in English and Chinese, few are biliterate, since most international schools provide much less academic support in Chinese compared with the local schools in Hong Kong.

Theoretical Framework

Two conceptual lenses inform this study: the Continua of Biliteracy (Hornberger, 1989) and positioning theory (Davies and Harré, 1990). The Continua of

Biliteracy was proposed by Nancy Hornberger (1989) to address biliteracy problems that ethnic minorities had encountered in the United States, and was expanded in Hornberger's later works on multilingual language policies and HL learner identity (Hornberger, 2002; Hornberger and Wang, 2008). This framework adopts an ecological perspective of bilingual identity formation by incorporating both internal and external qualities of human identity that constitute an individual's sense of self as a member of his or her social group (Hornberger and Wang, 2008). It is structured along four sets of interrelated continua: *context*, *content*, *media*, and *development*, constituting the dynamic and sometimes contested spaces in HL learners' linguistic experiences (Hornberger and Link, 2012).

Figure 1.1 shows a model that HL learners develop their HL, which is also considered as L1, and their L2 in linguistic *contexts* ranging from micro to macro, monolingual to bilingual, and oral to literate settings. Their L1 and L2 practices are characterized by majority-minority, literary-vernacular, and decontextualized-contextualized *content*. The languages that they were exposed to, referred to as *media*, were featured by similar-dissimilar, convergent-divergent, and simultaneous-successive structures. The *development of* their language skills is embodied in the L1-L2, receptive-productive, and oral-written continua. This model offers "new spaces to be exploited for innovative programs, curricula, and practices that recognize, value, and build on the multiple, mobile communicative repertoires, translanguaging and transnational literacy practices of students and their families" (Hornberger and Link, 2012, p. 274). It also provides researchers with a tool to consider how a language learner or multilingual speaker moves along from one continuum to another, and how this change causes potential adjustments along

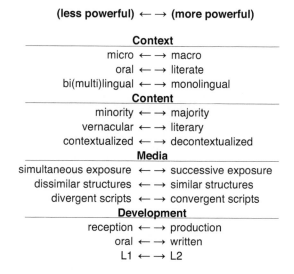

FIGURE 1.1 Continua of Biliteracy (Hornberger and Wang, 2008, p. 9)

16 Zhen Li

other continua and the opportunities for participation and success in language learning (Creese and Martin, 2003). The oppositional elements at both ends of each continuum reveal the power relations between the L1 and L2 contexts, which are crucial for shaping the identities of HL learners. In investigating CHL learner identity through this model, the ways in which learners and institutions negotiate the power relations, and why one language becomes more dominant than another in CHL learners' lives, can be seen.

The second conceptual lens is based on positioning theory (Davies and Harré, 1990). Drawing on the epistemology of social constructivism, the concept of positioning has been used as an analytical approach to examine identity construction in narrative discourse (e.g., Davies and Harré, 1990; van Langenhove and Harré, 1999). Position, as defined by van Langenhove and Harré (1999), refers to "a metaphorical concept through reference to which a person's moral and personal attributes as a speaker are compendiously collected" (p. 17). Positioning pertains to the "discursive construction of personal stories that make a person's actions intelligible and relatively determinate as social acts, and within which the members of the conversation have specific locations" (van Langenhove and Harré, 1999, p. 17). Some researchers adopted positioning as an analytical approach to examine the identity or language ideology of L2 language learners, HL learners, or bilingual speakers (e.g., McNamara, 2012; Norton and Toohey, 2011). The concept of positioning makes identity a visible construct and reveals the shifting nature of identity in conversational texts. In this study, the CHL learners' narratives about their experiences learning Chinese are expressed in their positions. They may also change their positions from time to time to negotiate their identities with other characters in their stories, or even with the interviewer (van Langenhove and Harré, 1999).

The Study

The Setting

As one of the few highly urbanized and populated cities in Asia, Hong Kong is governed as a Special Administrative Region (SAR) under the People's Republic of China (PRC). According to the 2011 Census (2012), Hong Kong has a population of 7.07 million with around 6.4% non-ethnic Chinese people. The Hong Kong government adopted a "biliterate and trilingual" education policy after the handover to the People's Republic of China from the British colonial governance in July 1997. This policy attaches importance to the biliterate competence in traditional written Chinese and English, and trilingual skills of spoken Putonghua, Cantonese, and English. However, due to the strong influence of the Cantonese-speaking culture, most residents in Hong Kong still speak Cantonese as their first language. In addition, English has always enjoyed a high status in the territory. The international schools and universities in Hong Kong still take pride in their use of English as the medium of instruction (Danielewicz-Betz and Graddol, 2014).

Hong Kong has 51 international schools, including 20 primary schools, eight secondary schools, 22 primary-cum-secondary schools, and one special school. In 2015, the total capacity in the international schools was approximately 41,106 students (Hong Kong, Education Bureau, 2016a). Compared to the local schools that accommodate 317,119 primary school students and 336,079 secondary school students (Hong Kong, Education Bureau, 2016b), the international schools form a much smaller sector. However, international school education has been gaining increasing popularity among the local Hong Kong families, especially since the political handover in 1997. Today an increasing number of Hong Kong parents choose the international school system over the local school system as they believe the international schools can equip their children with native-like English language skills that are crucial for achieving their future educational and career goals (Ng, 2011).

The study reported in this chapter is part of a larger investigation of CHL learners at a major English-medium university in Hong Kong. All lectures in the university are delivered in English, except for some in the Department of Chinese. Although the students in this university are fluent in English, Cantonese remains the first language of the majority of them. The university runs a CFL program, which provides lessons in Putonghua and simplified characters for international students from all faculties. Each year around 1,000 international students take the CFL classes. About 25% of the students are from CHL backgrounds.

The Participants

The participants were recruited primarily from the university CFL courses between 2012 and 2013. As can be seen in Table 1.1, the five participants, including two female and three male CHL learners, were all educated in English-medium international schools throughout almost all their formative years in Hong Kong. The five participants were all born of ethnic Chinese parents. Mike, Reyna, and Jason's parents are native Cantonese speakers and also speak English as their second language, while Tom and Ada's parents are bilingual speakers of Mandarin and English. Although Tom and Ada were born in Singapore, they could not remember anything about it because they had spent most of their K-12 years in Hong Kong. The frequency of speaking Cantonese or Mandarin at home, as the participants reported, differed from one to another. During the time of data collection, all participants were undergraduates studying in Hong Kong, taking the university CFL classes at intermediate or upper-intermediate levels.

Data Collection

Data were obtained from a larger study with 16 university CHL learners in Hong Kong between 2012 and 2015, and were based on narrative interviews with each

TABLE 1.1 Self-reported sociolinguistic backgrounds of the participants

Name	Gender	Place of origin	International schooling experience	Languages spoken at home	Experience learning Chinese
Mike	M	Hong Kong	International primary and secondary schools in Hong Kong	Mostly Cantonese, sometimes English	Mandarin in mixed CFL classes in Years 1–12
Tom	M	Singapore	International primary and secondary schools in Hong Kong	Mixture of English and Mandarin	Mandarin in mixed CFL classes in Years 1–12
Ada	F	Singapore	Grades 1–4, 7–13 in international primary school in Hong Kong; Grades 5–6 in Canada	Mostly English, occasionally Mandarin	Mandarin in mixed CFL classes in Years 3–4 in primary school, and Years 7–12 in secondary school
Reyna	F	Hong Kong	International primary and secondary schools in Hong Kong	Mostly Cantonese, occasionally English	Mandarin in mixed CFL classes in Years 1–12
Jason	M	Hong Kong	International primary and secondary schools in Hong Kong	70% English, 30% Cantonese	Mandarin in mixed CFL classes in Years 1–10; private Mandarin tutoring

individual participant. Since all of them reported that they felt most comfortable expressing their feelings in English, the interviews were conducted primarily in English, occasionally code-switched to Mandarin or Cantonese, and lasted approximately 60 to 90 minutes each. The interview questions focused on the participants' experiences learning Chinese in various institutional contexts, their motivations for learning Chinese, and their changing attitudes towards learning Chinese. In this chapter, identity was constructed through the process of story-telling as opposed to anything predetermined, thus, how the narrators position themselves through their narrating processes is perceived as the key to understanding identity in narratives. The narrative stories are seen as "interactional accomplishments" (Bamberg, 1997). That is to say, the telling of identity itself is co-constructed in the interactive dialogue between the interviewees and the interviewer (Kasper and Prior, 2015, p. 229).

Data Analysis

In the data analysis, I focused on the narrators' experiences learning Chinese during their international schooling and university study. I informed all the participants that there was an open access to the original transcription and audio tapes of the interviews. In addition to this open access to the original data, I member-checked the key points in their narratives to ensure the validity of my data interpretation.

The data were manually transcribed and coded. During the coding process, I first categorized the data and made notes on the categories that I grouped into broader themes, highlighting the main concepts that are relevant to the participants' individual experiences and identity positioning. The positioning analysis was based on a narrative-in-interaction perspective to analyze how each participant positioned themselves in their story worlds (Georgakopoulou, 2006).

Results

The narrative data suggest that the participants negotiated their identities across dynamic multilingual spaces, which interplayed with their bilingual development. Their stories range from how the participants *develop* their bilingual and biliterate skills along the continua of Chinese-English, receptive-productive, and oral-written language skills in *contexts* encompassing school, home, and university linguistic practices. The long-term experience learning Mandarin Chinese in mixed CFL classes from primary to secondary school and to university in Hong Kong constituted a dynamic continuum of contextual and developmental elements, which shaped their identities as CHL learners. What follows provides a detailed analysis of their narrative discourses that are relevant to their identity construction along the continua of context and development.

20 Zhen Li

Continua of Bilingual Spaces during International Schooling

The participants' experiences of learning Chinese in formal classroom contexts were almost exclusively from the CFL classes that they took when they attended international schools, except for Jason, who took private Mandarin class with a Mandarin tutor throughout most of his primary and secondary education. The participants taking the CFL classes reflected low motivation in learning Mandarin and feelings of being misplaced at class levels that did not meet their learning needs. As shown in Table 1.1, the participants were educated in international schools that offer formal English literacy education, while they were exposed to oral Cantonese or Mandarin, and English at home. These unbalanced power relations between school and home linguistic contexts became the primary factor that nurtured the participants into CHL speakers who were English-dominant.

Example 1: Interview with Mike

01	I:	Did you have Chinese classes in those schools?
02	M:	Yes, Mandarin classes.
03	I:	How often was it?
04	M:	Like twice a week. I think twice a week for one and a half hours.
05	I:	How did you feel about it? What's the best thing and worst thing about it?
06	M:	The best thing was some were easy as compared to foreigners, the worst thing was I didn't
07		learn that much, sometimes.
08	I:	Do you find it helpful for you?
09	M:	Yes, I think it was helpful cos I don't know Mandarin. I only know Cantonese as I speak
10		Cantonese. And I learned some characters as well, I mean . . . yeah . . . I don't really know
11		characters. It was easy for me to get like . . . when she taught us, it was easy for me to grasp
12		because I already knew Cantonese right?

Example 2: Interview with Jason

01	I:	How often was the Chinese class in your primary and secondary schools?
02	J:	Primary . . . I don't remember . . . Maybe once a week.
03	I:	Once a week? The school class?
04	J:	It was the school class. I mean that Mandarin is not even . . . I don't think it even really matters.

05		It was *so* basic. I really . . . Most of my learning were really from my home tutor.
06		He taught me a lot. But . . . He was a good teacher. But . . . and then because of that,
07		I did quite well on the high school one. So I really didn't feel like I need it.
08		So I just chose something else and sticked with the home tutor.

Example 1 and 2 are respectively Mike and Jason's descriptions about their experiences learning Mandarin Chinese during their school years. The main characters in Mike's narrative are his former classmates in primary and secondary schools. Mike referred his non-Chinese speaking classmates as "foreigners" (line 06). And then he commented that the worst thing about the classroom Chinese language learning throughout his formative years was that he "didn't learn that much" (lines 06–07), because he perceived that the class level was too easy for him. This indicates the Mandarin Chinese class that Mike took in schools was tailored for students from a non-Chinese background as opposed to CHL learners. An additional character in this narrative was Mike's teacher, who was mentioned as the third person pronoun *she* (line 11). This character appeared only once, reflecting Mike's vague impression about his school Chinese language classes, as he commented that the outcome of learning Chinese at school was merely learning some basic knowledge of Mandarin Chinese and "some characters" (line 10). He didn't seem to acknowledge the CFL class learning and commented that "it was easy" (line 11) for him since he was a Cantonese speaker.

Jason's narrative also reveals similar opinions about the minimal benefits of learning Mandarin in international schools. This point of view was reported clearly through his comments like "I don't think it even really matters" (line 04) and "it was so basic" (line 05). However, slightly different from Mike's storytelling, Jason brought in another character—his home tutor. In another narrative, Jason stated that he had a home tutor once a week for eight years to teach him conversational Mandarin. He appreciated the outcome of home tutoring and contrasted the uselessness of school classes (lines 05–08), which again proved his standpoint on the uselessness of formal Chinese language learning at school.

Example 3: Interview with Ada

01	I:	Was it helpful for you?
02	A:	I think, I think it wasn't . . . that . . . helpful, because . . .
03	I:	Why?
04	A:	Er . . . it didn't really improve . . . or maybe it was just me, but like . . . yeah, I feel like my level
05		didn't . . . cos I studied it for . . . from grade 7 to grade 12, but it still didn't improve much [laughs].

06	I:	Oh, like, in terms of speaking or writing?
07	A:	Especially reading, reading and writing, yeah. My
		speaking improved a bit, but . . . reading and
08		writing is still, yeah.
09	I:	What is the reason that you think you didn't improved a
		lot in your secondary school?
10	A:	Cos there's two streams of Chinese, er, and I was in the
		stream of Chinese for the foreign language
11		speaker, so I think maybe, it was just at a slower pace, cos
		all the other secondary schoolers are . . .
12	I:	At a very basic level?
13	A:	Yeah.
14	I:	So were most of the other classmates' Chinese levels
		lower than yours?
15	A	Yeah. Yeah.

In Example 3, Ada also considered herself as a misplaced learner in a class level that was too easy for her (lines 10–15). She "didn't improve much" (line 05) during the six-year experience learning Chinese in the school CFL class. This sense of low achievement in Chinese was related to the fact that the school CFL class did not equip her with strong "reading and writing" (lines 07–08) skills. She consolidated her position as a misplaced learner by positioning "all the other secondary schoolers" (line 11) as learners with lower proficiency.

To sum up, the participants' narratives about Chinese language learning during their K-12 years reflect the juxtaposition between the continua of context and development. As shown in Figure 1.2, the unbalanced power relations

(less powerful) ← → (more powerful)

Context

micro (home) ← → macro (school)
oral (Chinese, English) ← → literate (English)
bilingual (Chinese, English) ← → monolingual (English)

Development

receptive (Chinese, English) ← → productive (English)
oral (Chinese, English) ← → written (English)
L1 (Chinese) ← → L2 (English)

FIGURE 1.2 Context and development continua during K-12 study, adapted from Hornberger and Wang (2008)

between the home and school contexts contributed to the fact that the literacy development in Chinese is much weaker than that in English. Their identities were positioned in the dynamic power relationship between the dominant languages used at home and school, the bilingual context at home and the monolingual context at school, and their receptive development of Chinese and productive development of English. Additionally, the self and other positioning in their narratives also uncovered their positions as misplaced CHL learners, which strongly affected their language learning outcome and motivation.

Changing Continua during School–University Transition

The participants' narratives about their experiences learning Chinese at the university context reflect a process of reconstructing themselves as learners of Chinese. All participants stated that they became much more motivated to learn Chinese after they attended the university. The university CFL classes, as reported by the participants, also targeted speakers from non-Chinese backgrounds and were similar to those offered by the international schools. Instead of feeling being misplaced and de-motivated, the participants showed more intrinsic motivation after going to university. The narratives show that the participants' motivational change is essentially related to the change of the linguistic contexts, and their association of learning Chinese with better career opportunities. Figure 1.3 shows the changing continua of context and development from school to university. The participants reported that the university environment is more liberal in terms of language policy. In addition, they enjoyed greater contact with more native Chinese-speaking peers in university. This change in the linguistic environment exerted considerable influence in their reconstruction of their selves in terms of Chinese language learning.

(less powerful) ← → (more powerful)

Context

micro (home) ← → macro (university)
oral (Chinese, English) ← → literate (English)
bilingual (Chinese, English) ← → <u>bilingual (Chinese and English)</u>

Development

reception (Chinese, English) ← → <u>production (Chinese and English)</u>
oral (Chinese, English) ← → written (English)

FIGURE 1.3 Context and development continua during university study, adapted from Hornberger and Wang (2008)

24 Zhen Li

Example 4: Interview with Ada

01   I: Were you interested in learning Mandarin when you were in high school?
02   A: Not as much as now, yeah.
03   I: When did you become more interested in learning Mandarin? And why?
04   A: Probably . . . well, when I started it in university, cos in high school, most of my friends just speak
05   English. I think there was a policy that . . . er, not policy, but like you are expected to speak English
06   in an international school. And teachers don't like it if you speak Cantonese, so everyone just
07   speaks English, so there was not really much pressure to speak other languages. But when I started
08   it in university, everyone else is like, "oh, you lived in Hong Kong for so long, but you don't speak
09   Cantonese" [laughs]. Yeah.
10   I: Are you regretful about that?
11   A: Yeah.
12   I: Really?
13   A: Yeah. I think it would be easier to learn Chinese when I was younger.

In Example 4, Ada explained why she became more motivated in learning Chinese after she attended university. In lines 04–09, she described the discrepancies between her former school situation and the current university one. In her former school context, everyone was "expected to speak English" (line 05). She also reported that the teachers "don't like it if you speak Cantonese" (line 06). This position of the teachers as promoters of the monolingual policy reflects the power of international schools in terms of their monolingual practice.

In the narrative, Ada addressed the issue of cultural identity. When she was in the international school, no one questioned her identity as ethnically Chinese. However, after she attended university she found that many people assumed she was a native Chinese speaker. She used direct reported speech in lines 08–09 to provide an example of how other university students were surprised by her identity as a local Hong Kong resident whose knowledge of Cantonese was insubstantial. This social positioning about Ada led to the following narrative about her motivational change.

Example 5: Interview with Ada

01   I: What did you say about the reason you feel more motivated in learning Chinese now?

"Local-Born" CHL Learners in Hong Kong **25**

02	A:	Oh, ur, because . . . a lot of people . . . when I talk to them, er, they'll say . . . like to ask me where I
03		am from, and then I'll say Singapore and Hong Kong, and they'll be like "oh yes, you can speak
04		Mandarin, you can speak Cantonese" [laughs], so it's kind of like, I'm expected to know the language
05		but I don't.
06	I:	I see. Any other reasons beyond that?
07	A:	Oh yeah, job, job, job opportunities, yeah.
08	I:	How did you realize that speaking good Mandarin will bring you more job opportunities?
09		If you look at the job listings online, the vast majority all need Chinese or Cantonese, or both.

Example 6: Interview with Mike

01	I:	Has your learning objective ever changed in different stages of your life?
02	M:	What? Mandarin?
03	I:	Yeah, Chinese learning.
04	M:	Yeah, I think so. When I was young, I was like "OK, it's good to know some". And then it's not
05		really important though. And then I thought I'd learn it later. And then in secondary school I was
06		like "it's so hard to learn it." And now it's like I should learn it more.

In Example 5, Ada repeatedly mentioned that the influence from native Chinese-speaking peers whose positioning on her questionable identity prompted her to be more motivated in learning Chinese (lines 02–04). Interestingly, in both Example 4 and Example 5, Ada used "Cantonese," "Mandarin," and "Chinese" interchangeably, showing a blurred positioning about these terms. For instance, in lines 03–04, Ada said her university peers assumed she speaks "Mandarin" or "Cantonese," while in line 08, Ada mentioned "Chinese or Cantonese" instead of "Mandarin or Cantonese" as important language skills in terms of future job-hunting. The blurred positioning on the "Chinese," "Cantonese," and "Mandarin" also appeared numerous times in narratives of the other participants. This partly echoes Li and Zhu's (2010) findings that the current linguistic hierarchies among the Chinese language varieties have been changing toward a more translingual perspective with great flexibility. However, in addition to valuing Mandarin as the standard Chinese language and the significance of Chinese literacy skills (Li and Zhu, 2010), the participants in this study also value the oral skills of Cantonese, which is an integral part of their socialization with local Cantonese-speaking students.

26 Zhen Li

Example 7: Interview with Tom

01	I:	So were you always interested in learning Chinese?
02	T:	No . . . I don't think so. I think in primary school you are too young to know what you are interested
03		in. You just study it in school . . . You don't think.
04		Then in secondary school, I was like: why do I have to go to a Chinese tuition class?
05		My mom forced me to do it at home. I didn't like it cause I didn't want to study basically.
06		And then . . . probably . . . maybe when I get back to university again, and then I think I should
07		study Chinese, because it's quite important.
08	I:	So you think you had a stronger motivation in university as compared to . . .?
09	T:	Umm! To high school, Umm!
10	I:	So what do you think the reason that makes you feel Chinese is more important now?
11	T:	[laughs] There are economic reasons I think. China is the second largest economy.
12		But I think also cos . . . I'm Chinese. And . . . to me it's important to learn . . .
13		to learn your heritage, your own language, and understand it.

A similarity conveyed by Examples 6 and 7 is that both Mike and Tom reported that they became more motivated in learning Chinese after they attended university. In Example 6, Mike recalled his attitude towards learning Chinese changed over several stages in his life. He believed Chinese learning was "not really important" (lines 04–05), and "so hard to learn" (lines 05–06) when he was in secondary school, and "should learn it more" (line 06) after he attended university. Mike's change of opinion conveys a transformed positioning toward Chinese language learning and a reconstructed belief about its importance of learning Chinese across his K-12 and university education. It also indirectly reflects the dynamic relationship between the translingual contexts, bilingual and bilateral development, and his identity negotiation.

In Example 7, Tom discussed the role of his parents in his journey to learn Chinese. He initiated the topic about his mom pushing him to learn Chinese during his K-12 years in international schools. In this way, Tom could contrast the previous learning experience of being "forced" (line 05) in comparison to a more self-initiated learning experience after he entered university. He explicitly stated that the main reason for his changed motivation for learning Chinese is due to China's economy and the importance of one's own HL. Like many other

CHL learners, not only the transformed positioning toward the Chinese language and Chinese language learning stemmed from a realization of the growing power of the Chinese economy, but also a reconstructed perspective about the importance of their cultural and linguistic heritage.

Discussion and Conclusion

This chapter has examined how five Hong Kong-Chinese CHL learners constructed their identities in their narratives about experiences learning Chinese across complex sociolinguistic landscapes, from their K-12 years to university study. Raised in English-medium international schools and bilingual Chinese families, these "local-born" CHL learners reconstructed their identities as learners of Chinese spanning their transition from school to university. Previous research, which conceptualized CHL learner identity as a product of immigration and diaspora experiences, often overlooked how identity developed across changing institutional contexts. Similar to CHL learners who grew up in North American or other non-Chinese-speaking countries, the "local-born" CHL students still had a cross-lingual childhood of being exposed to Chinese predominantly at home, and to English at school.

This chapter has expanded the traditional concept of CHL learners as second-generation Chinese immigrants by exploring another subcategory of CHL learners in Hong Kong context. Although the "local-born" CHL learners have never been raised in overseas countries, they still need to negotiate transitions among multiple contexts that are linguistically, culturally, and ideologically different from one another (Bray and Yamato, 2003). Some findings in this chapter are unique to Hong Kong. They are related to the discrepancies between the international school and the university contexts, between their different language policies and sociolinguistic landscapes. It is evident from the data that the process of learning Chinese is juxtaposed with identity construction and motivational change. Institutional contexts could strongly affect how CHL learners position themselves as well. As noted by Norton and Toohey (2011), language learner identity is no longer a static substance in today's world, which is characterized by boundary-crossing and multilingualism. Many CHL learners who did not cross the national borders from K-12 to higher education still experienced significant identity transformation through crossing institutional borders during the school–university transition. Reconstruction of learner identity, as shown in the above analysis, is not only a result of CHL learning per se but is also associated with peer socialization and contextual change.

The small sample size may not precisely exhibit the entire "local-born" CHL learner population in Hong Kong, and some variables such as gender, language proficiency, school-type were not included in the analysis. However, the findings from the study can shed some light on the topic. Although born and raised in the territory of China, some Chinese students' L1 literacy development may still

28 Zhen Li

be constrained by K-12 institutional context. As the population of CHL learners has been expanding globally, this research could be extended more widely. It would be instructive to investigate more "local-born" CHL learners from more types of schools. A larger part of the picture could be seen if similar studies could be carried out in Mainland China or elsewhere.

References

2011 Census. (2012). *Thematic report: Ethnic minorities*. Hong Kong, China: Census and Statistics Department.

Bamberg, M. (1997). Positioning between structure and performance. *Journal of Narrative and Life History*, 7, 335–342.

Bray, M., and Yamato, Y. (2003). Comparative education in a microcosm: Methodological insights from the international schools sector in Hong Kong. In M. Bray (Ed.), *Comparative education: Continuing traditions, new challenges, and new paradigms* (pp. 51–73). Dordrecht, Germany: Kluwer Academic Publishers.

Canagarajah, A. S. (2013). *Literacy as translingual practice: Between communities and classrooms*. New York, NY: Routledge.

Creese, A., and Martin, P. (2003). Multilingual classroom ecologies: Inter-relationships, interactions and ideologies. *International Journal of Bilingual Education and Bilingualism*, 6(3–4), 161–167.

Danielewicz-Betz, A., and Graddol, D. (2014). Varieties of English in the urban landscapes of Hong Kong and Shenzhen. *English Today*, 30(3), 22–32.

Davies, B., and Harré, R. (1990). Positioning: The discursive production of selves. *Journal for the Theory of Social Behaviour*, 20(1), 43–63.

Forse, C. (2010). Fit for purpose? Why Chinese families choose international schools in Hong Kong. In J. Ryan and G. Slethaug (Eds.), *International education and the Chinese learner* (pp. 59–72). Hong Kong: Hong Kong University Press.

Georgakopoulou, A. (2006). The other side of the story: Towards a narrative analysis of narratives-in-interaction. *Discourse Studies*, 8(2), 235–257.

Hong Kong, Education Bureau. (2016a). International Schools in Hong Kong. Retrieved from http://edb.hkedcity.net/internationalschools/statistics_at_a_glance.php?lang=en.

Hong Kong, Education Bureau. (2016b). Student enrollment statistics, 2015/16: Kindergarten, primary and secondary levels. Retrieved from www.edb.gov.hk/attachment/en/about-edb/publications-stat/figures/Enrol_2015.pdf.

Hornberger, N. H. (1989). Continua of Biliteracy. *Review of Educational Research*, 59(3), 271–296.

Hornberger, N. H. (2002). Multilingual language policies and the continua of biliteracy: An ecological approach. *Language Policy*, 1(1), 27–51.

Hornberger, N. H., and Link, H. (2012). Translanguaging and transnational literacies in multilingual classrooms: A biliteracy lens. *International Journal of Bilingual Education and Bilingualism*, 15(3), 261–278.

Hornberger, N. H., and Wang, S. C. (2008). Who are our heritage language learners? Identity and biliteracy in heritage language education in the United States. In D. M. Brinton, O. Kagan, and S. Bauckus (Eds.), *Heritage language education: A new field emerging* (pp. 3–38). New York, NY: Routledge.

Igarashi, H., and Saito, H. (2014). Cosmopolitanism as cultural capital: Exploring the intersection of globalization, education and stratification. *Cultural Sociology, 8*(3), 222–239.

Jabal, E. (2010). Being, becoming, and belonging: Exploring Hong Kong-Chinese students' experiences of the social realities of international schooling. In J. Ryan and G. Slethaug (Eds.), *International education and the Chinese learner* (pp. 73–88). Hong Kong, China: Hong Kong University Press.

Kasper, G., and Prior, M. T. (2015). Analyzing storytelling in TESOL interview research. *TESOL Quarterly, 49*(2), 226–255.

Li, W., and Zhu, H. (2010). Voices from the diaspora: Changing hierarchies and dynamics of Chinese multilingualism. *International Journal of the Sociology of Language, 2010*(205), 155–171.

Li, W., and Zhu, H. (2013). Translanguaging identities and ideologies: Creating transnational space through flexible multilingual practices amongst Chinese university students in the UK. *Applied Linguistics, 34*(5), 516–535.

Li, Z. (2014). Teaching Chinese in Hong Kong international schools: Opportunities and challenges. *International School Magazine, 17*(2), 42–43.

McNamara, T. (2012). Poststructuralism and its challenges for applied linguistics. *Applied Linguistics, 33*(5), 473–482.

Mu, G. M. (2014). Learning Chinese as a heritage language in Australia and beyond: The role of capital. *Language and Education, 28*(5), 477–492.

Ng, V. (2011). The decision to send local children to international schools in Hong Kong: Local parents' perspectives. *Asia Pacific Education Review, 13*(1), 121–136.

Norton, B., and Toohey, K. (2011). Identity, language learning, and social change. *Language Teaching, 44*(4), 412–446.

Rothman, J. (2009). Understanding the nature and outcomes of early bilingualism: Romance languages as heritage languages. *International Journal of Bilingualism, 13*(2), 155–163.

Schmidt, M. (2010). Educating Chinese learners for social conscience in Hong Kong: An international school perspective. In J. Ryan and G. Slethaug (Eds.), *International education and the Chinese learner* (pp. 89–108). Hong Kong: Hong Kong University Press.

van Langenhove, L., and Harré, R. (1999). Introducing positioning theory. In R. Harré and L. van Langenhove (Eds.), *Positioning theory: Moral contexts of intentional action* (pp. 14–31). Malden, MA: Blackwell.

2

CHINESE INTERNATIONAL STUDENTS IN ENGLISH-MEDIUM PROGRAMS IN JAPAN

Experiences and Life Strategies

Hanae Tsukada

The history of Chinese students going to Japan to study dates back to the late 1800s, with the estimated number reaching 8,000–10,000 before the relationship between the two countries became strained by repeated wars (Takeda, 2006; Tsuboya, 2008). Following the normalization of the bilateral relationship in 1972 and the Japanese government's policy initiatives to increase the number of international students in Japanese higher education institutions (HEIs), the massive influx of Chinese students into Japan started in the 1980s. As of May 2014, 94,399 students from China (including Macau and Hong Kong, but not Taiwan) were enrolled in Japanese HEIs, accounting for more than 50% of the country's entire international student population (Japan Student Services Organization, 2015).

Traditionally, Japanese has been the language of instruction in Japanese HEIs. However, there is a new language option for international students to study in Japan: English as a medium of instruction (EMI) is now part of Japan's strategy for the internationalization of higher education. In 2008, the Japanese government launched the 300,000 International Student Plan with the goal of increasing the number of international students to 300,000 by the year 2020. This new policy proposes to increase the number of courses conducted in English in order to attract more international students, and envisages retaining them after graduation to feed Japan's labor force. As a supporting program for this international student policy, the Project for Establishing University Network for Internationalization was launched in 2009. By the end of the five-year program in 2013, this project had created 148 English-medium programs in Japanese universities (Japan Society for the Promotion of Science, 2015).

Tsuneyoshi (2005) refers to this zealous internationalization effort through the promotion of increased use of EMI as "Englishization." On the one hand,

Englishization suggests that new educational opportunities are opening up in Japan to a new group of international students from China and elsewhere who could not study in Japan in the past due to a lack of Japanese-language skills. On the other hand, English does not represent the linguistic diversity of the residents of Japan, including the international student population. As of 2015, Chinese and Koreans are the largest groups of registered foreigners in Japan, accounting for 30.2% and 22.9%, respectively, followed by the Philippines (10.3%) and Brazil (8.0%) (Immigration Bureau, Ministry of Justice of Japan, 2015). International students account for 10.4% of these registered foreigners in Japan, and over 90% of international students come from other Asian countries (Japan Student Services Organization, 2015). When Englishization is promoted as a way to increase the number of international students, regardless of Japan's actual linguistic diversity, the implications for international students' experiences in Japan are of particular interest. Since English is neither a mother tongue for these students, nor a common language in Japan, how do these students experience complex language situations created by Englishization in Japanese HEIs and society?

In addition, what do international students expect to gain from English-medium programs in Japan? The literature shows that students' pursuit of education overseas is a strategy for developing transnational life options to help them navigate the challenges they expect to face in their lives and the life opportunities they imagine will be open to them by studying overseas (Baas, 2010; Fong, 2011; Ong, 1999). In the same vein, studies demonstrate that international students in Western English-speaking countries seek to gain privileged access to the global labor market, where Western educational qualifications and English have privileged value (Doherty and Singh, 2005; Matthews and Sidhu, 2005; Waters, 2006b, 2006a). As I will discuss in this chapter, scholars have also studied the transnational life strategies Chinese students have crafted for themselves by studying in Japan (Fong, 2011; Liu-Farrer, 2009; Tsuboya, 2010), but few have focused on Chinese students attending English-medium programs in Japan. Hence, little is known about how these programs are related to Chinese students' life strategies and experiences.

Based on a qualitative study with Chinese students in two English-medium programs in Japan, this chapter will examine these students' experiences and life strategies, with a particular focus on the implications of language. Specifically, this chapter asks: 1) How do these students experience the language landscapes created by Englishization in Japanese HEIs and society? and 2) How is their participation in their English-medium programs in Japan related to their life strategies? By exploring these two questions, the chapter aims to understand not only these Chinese students' experiences and life strategies but also the meaning of Englishization in Japan, both the challenges and opportunities it creates. Before I present the study and its findings, I review the relevant literature on Chinese international students in Japan, and in English-medium programs in non-English-speaking countries.

Chinese International Students in Japan and English-Medium Programs

The literature shows that Chinese people's choice to study in Japan reflects their strategies to navigate the uneven socioeconomic and academic systems within China and other countries. For example, Chinese students' outflows to Japan and Western countries can be attributed to an insufficient number of HEIs in China to meet the demand for higher education (Liu-Farrer, 2009; Tsuboya, 2010). In addition, Fong's (2011) study shows her Chinese student participants' desire and strategies for socioeconomic mobility through studying in developed industrial countries, such as the United Kingdom, Australia, Ireland, and Japan. They believe that studying in one of those countries will lead them to a "better life" with improved socioeconomic conditions and freedom. However, for many of them, the cost of education in English-speaking developed countries is too high, and Japan is the "most convenient, lowest cost, and easiest option" (Fong, 2011, p. 46). Compared to countries that set strict restrictions on international students' employment, Japan is one of the rare cases of a developed country allowing international students to work to finance their studies.

The literature confirms that for many Chinese students who decide to go to Japan, destination is a secondary concern. In Tsuboya's (2008) survey of Chinese people living in Japan who initially arrived as students, the major reasons for choosing to go to Japan were not because of some specific attraction to Japan. Rather, when asked about their reason for going to Japan, more than 50% answered, "to acquire specialized knowledge." This reason exceeded Japan-specific reasons, such as "wanted to study Japanese" or "wanted to work in Japan," which accounted for less than 20% of the total. As for their reasons for leaving China, over 40% said they "wanted to see the outside world; wanted to go anywhere overseas," and over 20% noted their dissatisfaction with social and labor conditions in China. Tsuboya's follow-up interviews with transnational Chinese people support the assertion that it is not a specific attraction to Japan, but rather a dissatisfaction with socioeconomic conditions in China that motivates Chinese people to leave China.

Studies about the experiences of Asian international students in Japan, particularly Chinese students, consistently address language as one of the major challenges, among others, such as securing time for studies while working a part-time job, and discrimination against non-Japanese Asians in Japan (Asano, 1997; Duan, 2003; Ge, 2010; Suhara, 1996). As Liu-Farrer (2009) notes, many Chinese international students in Japan, especially those who have little Japanese skills and who enroll in Japanese-language schools, serve as unskilled, low-wage labor in Japan. In addition, studies by Asano (1997) and Ge (2010) show that Chinese international students who are in the field of science at Japanese universities tend to have less command of Japanese, and hence have difficulties developing relationships with their Japanese counterparts, especially compared to Chinese students in the humanities field.

34 Hanae Tsukada

Despite these challenges, some Chinese students succeed in attaining trans-national life paths and economic mobility through their studies in Japan (Liu-Farrer, 2009, 2010; Tsuboya, 2008). They become skilled laborers who facilitate transnational economic relations between China and Japan by using their bilingual and bicultural competencies, as well as the specialized knowledge and skills they acquired in Japanese HEIs. However, their professional successes in Japan can be layered with a sense of marginalization because of Japanese society's prejudice against immigrants from developing countries (Liu-Farrer, 2010).

While these prior studies provide a valuable overview of Chinese international students in Japan, they tend to be contextualized in traditional educational and social contexts where Japanese is the dominant, and often the only, language of communication. There are few studies about international students, let alone Chinese international students, in English-medium programs in Japan, and even in other non-English-speaking countries more broadly. However, among the notable exceptions, a study in Korea reports that international students' expectations of practicing Korean were unmet due to their program's use of English (Jon et al., 2014). In addition, other studies of English-medium programs in Korea and Thailand address international students' appropriation of English for their advantage, ranging from facilitating communications with people of varying linguistic backgrounds to positioning themselves as superior to those with lower English skills (Kim et al., 2014; Phan, 2009). These findings show an interesting contrast to a body of research on international students in English-speaking countries, where international students are expected to master the language of their host countries (i.e., English), and where they find themselves, as non-native English-speakers, at the margins of their host societies (Lee and Rice, 2007; Sawir et al., 2008). When Japan implements Englishization, it is important to examine the implications of English for international students' lives in Japan and their life strategies.

The Study

The data for this chapter is drawn from a broader study that included interviews with faculty, staff, and international students, and examined the intersection of the internationalization of universities and international students' experiences in Japan. However, the findings presented in this chapter are limited to the student interviews.

The study deployed a case study design (Gerring, 2007; Yin, 2003) and selected two private HEIs in Japan: International College (IC) of Kasuga University and Hokuto Global University (HGU). The names of the institutions and participants in this chapter are pseudonyms. IC is an undergraduate college that specializes in international studies within Kasuga University, a large and prestigious comprehensive university located in an urban area of Japan. In contrast, HGU is a smaller and less prestigious university established specifically as an international university in rural Japan. At both IC and HGU, approximately 30–40% of the students are international students, which is among the highest in the Japanese higher education system. Both institutions allow students to complete their degree programs in English, which is still rare in Japan. Both of these institutions have served as models that have been emulated under recent Japanese internationalization policies and programs.

IC and HGU have different language-of-instruction systems, but for the majority of international students at both institutions, English is the primary language of instruction, and they are required to take an equal number of credits in Japanese language as an additional language. At IC, English is the primary language of instruction for all students, but students are divided into native Japanese speakers and non-native Japanese speakers. Approximately 30% of IC students are non-native speakers, and they are required to take 24 credits of Japanese courses. In contrast, HGU has a bilingual system in which both English and Japanese are the mediums of instruction and campus communication. HGU students choose either a Japanese track or an English track, and more than 80% of international students are enrolled in the English track. The students in the English track can complete their coursework in English, while still being required to take at least 24 credits of Japanese language courses.

The study statistically targeted the most representative international student population in the Japanese higher education system, namely, self-funded, degree-seeking undergraduate students from China (including Macau and Hong Kong) who were majoring in humanities and social sciences at private universities (Japan Student Services Organization, 2010). To limit the background variables and determine the focus and scope of the study, I narrowed this group of students further to those who were in their third or fourth year of study and who were from Mainland China. Twenty-seven students (15 at HGU and 12 at IC) who fulfilled the above sampling criteria participated in the study. There were more female participants than male participants; ten females and five males at HGU, and nine females and three males at IC. They were between 20 and 23 years old at the time of their interviews. All of the HGU student participants except one were enrolled in the English track, and I removed the accounts of the one Japanese-track HGU student from the analysis for this chapter.

I conducted semi-structured interviews in either English or Japanese, according to the participant's preference. Each interview lasted approximately 60 to 90 minutes. Interviews covered participants' motivations for going to Japan and their respective host institutions to study, their on- and off-campus experiences in Japan, and their future prospects. I transcribed the interviews in the language of the interview. Due to a lack of prior studies about international students' experiences in similar institutional settings in Japan, I coded interview data inductively following the data analysis process developed by Auerbach and Silverstein (2003). I compiled repeating ideas and then grouped them into themes and sub-themes. I first analyzed data from HGU students and IC students separately. I then combined these two student groups' data to identify differences and consistencies between the groups.

Before presenting the findings, I will describe the scope and focus of this chapter. First, to limit the scope of the analysis, I present only my findings on the implications of language for student participants' experiences in Japan and their life strategies. Second, the focus of the original study was not on teaching and learning at the case institutions, and my investigation therefore did not extend into the classroom. Accordingly, the goal of this chapter, as well as of the study as a whole, was not to assess the effectiveness of EMI at the case institutions, or in Japan in general.

Results

I present the findings in three parts: first, student participants' decisions to enroll in an English-medium program in Japan as their life strategy; second, students' experiences in Japan, with a particular focus on the implications of language; and third, students' future prospects after graduation and how their language skills are related to their future outlook.

Decisions for Enrolling in English-Medium Programs in Japan as Life Strategies

The student interviews showed how these Chinese students, who grew up with privileged access to English education, strategically and opportunistically chose to go to English-medium programs in Japan in order to further advance their privilege by learning Japanese as an additional foreign language. However, the data suggest a slight socioeconomic class gap between HGU and IC students.

Enhancing Privilege: Japanese Language as a Competitive Edge

The majority of student participants at both HGU and IC come from a relatively privileged segment of the Chinese population, a segment for whom access to English education and global mobility is common, and even taken for granted. They grew up in affluent coastal Chinese cities and learned English from an early age. Eleven participants, ten of whom are HGU participants, attended high schools that are so-called "foreign language schools" that emphasize foreign language education, especially English. Many others attended high schools that they described as top-level in their regions and whose graduates often go to foreign universities, particularly in English-speaking countries.

For these students, EMI at HGU and IC was one of the common factors motivating and enabling them to go to Japan. The majority had little command of Japanese before arriving in Japan, and they were interested in the opportunity to learn Japanese while taking subject courses in English. For example, one IC student explains:

> I really wanted to try a different kind of culture and try to learn another new language, because I have been studying English for about 20 years before I came to Japan . . . I was really interested in [studying at IC] because I really didn't want to give up my English, and using English to study in Japan, I think, is . . . really a good experience.
>
> (Mao Mao, female, IC)

Few students in this study, at the time they went to Japan, had concrete goals or plans for their lives after graduation. However, many students, particularly those at HGU, envisaged that a combination of language skills—Chinese, English, and Japanese—would help them stand out in the competitive labor market in China or elsewhere. For example, Xiazhi (male, HGU) explained:

> I may not be able to beat Chinese students from top Chinese universities in many areas, but I thought that if I learn Japanese, I might be able to beat them. Everyone can speak English, of course, but there are not so many people who can speak Japanese.
>
> (Japanese interview translated into English by author)

As this quote illustrates, student participants saw English proficiency as something that everyone had, suggesting their privileged social location. Building on this privilege, they took the opportunity to further develop their competitive edge in the future job market by gaining a new skill (i.e., Japanese) that their future competitors were not likely to possess.

Different Motivations for Going to HGU and IC: A Slight Class Gap

As seen above, the opportunity to learn Japanese was a major attraction for student participants, but Japan was not initially their ideal study destination. The majority deemed English-speaking Western countries as ideal destinations for their education. However, they were attracted to different characteristics of HGU or IC, rather than to Japan as a country, and the different institutional attractions suggested a slight class gap between the students.

For many HGU student participants, their admission to HGU meant a convenient and strategic solution to their challenging life circumstances in China. Their high schools in China had strong connections with HGU, and they were first enticed by the opportunity to study in Japan when they came into contact with HGU at their high schools. When asked to explain why they chose HGU,

38 Hanae Tsukada

many mentioned their anxiety about China's nationwide university entrance exam, the *gao kao*, which is fiercely competitive and offers no guarantee of post-graduation employment, even for graduates from top-tier universities in China. A participant explains:

> If I stay in my home country, I'll face a really huge competition in . . . a national college entrance examination. It's a large pressure. That does not necessary guarantee, after you finish a degree at a Chinese institute, a very promising future, I guess, because of simply the competition.
>
> (Xiao Ming, male, HGU)

HGU participants were admitted to HGU before the *gao kao* even took place. HGU's generous scholarships were also a big attraction—80% of them received a tuition reduction of 50% or higher. They took advantage of this conveniently timed and well-funded international education opportunity in Japan.

In contrast, the vast majority of IC participants were attracted to Kasuga University's prestige more than anything else. "Because it's famous [*yūmei dakara*]" was the most common explanation given when asked why they decided to go to IC. According to them, Kasuga University is well-known in China, and they assessed that IC was the most famous, and therefore the best, choice for them out of the universities to which they had been admitted or to which they were likely to be admitted in China, Japan, and other countries.

Compared to HGU participants, for most IC participants, going to IC was more a *choice* representing their desire for prestige than a *solution* to challenging life circumstances. The estimated annual expenses at IC are 525,820 Yen (approximately US$5,128) higher than at HGU,[1] and only half of the IC participants received a scholarship or a 20–50% tuition reduction from Kasuga University. However, there were only a few IC participants who mentioned financial issues as a matter of concern in their selection of a university, suggesting that the majority of IC students could afford to pursue their desire for a prestigious university education with few financial constraints. This difference between HGU students and IC students suggests that while the English-medium programs at both HGU and IC attract students from relatively privileged backgrounds in China, these institutions of varying levels of academic prestige further sort the students by socioeconomic class.

Experiences in Japan

As mentioned above, HGU has a bilingual system, and IC adopts English as a lingua franca. Although there were differences between the two systems, students' stories at both institutions consistently demonstrated the dominance of the Japanese language and the limited usefulness of English in every sphere of their lives outside their institutions. While some students expressed their disappointment and struggles with this reality, many took advantage of the abundance of Japanese-learning opportunities in their everyday lives.

The Significance of Japanese and the Limited Usefulness of English

Students at both institutions repeatedly described that Japanese was the primary language outside their classrooms in Japan. Even at IC, which is located in a metropolitan city that attracts a lot of international tourists, expatriates, and immigrants, IC participants still described the dominance of Japanese language in their lives outside IC. Even on the Kasuga University campus, once stepping outside IC, Japanese is the main language in every aspect of campus life. Although English is the language of instruction throughout IC, one-third of IC participants lamented that their English skills had either deteriorated or had not improved as much as they had hoped, and they attributed this to their limited opportunities to use English in Japan. One of them, Yong Ling (female, IC), expressed her disappointment at the lack of opportunities to improve her English, in contrast to the abundance of opportunities to learn Japanese:

> [EMI] is . . . one of the reasons why I chose IC because I wanted to improve my English in Japan. But [pause] I just can't learn English from my classes or lectures or seminars, but I can learn Japanese everywhere. When you are, for example, watching TV, traveling, also doing a part-time job, anywhere I can learn *a lot of* Japanese. English, . . . how can I learn it? I just can't [by] reading a book or something or writing essays.

This comment not only shows the reality of language use in Japan, but also suggests a limitation of Englishization in Japan: Englishization promises the use of English and enables students like her to study in Japan, and yet the actual usefulness of English tends to be limited to academic settings.

Although English is rarely used in Japanese society, something with which some students were disappointed, many took advantage of the opportunity to learn Japanese. Besides taking the Japanese language courses required by their degree programs, how and to what extent students were invested in mastering Japanese varied greatly. However, overall, their stories at both HGU and IC suggest that mastering Japanese is often, if not entirely, the key to participants' sense of success and inclusion in Japanese society. Zing's (female, HGU) story about her part-time job experience at a restaurant is representative:

> I practiced my Japanese a lot there [at the restaurant], and my Japanese really improved. I feel like I entered Japanese society when I started working there. Like other foreign staff members, at first I was not allowed to take orders from customers, but I became the first foreign staff member whom

the restaurant allowed to take orders. The owner and other staff were really nice to me, and I had such a fantastic time there.

(Japanese interview translated into English by author)

Like Zing, students often linked the improvement of their Japanese skills to a sense of inclusion in Japan, and hence a sense of accomplishment and confidence.

Questions of Englishization in Japan

From above, it is clear that students' improved Japanese skills helped them participate in Japanese society. In addition, some students connected their Chinese skills to work opportunities in Japan, such as jobs that involved Chinese business counterparts or clients. Moreover, for many students, Chinese was the basis of their close friendships with their peers from Taiwan as well as from Mainland China. As such, English, Japanese, and Chinese were part of their daily lives in Japan.

However, some students' stories raised questions about the extent to which Japanese society is fair and inclusive of people with different linguistic backgrounds. For example, students who participated in the economic sphere in Japan, including through part-time jobs, internships, career development programs for international students, and job-hunting, consistently stated that the Japanese language and cultural norms were central in that sphere. For example, Qiang (male, IC), who was seeking a job in the international financial industry in Japan, described his puzzling job-hunting experience as follows:

[The companies] do have recruitment activities in Japan, and their official language is English, and they use English for everything within the company, but the [recruitment] process is always carried out in Japanese . . . I need to compete with Japanese people using Japanese. . . . I feel there isn't a point of testing people only in Japanese.

It is not known to what extent this story represents language use in hiring and daily work practices in Japan, including in the transnational business sector. However, his account illuminates how the Japanese language and native-Japanese speakers can be prioritized in Japan, despite the promotion of Englishization in the country.

While many students adjusted to the Japanese-speaking and English-speaking environments in Japan without too many questions or emotional struggles, a few participants' comments suggested that Englishization in Japan offers a rather limited space for people of various linguistic backgrounds. For example, Jie (female, HGU) found herself lost in the English-or-Japanese environment on her campus. Asked how she thought her experiences in Japan have changed her self-perception, she responded, "It makes me feel less confident." She continues:

Jie:	I kind of feel like, if I were a native speaker of . . . not Chinese but English, then perhaps I would be looked like in different ways. But I'm neither a native speaker of Japanese nor English. That makes me be in another position to be looked at.
Author:	What position?
Jie:	Like a totally different, like a third position. I'm neither this nor that.

These comments illustrates that Jie was affected by what Hashimoto (2013) critiques as a limited sense of bilingualism (i.e., only Japanese and English) established by Englishization in Japan, which not only fails to acknowledge non-English-speaking bilingual or multilingual speakers like her, but also categorizes all non-Japanese speakers as English speakers.

Future Prospects: The Process of Becoming Transnational

While HGU and IC students had different motivations for going to their respective institutions, the study did not find a particular difference in how these students envisioned their lives after graduation. Although each student's future outlook varied greatly from one to the other, there was some consistency in the tentativeness of their plans, which encompassed a wide array of alternative possibilities and options that transcended national borders. This suggests that, as Baas (2010) describes, they are "*in* the process of becoming transnationals" with flexible life options (p. 12, emphasis in original).

For many participants in this study, to live as transnationals was not an explicit pre-existing goal that brought them to Japan, but rather an emerging life option. They saw this open-ended future outlook as one of the most valuable outcomes of their experience in Japan, including their acquisition of the Japanese language. For example, Xiao Han (female, IC), who was applying for a job at a multinational corporation branch in Japan at the time of her interview, discussed how her experiences in Japan opened up new life options:

> If I had stayed in China, I probably would have gone straight to a grad school, and . . . I don't know if I would have gone to a multinational corporation. . . . The best thing for me about having come to Japan is that I have gotten a chance to enter a multinational corporation, and I have acquired Japanese language skills, too. Speaking of my career, I think my life has changed.
>
> (Japanese interview translated by author)

She anticipates that once she enters the company, she may be able to work at their branch in China in the future. As Baas (2010, p. 176) contends, "temporariness" and "indefiniteness" are what international students, including participants in this study, are aiming to gain control of through their participation in international education.

Discussion

Based on interviews with Chinese students in English-medium undergraduate programs at HGU and IC, this chapter showcases the development of their life strategies through their participation in these English-medium programs and their experiences in Japan, with particular attention to the implications of language. Due to a lack of similar studies and the small size of the present study, these findings raise more questions than provide clear and definitive answers. However, in this final section of the chapter, I discuss some implications of the key findings and remaining questions as a way to suggest critical reflections and areas for future research.

First, one of the most outstanding findings from student interviews is the limitations and contradictions of Englishization in Japan. As mentioned earlier, Englishization was introduced to Japanese HEIs as a way to increase the number of international students in Japan, and this policy strategy is also found in other countries like Korea and China (Jon and Kim, 2011; Kuroda, 2014). Indeed, EMI succeeded in attracting the Chinese student participants in this study who would not otherwise have considered going to Japan to study. EMI undoubtedly removed a language barrier for those students and broadened their life chances. However, what was equally clear in this study was that English served as little more than a bridge to a new opportunity in Japan. Consistent with studies that demonstrate the use of English limited to specific purposes and the importance of local languages in non-English-speaking countries (Amelina, 2010; Kubota, 2011), this study found the crucial role of Japanese language for student participants' social and economic integration into Japan. Once outside their institutions, students struggled with having to compete with their Japanese counterparts in Japanese and with finding a space for themselves as native speakers of neither English nor Japanese.

To be sure, this study's findings cannot be generalized to all English-medium programs in Japan, let alone to other country settings. In addition, both HGU and IC are not entirely focused on English. Both institutions require students whose mother tongue is not Japanese to take a certain number of Japanese-language courses. Moreover, my intention is not to dismiss Englishization entirely or to advocate for a Japanese-only monolingual campus environment. Nevertheless, the dilemmas of Englishization addressed by this study's participants require us to ask: To what extent is Englishization actually functioning to include and connect people of various linguistic backgrounds in non-English-speaking countries? Engaging with this question is important for educators and researchers whose work focuses on international students from China and elsewhere, as Japan and other non-English-speaking countries continue to promote Englishization with the goal of attracting more students from around the world.

Yet, it is equally important to recognize that student participants are not passively affected by the flaws of Englishization in Japan. Another important finding of this study is participants' opportunistic and strategic ways of developing their transnational life paths by taking advantage of the opportunities presented to them to study in Japan, despite the fact that Japan was not originally their most ideal study destination. They did so in order to earn an extra qualification—Japanese language skills—that their future competitors in the employment market were not likely to have. Once in Japan, some felt disappointed by a lack of opportunities to maintain or improve their English skills, and/or felt overwhelmed by the dominant power of Japanese. But many of them overcame, or actively capitalized on, this reality, as the opportunities to learn Japanese were everywhere. They invested in learning Japanese not only to integrate themselves socially and economically into Japanese society but also to enhance their positional advantage in the global employment market.

These students' strategic participation in English-medium programs in a non-English-speaking country like Japan adds new knowledge and questions to the existing body of literature. First, as mentioned earlier, numerous studies have focused on international students' pursuit of education in Western English-speaking countries to earn Western educational credentials and English skills, both of which have privileged value in the competitive labor market (Doherty and Singh, 2005; Matthews and Sidhu, 2005; Waters, 2006a, 2006b). Moreover, as Waters (2009) addresses, against the backdrop of the expansion of international education opportunities around the world, there is an emerging trend by which students seek to add unique qualifications to their overseas degrees. Waters (2009) found that middle-class students from Hong Kong pursued Masters of Business Administration (MBA) degrees in Canada to supplement their overseas undergraduate degrees and to enhance their employability in the global economy. My study's participants' strategic pursuit of Japanese language skills as a competitive edge highlights the role of foreign language skills other than English in the life strategies of globally mobile Chinese-heritage students. As EMI spreads across non-English-speaking countries, how students incorporate their host countries' languages, as well as English, into their life strategies is an important area of future research. Especially, in light of the dominance of English in the world, it is important to investigate how and to what extent language skills other than English benefit (or do not benefit) transnational Chinese-heritage students' lives.

Second, the literature suggests that EMI in non-English-speaking countries privileges those students who already have a high command of English, and, consequently, reproduces inequality between those who have English proficiency and those who do not (Hu et al., 2013; Jon and Kim, 2011). Consistent with the literature, this study also found that Chinese students who grew up with privileged access to English education from an early age gained opportunities to study in English-medium programs. Moreover, by building on this privilege, these students pursued opportunities to learn Japanese while taking subject courses in English. The English-medium programs at both HGU and IC made possible not only the reproduction but also further enhancement of these students' privilege.

Scholars have studied how Chinese international students in Japan develop their transnational life paths based on their bilingual and bicultural competencies in Chinese and Japanese (Liu-Farrer, 2009, 2010; Tsuboya, 2008). The emergence of this new group of Chinese students who enroll in English-medium programs in Japan raises questions regarding if and how this new student group's English skills make their life paths different from the paths of those Chinese international students who study in traditional Japanese university settings, where Japanese is the primary language of instruction. Longitudinal studies about this new group of Chinese students would serve as an important point of comparison for the existing body of literature about Chinese students in Japan. An analysis of the implications of students' socioeconomic backgrounds for their life paths would make a particularly significant contribution to the literature.

Conclusion

This study illuminated the emergence of a new group of Chinese students in newly developing English-medium programs in Japanese HEIs. Like an earlier generation of Chinese students, participants in this study were not attracted to Japan as a study destination. However, rather than being driven by a desire to leave China, this new group of students strategically and opportunistically chose English-medium programs in Japan with the aim of enhancing their positional advantage in the future labor market by acquiring Japanese as a foreign language in addition to English, which they assumed everyone already had.

Participants' accounts of their experiences in Japan revealed the scarce use of English outside of their institutions and the dominance of Japanese in their everyday lives, regardless of the promotion of Englishization in Japan. While they discussed their struggles with this linguistic reality, they took advantage of the abundant opportunities to improve their Japanese and developed transnational life prospects, which many saw as one of the most valuable outcomes of their education in Japan. How the transnational life strategies of this new group of Chinese students unfold has yet to be seen. Future studies should focus on how these students' socio-economic backgrounds and the power of Japanese and Chinese relative to English are related to the life strategies that they develop and their actual experiences.

Note

1   Calculated based on the respective institutions' brochures for prospective students. HGU: tuition 1,349,000 Yen plus 1,327,680 Yen for living expenses. IC: tuition 1,602,500 Yen plus 1,700,000 Yen for living expenses.

References

Amelina, M. (2010). Do other languages than English matter? International career development of highly-qualified professionals. In B. Meyer and B. Apfelbaum (Eds.),

Multilingualism at work: From policies to practices in public, medical and business settings (pp. 235–252). Amsterdam, The Netherlands: John Benjamins Publishing.

Asano, S. (1997). *Nihon de manabu ajiakei gaikokujin: Kenshūsei, ryūgakusei, shūgakusei no seikatsu to bunka hen-yō [Foreigners from Asian countries studying in Japan: Acculturation and life changes of trainees, international students, and precollege students]*. Okayama, Japan: Daigaku Kyōiku Shuppan.

Auerbach, C. F., and Silverstein, L. B. (2003). *Qualitative data: An introduction to coding and analysis.* New York, NY: New York University Press.

Baas, M. (2010). *Imagined mobility: Migration and transnationalism among Indian students in Australia.* London, UK: Anthem Press.

Doherty, C., and Singh, P. (2005). *International student subjectivities: Biographical investments for liquid times.* Presented at the AARE Education Research Conference, Sydney, Australia. Retrieved from http://eprints.qut.edu.au/2868.

Duan, Y. (2003). *Gendai chūgokujin no nihon ryūgaku [The modern Chinese's study abroad in Japan].* Tokyo, Japan: Akashi Shoten.

Fong, V. L. (2011). *Paradise redefined: Transnational Chinese students and the quest for flexible citizenship in the developed world.* Stanford, CA: Stanford University Press.

Ge, W. (2010). Zainichi chūgokujin ryūgakusei. kenshūsei no ibunka tekiō [Cultural adjustment of Chinese international students and trainees in Japan]. *Chūgoku 21, 33,* 121–136.

Gerring, J. (2007). *Case study research: Principles and practices.* Cambridge, UK: Cambridge University Press.

Hashimoto, K. (2013). "English-only," but not a medium-of-instruction policy: The Japanese way of internationalising education for both domestic and overseas students. *Current Issues in Language Planning, 14*(1), 16–33.

Hu, G., Li, L., and Lei, J. (2013). English-medium instruction at a Chinese University: Rhetoric and reality. *Language Policy, 13*(1), 21–40.

Immigration Bureau, Ministry of Justice of Japan. (2015, October 16). Heisei 27 nen 6 gatsumatsu genzai ni okeru zairyū gaikokujinsū ni tsuite [Statistics of registered foreign nationals as of the end of June 2015]. Retrieved from www.moj.go.jp/nyuukokukanri/kouhou/nyuukokukanri04_00054.html.

Japan Society for the Promotion of Science. (2015). Jigo hyōka kekka [Final assessment results: Project for Establishing University Network for Internationalization]. Retrieved from www.jsps.go.jp/j-kokusaika/jigo_kekka.html.

Japan Student Services Organization. (2010). International students in Japan 2010. Retrieved from www.jasso.go.jp/statistics/intl_student/data10_e.html.

Japan Student Services Organization. (2015). International students in Japan 2014. Retrieved from www.jasso.go.jp/en/about/statistics/intl_student/data2014.html.

Jon, J.-E., and Kim, E.-Y. (2011). What it takes to internationalize higher education in Korea and Japan: English-mediated courses and international students. In J. D. Palmer, A. Roberts, Y. H. Cho, and G. S. Ching (Eds.), *The Internationalization of East Asian higher education: Globalization's impact* (pp. 147–171). New York, NY: Palgrave Macmillan.

Jon, J.-E., Lee, J. J., and Byun, K. (2014). The emergence of a regional hub: Comparing international student choices and experiences in South Korea. *Higher Education: The International Journal of Higher Education and Educational Planning, 67*(5), 691–710.

Kim, J., Tatar, B., and Choi, J. (2014). Emerging culture of English-medium instruction in Korea: Experiences of Korean and international students. *Language and Intercultural Communication, 14*(4), 441–459.

46 Hanae Tsukada

Kubota, R. (2011). Questioning linguistic instrumentalism: English, neoliberalism, and language tests in Japan. *Linguistics and Education, 22*(3), 248–260.

Kuroda, C. (2014). The new sphere of international student education in Chinese higher education: A focus on English-medium degree programs. *Journal of Studies in International Education, 18*(5), 445–462.

Lee, J., and Rice, C. (2007). Welcome to America? International student perceptions of discrimination. *Higher Education, 53*(3), 381–409.

Liu-Farrer, G. (2009). Educationally channeled international labor mobility: Contemporary student migration from China to Japan. *International Migration Review, 43*(1), 178–204.

Liu-Farrer, G. (2010). Between privilege and prejudice: Chinese immigrants in corporate Japan's transnational economy. In P. Kee and H. Yoshimatsu (Eds.), *Global movements in the Asia Pacific* (pp. 123–145). Singapore: World Scientific.

Matthews, J., and Sidhu, R. (2005). Desperately seeking the global subject: International education, citizenship and cosmopolitanism. *Globalisation, Societies and Education, 3*(1), 49–66.

Ong, A. (1999). *Flexible citizenship: The cultural logics of transnationality.* Durham, NC: Duke University Press.

Phan, L. H. (2009). English as an international language: International student and identity formation. *Language and Intercultural Communication, 9*(3), 201–214.

Sawir, E., Marginson, S., Deumert, A., Nyland, C., and Ramia, G. (2008). Loneliness and international students: An Australian study. *Journal of Studies in International Education, 12*(2), 148–180.

Suhara, S. (1996). *Ajiajin ryūgakusei no kabe [Barriers for Asian international students].* Tokyo, Japan: Nihon hōsō shuppan kyōkai.

Takeda, S. (2006). *Nihon no ryūgakusei seisaku no rekishiteki suii: Taigai enjo kara chikyū shimin keisei e [Historical transition of the roles of Japan's international education policy: From foreign aid to global citizenship]* (pp. 77–88). Tokyo: Nihon University, Graduate School of Social and Cultural Studies.

Tsuboya, M. (2008). *"Eizokuteki sojonā" chūgokujin no aidenthithī: Chūgoku karano nihon ryūgaku ni miru kokusai imin sisutemu [The identities of the "permanent sojourner" Chinese: International migration system observed in the student flow from China to Japan].* Tokyo, Japan: Yūshindō.

Tsuboya, M. (2010). "Eizokuteki sojonā" toshite no chūgokujin ryūgakusei: 1980 nendai no "ryūgaku būmu" kara shin sedai no shutsugen e [Chinese international students as "permanent sojourners": The shift from the study abroad boom in the 1980s to the emergence of a new generation]. *Chūgoku 21, 33*, 137–154.

Tsuneyoshi, R. (2005). Internationalization strategies in Japan: The dilemmas and possibilities of study abroad programs using English. *Journal of Research in International Education, 4*(1), 65–86.

Waters, J. L. (2006a). Emergent geographies of international education and social exclusion. *Globalisation, Societies and Education, 38*(5), 1046–1068.

Waters, J. L. (2006b). Geographies of cultural capital: Education, international migration and family strategies between Hong Kong and Canada. *Transactions of the Institute of British Geographers, 31*(2), 179–192.

Waters, J. L. (2009). In pursuit of scarcity: Transnational students, "employability," and the MBA. *Environment and Planning A, 41*(8), 1865–1883.

Yin, R. K. (2003). *Case study research: Design and methods* (3rd ed.). Thousand Oaks, CA: Sage.

3

LEARNING CHINESE AS A HERITAGE LANGUAGE BY TWO MULTILINGUAL YOUTHS IN INDONESIA

Anita Lie

The Chinese in Indonesia have become the subject of numerous research studies. Most of these studies investigate the political, economic and social aspects of the Chinese population (Giblin, 2003; Hoon, 2006, 2008; Wibowo, 1999; Coppel, 2012; Mahfud, 2013; Sai and Hoon, 2013). In addition, Dawis (2008) studied the education of Chinese Indonesians during the post-Suharto era, Oetomo (1987) explored the language and identity of the Chinese in the town of Pasuruan during the Suharto administration, and Kuntjara (2009) specifically examined the hybrid language and culture of four Chinese Indonesian women in Surabaya.

The lives of the Chinese Indonesians have been marked by their struggle to survive and to adjust to the local life while having to make political decisions about whether to maintain their own Chinese tradition—including the language—in the new land, or to abandon it and embrace the new cultures or blend their Chinese culture with the local cultures. As is widely reported, President Suharto engineered political, legal, and cultural discrimination towards the Chinese during his 32 years of authoritarian rule and made them an easy target of racial and class violence. In 1966, the Suharto administration closed all Chinese-medium schools. Between 1966 and 1998, the regime's assimilationist policy to solve the so-called "Chinese problem" banned Chinese printed media and any public expression of Chinese religious beliefs and culture, as well as suspended diplomatic ties with China (Giblin, 2003; Hoon, 2006, 2008; Wibowo, 1999; Coppel, 2012; Mahfud, 2013; Sai and Hoon, 2013).

As a result, the younger Chinese Indonesians were publicly deprived of the opportunity to maintain their cultural heritage during the Suharto administration. Chinese names had to be legally changed into Indonesian names. Somehow, some of the Chinese managed to cling to their Chinese ancestry by maintaining their cultural identity as Chinese in the private spheres of close friends and relatives.

48 Anita Lie

Children were called by their Indonesian names in schools and adults had their Indonesian names on their ID cards while families, friends and relatives continued to call them by their Chinese names. In those personal circles, kinship terms such as 大哥, 大姐, 小弟, 小妹, 叔叔, 阿姨 (big brother, big sister, little brother, little sister, uncle, and aunty) were still used.

Following the May 1998 anti-Chinese riots and the dramatic political reform after President Suharto was toppled, discourses of multiculturalism have circulated among academics and social activists. Along that line of progress, the Chinese in Indonesia have gradually emerged from the political backstage and enjoyed the freedom from the Suharto regime's pressure to assimilate this minority into the national norms. Part of this freedom includes the opportunity to explore their Chinese heritage and identity for which the Chinese of Indonesia feel indebted to President Abdurrahman Wahid who made friendly gestures towards the minority group including the lift on the 1978 official ban on Chinese language use. Since then, a revival of Chinese language and culture has emerged among Chinese Indonesians. Chinese-language media and publications have been widely circulated even though many Chinese Indonesians—particularly those who were born and grew up during Suharto's era—no longer speak or read Chinese (Hoon, 2006). Chinese-medium schools and after-school Chinese language courses have opened and been flooded with children and youths. After 1998, parents have sent their high-school and college graduating children to study in China.

Currently, while the doors to rediscover the Chinese cultural heritage and learn the language have been widely opened, the young Indonesians are also experiencing massive Western influence through popular sociocultural icons. Moreover, English has been taught as a foreign language in the formal curriculum in Grades 7 through 12 as well as at the university level. Many private schools have added English in their curriculum as early as pre-kindergarten. Furthermore, English-medium formal schools and after-school English courses have been flourishing and attracting children of the middle-class families, including the Chinese Indonesians. English has gained an increasing popularity to be used as a language of prestige particularly among the young middle class. Therefore, families have to make decisions in which additional language(s) their children should invest their time and energy. These decisions in the language learning investment differ between the older and younger generations. While the older Chinese see the investment as cultural needs, the younger learners' investment is based more on instrumental purposes in the context of global competitions between the superpowers of the West and China rather than on cultural needs. Some of the Chinese who decided to abandon their cultural heritage during the repressive Suharto administration and some indigenous Indonesians have also jumped into the bandwagon of learning Chinese hoping that the investment would eventually lead to better job and business prospects in the future.

As a Chinese descent who grew up during the repressive regime of Suharto, I was deprived of the opportunity to learn Chinese as my heritage language and am now delighted to see the revived interest in learning Chinese among the young people. My experience has prompted me to study the learning of Chinese by younger Chinese Indonesians. It is interesting to investigate how the young Chinese Indonesians grab the opportunity to learn their heritage language currently and how they struggle to master the language. This research focuses on Chinese-heritage language (CHL) learning by two multilingual youths. In addition to Indonesian (the national language), Javanese (the local language), and English, these youths used Chinese with their parent and grandparents. This study explores the intergenerational literacy practices in a family of Chinese descent and the relationship of cultural identity and heritage language learning as well as the emotional needs involved in learning CHL.

Theoretical Framework

This research is informed by the sociocultural approach and previous research on Chinese Indonesians. The sociocultural approach to literacy that has built up the conceptual framework of this research is that "literacy is a social practice which has many specific manifestations" (Cairney and Ruge, 1998, p. 8). The social practices are integrated within specific literacy events. Literacy events build up literacy practices of a particular group. To understand literacy fully, therefore, we need to understand the groups and institutions engaging in specific literacy practices (Au, 1995; Gee, 1990). As a number of researchers have indicated, literacy practices are culturally defined and continuously negotiated through the interactions of students and teachers at school and of family members at home (Li, 2006; Cairney, 2009). On a different note, Norton (2012) argues to distinguish investment from motivation to capture the complex relationship of language learners to the target language and their sometimes ambivalent desire to speak it. The notion of investment conceives of the language learner, not as a historical and unidimensional product, but as having a complex social history and multiple desires.

In this study, intergenerational literacy practices were identified through the manifold literacy events engaged in by and for the two multilingual youths within their family circles. Families can be understood as sociocultural spheres in which opportunities for literacy learning are created through resources and experiences, members' literate behaviors and achievements are recognized and celebrated through literacy events, and the models of literacy are demonstrated by the more literate members of the family. As Hannon (1995, p. 104) suggests, "The family's literacy values and practices will shape the course of the child's literacy development in terms of the opportunities, recognition, interaction and models available to them." Research into family literacy practices across cultural groups, then, has the potential to contribute a great deal to our understanding of the relationship between literacy practices at home and the transformation of cultural identity in CHL learning.

50 Anita Lie

Furthermore, Hoon (2008) presents the identity of the Chinese in post-Suharto Indonesia from historical, cultural, and political perspectives and dedicates a small section on the Chinese-language education as idealism or pragmatism. He quotes Kusuma who estimated that "there were more than three million people learning Mandarin in Indonesia." Dawis (2008) puts forward the burgeoning development of Chinese-medium schools and language centers in the post-Suharto era.

There has not been any documented study specifically dedicated to the learning of CHL taking place in Indonesia. Studies on CHL learning in other countries happen to have participants originating from Indonesia. Mu (2015) studies Chinese Australians' learning of Chinese and one of his participants, Adam, was born in Indonesia, moved to Australia at the age of 12 and lived in Singapore for a year on an exchange program. Adam was growing up during the Suharto era and thus learning Chinese was almost impossible. Similarly, in Duff and Li's study (2014), one of the participants was a student who had been denied his opportunity to learn Chinese during his youth in Indonesia and found his inability to speak Chinese interfered with his Chineseness. These two studies confirm the challenges of learning CHL prior to the end of Suharto administration.

Method

The Participants

The two participants were brother and sister Zeth (16 years old) and Lea (13 years old). They were both ethnically Chinese and grew up in a middle-class family who highly valued their Chinese heritage. Their mother invested in sending them to a more costly trilingual school—Xin Zhong (新中三语学校), that was founded in 2004 by a group of former teachers and alumni of the old Xin Zhong School. The school used Indonesian, English, and Chinese, which was the most predominant language of instruction. Indonesian is used in Indonesian language class and history; English is used in science classes; Chinese is used in civics and character education. The school board hired several native speaker teachers from Guangdong, China. Zeth and Lea spoke Chinese with the Chinese teachers, English with their Indonesian teachers, mostly Indonesian with their schoolmates. When they were in Grade 5 at Xin Zhong School, they took the Youth Chinese Test (YCT) Level 4 and the Intermediate Level of the Speaking Test. The YCT is an international standardized test of Chinese language proficiency for young international learners. Zeth's total written test score of listening, reading, and writing was 211 and his speaking score was 81 while Lea's total score was 264 and her speaking score was 75.[1]

After completing elementary school, Zeth and Lea continued to a national high school where the language of instruction is Indonesian. At the time of the interview, Zeth was in Grade 11 and Lea in Grade 8. They attended English class five to six hours a week and Chinese only three hours a week in school. English is part of the formal national curriculum but Chinese is extra content added by the school as their local curriculum.

The two youths lived with their mother in a house adjacent to that of their grandparents. At home they talked with their mother in English, Indonesian, or Chinese and mostly Chinese with their grandparents. In addition, ever since they were in kindergarten, each of them had separately been taking one hour of Chinese lessons per week with their grandmother who was a Chinese teacher at an elementary school and a junior high school from 1957 to 1962.

Data Collection

I have known the family well and visited them occasionally since 2004. The data for this study were drawn from observations, field notes, and family interactions from 2014 through 2016. The methods for the data collection were triangulated to reduce any bias on the part of the researcher. I visited the family a few times in a year. In January 2016, I conveyed my formal research intention to the family and obtained their written consent. The visits were conducted on a weekly basis from January through March 2016 with a one-week break in early March due to their mid-term exams. The ten-session interviews with the two participants— accompanied by their mother—were conducted over dinner on weekends. Each meeting lasted for 90 to 120 minutes. To verify the results of interviews with the two youths, I also conducted two interviews with the mother and both grandparents at their home while the children were in school.

Semi-structured interviews were conducted in English and Indonesian because my proficiency in Chinese is very limited. I allowed them to express themselves in any language in which they felt comfortable. Both participants opted to use English and Indonesian. The mother and grandmother assisted me in translating and interpreting Chinese into Indonesian. The interview questions concerned their experiences and feelings of learning CHL. The interviews were audio-recorded.

Data Analysis

Data in this study came primarily from observations that were recorded in fieldnotes and interviews that were audio-recorded, transcribed, and analyzed for themes related to the research questions. Each interview and family interaction was analyzed for meaningful units, which were then grouped and coded into conceptual categories, with an emphasis on the qualitative description of how and when Chinese-heritage learners alternated the three languages (Chinese, English, and Indonesian), how their linguistic choices revealed their ethno-linguistic and cultural identities, and how they overcame their emotional needs. This study focuses on particular recurring patterns of language use and practices

52 Anita Lie

and investigates the connection of the particulars to larger cultural patterns and to their ethnic identities (Erickson, 1996).

The particulars that I saw in the family literacy practices of CHL learning were experiences I never had in my own family. Yet, as a researcher of Chinese descent living in Indonesia, I shared the same historical and political experiences as the family and so was able to see the larger cultural patterns that this family was a part of. I was a few years older than the participants' mother. The mother and I belonged to the generation who was deprived of the opportunity to learn CHL. Yet, due to the grandparents' perseverance in maintaining their cultural heritage and capacity as former teachers of Chinese, the mother could speak Chinese at a functional level. This made her an outlier in our generation and enabled her to play a significant role as a bridge between two generations in the inter-generational literacy practices in her family. She also helped me a great deal by explaining the literacy practices provided for her children by the grandparents. On the other hand, my inability to speak Chinese well and deprivation of the experiences of CHL learning positioned me to analyze the data as an outsider and to group the data into the conceptual categories that led to the findings.

Results

Intergenerational Literacy Practices and the Learners' Cultural Identity Formation

The intergenerational literacy practices were shaped in this family through modelling and valuing, creating literacy events, and recognizing the learners' achievements (Hannon, 1995; Cairney and Ruge, 1998). Both Zeth and Lea had talked to their grandparents in Chinese since they were very young. At home, the grandparents attempted to model literate behaviors; sometimes, the grandfather took the effort to translate complex notions or concepts into Indonesian whenever he thought they needed it. They also shared Chinese folk tales. Both grandparents highly valued their Chinese cultural heritage and hoped their grandchildren would maintain this. The grandfather was actively involved as a senior leader in the Hainanese community in Surabaya.

The family subscribed to *Qiandao Ribao* (千岛日报), the Chinese daily newspaper and had access to China Central Television (CCTV). Zeth and Lea read the paper only occasionally, especially when their grandmother assigned them to. They used to watch cartoon series on CCTV, but at the time of the interview they felt they had outgrown the existing programs on CCTV. They also used books from the Singapore National Academy (SNA) where another granddaughter was studying. When the kids were still in the Chinese-medium elementary school, they used to review their homework with their grandmother almost every day.

A typical weekly lesson observed during this study was asking the participants to read a passage taken from the SNA course-book, then discussing the passage and answering questions about it. The grandmother then explained the new vocabulary, sentence patterns in the passage, and idiomatic expression. The lesson tended to focus on discrete linguistic features. Towards the end of the lesson, the grandmother read the Chinese Holy Bible and pointed out the wise verses. The grandmother expressed concerns over the challenges of delivering the lessons:

> They are both busy with homework and extracurricular from school. So I have to give in and postpone the lessons. Perhaps, they also get bored with learning Chinese. We don't have enough reading materials that are appealing to Zeth and Lea.
>
> (Personal communication, March 12, 2016)

Responding to the grandmother's concerns, the mother commented that the grandmother had managed to make them write numerous short paragraphs (brief essays) and showed me a big folder of the kids' published essays in the *Qiandao Ribao* (see a sample in Appendix A and B).

Both grandparents invested significantly in these two teenagers' heritage language learning by playing the role of teachers in the family. The mother showed her appreciation that both her parents were involved in their different ways:

> Nai-nai usually teaches them the grammar, vocabulary, and pronunciation and Ye-ye likes to tell them stories, folk tales, historical events, moral lessons, and the cultural wisdom.
>
> (Personal communication, March 12, 2016)

In this sense, the grandmother was more concerned with teaching them discrete linguistic units while the grandfather delivered a whole-language approach by passing on the historical and cultural context of the language.

In the meantime, the mother, who said that her Chinese proficiency was far below her children's—and yet whose Chinese proficiency was still much better than that of her peers—supported the heritage language learning in the best way she could by participating in the family conversations conducted in Chinese and motivating the children to persevere in learning Chinese. She expressed her determination:

> We are the lost generation because of Suharto. I want to make sure my kids can speak Chinese, not like us. It's hard to claim ourselves as Chinese if we don't even speak the language.
>
> (Personal communication, March 12, 2016)

Furthermore, she also served as a bridge between grandparents and grandchildren. She played the role of a mediator both ways. When Zeth and Lea were reluctant to take Chinese lessons, she motivated them to continue learning. On the other hand, there were also times that the grandmother felt frustrated and doubted whether her teaching was worthwhile.

> Sometimes my mom feels frustrated to see the kids unmotivated and once said about giving up the lessons. I then persuaded her to be patient and continue the lessons. I told her "the kids need you."
>
> (Personal communication, March 12, 2016)

She motivated her mother to bear the toil of teaching difficult Chinese lessons to teenagers who were yet to find the immediate relevance of the language in their lives.

The family also created special literacy events to perk up the daily literacy practices. In 2011, they took Zeth, Lea, and their mother to Hainan to visit relatives so "the kids could practice their Chinese, get to know relatives, and learn their roots" (Grandfather, personal communication, February 24, 2016). Zeth and Lea had the chance to speak more Chinese then but felt a bit nervous because they were afraid that their Chinese proficiency was not good enough. They loved the trip and enjoyed the attention from relatives in Hainan.

Another literacy event was the grandparents' 50th wedding anniversary celebration in 2010. All ten grandchildren performed in Chinese on stage either individually or collectively. Similarly, in November 2015, the big family celebrated the grandfather's 80th birthday with friends and relatives. The evening was a festive celebration and showcase of their Chinese cultural identity. All the grandchildren sang, danced, and shared the highlights of their experiences with their grandfather in Chinese. One granddaughter who was studying in the U.S. got to say her words of appreciation and birthday wish in fluent and excellent Chinese on Skype. While the grandchildren performed on stage to entertain the grandparents on those two occasions, the six children—all speaking Chinese—organized the program and event. They prepared their children well for those two events and made sure every one of them did their best on stage.

These two parties, along with the weekly lessons, family gatherings and interactions, Chinese language competitions, and the trip to Hainan, were literacy events, which as Cairney (2009) and Hannon (1995) define, shaped literacy practices across three generations in this family. The intergenerational literacy practices that were maintained purposively in their daily lives all those years were showcased among relatives and close friends during the wedding anniversary and the 80th birthday celebration. When asked how they felt, Zeth said, "I feel happy when I recollect about my grandpa's birthday." Lea said, "I think it's nerve-wrecking but it was fun. I was so touched by my grandpa's birthday celebration."

Achievements were recognized and shared in this family. Both grandparents and mother were proud of Zeth's and Lea's achievements as Chinese-heritage learners. Zeth and Lea won numerous Chinese language competitions. A couple of award certificates were displayed in the family living room and the rest were filed neatly in plastic folders as treasures.

The intergenerational literacy practices in which Zeth and Lea were engaged helped form their cultural identity as young Chinese Indonesians. When asked whether they saw themselves more as Chinese or as Indonesian, Zeth responded without any hesitation:

> I am Chinese because I was born Chinese. I look Chinese and my character is Chinese. I make friends with non-Chinese in school and at church. I get along well with them but I am definitely Chinese. I am proud to be Chinese. That's why I want to speak Chinese the best I could.
>
> (Zeth, personal communication, February 27, 2016)

And Lea associated her Chinese identity with her ability to speak Chinese as perceived by others:

> I am Chinese because my friends say so. Sometimes they make jokes about me being Chinese—my slanting eyes and fair skin. But I don't feel insulted by their jokes. We're friends. They also make jokes about me being Chinese because of my ability in speaking Chinese fluently. When the Chinese teacher talked to me in Chinese and I responded to her, my friends were all impressed even though it was just a very simple conversation. They were exaggerating when they said I was smart because I'm Chinese. Yet, I am proud, anyway.
>
> (Lea, personal communication, February 27, 2016)

The learning of CHL at home bore fruit in their above-average Chinese proficiency and this result helped the two participants affirm their cultural identity. This finding is consistent with those in previous studies that speaking a language helps shape cultural identity (Oetomo, 1987; Kuntjara, 2009; Norton, 2012). The relationship between heritage language learning and cultural identity formation works both ways (Cairney, 2009; Norton, 2012). The intergenerational literacy practices and investment in learning Chinese as a heritage language instilled in the two teenagers a sense of pride in their Chinese identity. Zeth and Lea were privileged to be growing up in an era of opportunities to reclaim the cultural identity by learning the heritage language.

Learners' Linguistic and Language Environment Challenges

The participants used the simplified version of Chinese. Lea thought—and this was affirmed by her mother—that her Chinese was as good as her English but Zeth thought that he was more proficient in English than in Chinese. Lea also

56 Anita Lie

demonstrated more enthusiasm as a Chinese-heritage learner; she was more studious and eager in doing the lessons with the grandmother, while Zeth sometimes expressed his reluctance and requested postponement of the lessons. In spite of the opportunities, however, these two teenagers faced linguistic challenges and language environment issues in learning CHL. Both Zeth and Lea agreed that linguistically Chinese was very difficult to learn. Zeth said, "Chinese is a difficult language. For instance, 长 [*chang*] can mean either long or growing depending on the pronunciation." Lea agreed to this and added, "Another difficulty is the idiomatic expression. Like *man tou da han* [满头大汗], which has multiple meanings."

The materials they learned did not correspond with the daily life topics they talked about. Lea said, "I never have the chance to say those idioms because it would sound funny." The connection between reading-writing and oracy development in Chinese remains an issue in the case of Zeth and Lea as they faced a shortage of relevant reading materials.

In addition to linguistic difficulties, learning a heritage language also posits a few language environment issues. The two participants would rather use English than Chinese. Zeth said that "everything sounds better in English." Lea nodded to that agreeably. The first challenge was to find the right circle of interlocutors to use the language with. The investment in Chinese acquisition at home and during their elementary school years had positioned Zeth and Lea far ahead in their Chinese proficiency of their peers in their current national school. Lea said that the Chinese instruction in her Grade 8 class was like her Grade 2 level. Her teacher noticed Lea's outstanding proficiency among her peers and spoke Chinese to her more intensively than to her classmates. Lea's friends disliked learning Chinese in school because the language was too hard to learn. Zeth and Lea felt proud that they could speak Chinese relatively well compared with their peers. Yet, this situation also prevented them from using this language in a natural setting with their peers.

The different proficiency levels between the two participants and their peers was not the only reason that they did not use the language in daily conversations in school. They recollected that even when they were still at Xin Zhong elementary school, they used Chinese only in the Chinese classrooms and with their Chinese teachers. Outside the classrooms, they spoke Indonesian with their schoolmates.

The big family gathered weekly and so both participants got to see their cousins. All the cousins were able to speak Chinese in varying levels of proficiency; two of them spoke Chinese at a higher proficiency level than Zeth and Lea did. It is interesting to note, however, that they were more keen on speaking Indonesian or English with their cousins.

So when and to whom did these two youths use Chinese? They used Chinese during the lessons and in conversations with their grandparents, their older relatives, or the grandparents' friends. The discourses then were limited to the here-and-now and daily activities topics. Grandma's formal teaching of classical idioms was not applicable in these daily conversation. Zeth said, "it sounds weird if I say what I learn from Nai-nai and the books. It's just too old-fashioned."

The forming of the two teenagers' cultural identity as well as their heritage language acquisition process intersected with age. When talking with adult speakers of Chinese, the limited shared interests due to the generation gap hindered extended communication beyond the daily activities and so further impeded vocabulary development in the heritage language. Yet, they felt reluctant to speak Chinese with interlocutors of their age group because they were not able to speak—in Lea's words—"something deep" in Chinese because of their peers' limited vocabulary.

When probed further to elaborate on their *everything-sounds-better-in-English* code, the second language environment issue was revealed. Zeth said, "I feel so distanced when speaking Chinese and can't find the right words. Easier to express myself in English." In their multilingual situations, the prevailing pop culture played a significant role in their choice of preferred language. "When they were younger, they used to love the Chinese cartoon such as *Xi Yang Yang* 喜羊羊 [*The Happy Sheep*] on CCTV. Now that they were in their teenage years, there's no more interesting program for them on CCTV" (Mother, personal communication, January 16, 2016). In their spare time, Zeth and Lea would rather watch English than Chinese movies. They both loved to play Japanese Visual Novels games with English subtitles. To their understanding, China had never released such appealing games.

In addition, the choice of a preferred language was also influenced by the dominant language use on the internet. Lea used English to connect with friends on social media. She has international friends from the U.S., Australia, and Malaysia in her Facebook, Instagram, and Path networks. She did not have any Chinese-speaking friends with whom she could connect virtually and had not invested in finding them.

The two CHL learners faced linguistic and language environment challenges in their process of forming their cultural identity and learning the language. The linguistic challenges related to the nature of the language and the dearth of relevant reading materials. The language environment challenges pertained to the prevailing pop culture and internet communication, which significantly affected teenagers' preferences of their language.

Learners' Psychological and Emotional Needs

The learners' emotional needs relate to their sense of affiliation, frustration, and boredom. Zeth did not think that Chinese proficiency was important in his life at the moment but believed that his ability to speak Chinese would be rewarding in the future. Lea said, "China economy is progressing faster than the rest of the world so I understand why Nai-nai and Mama push us to learn Chinese well."

58 Anita Lie

Both children realized that their Chinese was still not good enough and they needed to work harder to close the gap between their current proficiency level and what is required to function well in global competition in the future. Yet, Zeth and Lea felt reluctant to speak Chinese with their peers. Zeth loved hanging around with his friends and cousins and he could not bear the sense of distance with them when he spoke Chinese. His need of affiliation with his peers who did not feel comfortable speaking Chinese got in the way of his learning progress. He said "if I speak Chinese, I can't connect with my friends. They won't understand me. And besides, I can't say things in Chinese like in English."

Lea had mixed feelings about her Chinese proficiency. "I feel proud and happy that I can speak Chinese pretty well compared with my friends but I think they were exaggerating when they said my Chinese is good." She added, "I better not speak Chinese with my friends because they won't understand me and I don't want to be different." As teenagers, both participants dreaded the sense of dissociation with their peers. It is unfortunate that they cope with the need to affiliate with their peers by toning down their use of Chinese in conversation.

Zeth and Lea occasionally felt frustrated and bored with learning Chinese. Other than the future potential benefits, they did not have immediate incentive to maintain their investment in learning Chinese. Occasionally they skipped the Chinese lessons with their grandma because of demanding homework from school. After a one- or two-week break, most of the time it was their mother who made them have the lessons again.

Discussion

Learning Chinese as a Heritage Language and Forming Cultural Identity

Figure 3.1 sums up the interplay between learning CHL and the forming of cultural identity within the socio-cultural-political context in Indonesia. Living in an era of democracy in the making with changing socio-cultural-political forces, the two participants were privileged to have the opportunities to enhance their cultural identity by and through learning their heritage language as well as to continue their language learning as expected of them within their family literacy practices.

The forming of the two teenagers' cultural identity as CHL learners as well as their heritage language acquisition process found the impetus in the fact that they were ethnically Chinese and growing up in a family who highly valued their Chinese heritage. This process was further enabled through the family investment in their literacy practices. The investment was made possible by their middle-class capacity as a Chinese family. Their ethnicity, social class, and family literacy practices enabled them to learn CHL. Yet, their linguistic and language environment challenges were not susceptible of an easy solution in their language learning process. As learners, both participants did not have the appropriate media,

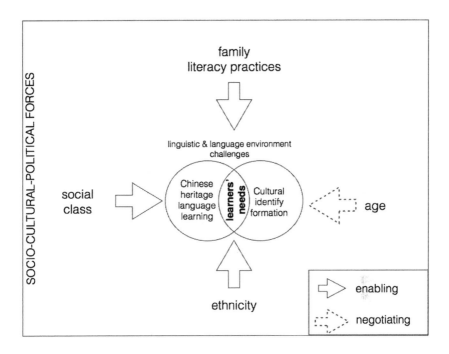

FIGURE 3.1 The interplay between learning Chinese as a heritage language and the forming of cultural identity

forum, and network of fellow learners to practice their Chinese because they were enrolled in a national school that burdened them with homework and tests. Outside school, they interacted with cousins—with whom they would not speak Chinese for reasons explained above—and church friends, most of whom did not speak Chinese. As a matter of fact, the process would remain a continuous negotiation as their heritage language learning was nuanced by their age identity, including all the implications of becoming teenagers. The age factor positioned the two participants to negotiate their CHL learning and cultural identity formation. They continuously negotiated to postpone the lessons with grandma, to choose situations where they would rather speak Indonesian or English, and to avoid opportunities to practice their CHL.

Pedagogical Implications

Based on the findings, this study put forward three implications for practitioners in the field of heritage language learning. First, family literacy practices could drive investment in heritage language learning and help the process by exposing the learners to rich learning environments and establishing a sense of cultural identity. However, the learners' motivations (and the mentors' as well) are not

60 Anita Lie

static as they embark on an uphill journey of maintaining their heritage language. As the learners mature, they will develop different interests and multiple desires as to what and how they like to learn. This may lead to boredom with the same old lessons. Therefore, it would be helpful to create age-relevant learning environments. Practitioners might want to organize out-of-class activities such as field trips to provide rich language environments for learners to practice their CHL. Second, Generation Z (those born after the turn of this century) is exposed to the internet and virtual communication that is heavily loaded with the pop culture of the West. Naturally, this exposure provides inevitable learning media and environments that may work against the heritage language learning. Taking advantage of the internet would help educators find more age-appropriate learning materials by connecting and sharing with other teachers of CHL. Third, to use the heritage language more in a natural setting, the learners need to have other interlocutors of their age group so they can interact based on common life experiences and interests as children, teenagers, or adults. Families that are committed to CHL learning may want to form associations or forums to provide opportunities for the children to meet, interact, and use their CHL in natural environments.

Conclusion

Extending the previous studies on language learning and identity (Oetomo, 1987; Norton, 2012), this study explored the complex interplay between the learning of CHL by two teenagers and the formation of their cultural identity by examining how their CHL learning led them to construct their identity as well as how their constructed identity affected their heritage language learning. The two teenagers were still negotiating their heritage language learning and cultural identity transformation along with their age. As teenagers, they faced the dilemma of distancing themselves from their peers when speaking Chinese or maintaining their investment in learning the heritage language.

Adolescent CHL learners like Zeth and Lea are still considered as outliers compared to their peers. Although 3 million learners of Mandarin were reported in Indonesia (Hoon, 2008), this number is very small in a country with a population of over 255 million. The Indonesian government had decided on English as the only foreign language in the official core curriculum. This curriculum policy has put approximately 94 million people as learners of English in view of the fact that people under 20 years old comprise 37% of the total Indonesian population (www.bps.go.id/linkTabelStatis/view/id/1532). In the context of global contestations between the superpowers of the West and China, families have to make decisions in which additional language(s) they should invest in for their children. While some of the older Chinese see CHL learning as a cultural need, the younger learners' motivation in learning Chinese is based more on instrumental purposes for better job and business prospects in the future.

The increasing importance of China in trade relations with Indonesia would create higher demand for young people with Chinese proficiency as well as more conducive language environment for learning CHL. This prospect would provide impetus for further investment in CHL learning. In light of the linguistic challenges in learning Chinese and the predominant use of English, however, it takes more than families' decisions to proliferate the Chinese language learners in Indonesia. English has gained its importance in the world today partly because organizations such as the British Council, USAID, Fulbright, and the former USIS managed to promote the language and culture through their massive investments as part of their diplomacy agenda after the era of Western colonization. By the same token, China has started promoting its higher education in Indonesia in the past decade and sponsoring roots-seeking summer/winter programs for children and youth of the Chinese diaspora. More massive, strategic, and comprehensive plans are needed to promote CHL learning and propel Chinese as an alternative foreign language in the curriculum.

The results and insights of this study are expected to contribute to our understanding of Chinese-heritage learners in Southeast Asia, particularly in Indonesia. Some caveats need to be given. First, the researcher's very limited Chinese proficiency might have hindered the collection and interpretation of the data pertaining to the participants' heritage language use. Second, the findings of this study are not generalizable to other groups of heritage language learners. For future research, it would be valuable to study the family–school connection in CHL learning in different age groups. It would be worthy to explore how school and family can support each other by accommodating specific needs of a particular age group and creating age-appropriate learning activities and materials. It would also be strategically beneficial to study curriculum policies and possibilities of promoting Chinese language in the official curriculum.

Note

1 The passing score of Level 4 YCT is 180. "Test takers who are able to pass the YCT (Level IV) can communicate in Chinese at a basic level in their daily, academic and professional lives. When travelling in China, they can manage most forms of communication in Chinese." http://english.hanban.org/node_8001.htm.

References

Au, K. (1995). Multicultural perspectives on literacy research. *Journal of Reading Behavior*, *27*(1), 85–100.

Badan Pusat Statistik (2016, September 29). *Persentase penduduk berumur 5 tahun ke atas menurut golongan umur, daerah tempat tinggal, dan partisipasi sekolah, 2000–2014* [Percentage of residents aged 5 and above based on age groups, areas of residence, and school enrollments, 2000–2014]. Retrieved from www.bps.go.id/linkTabelStatis/view/id/1532.

Cairney, T. (2009). Home literacy practices and mainstream schooling: A theoretical understanding of the field. In G. Li (Ed.), *Multicultural families, home literacies, and mainstream schooling* (pp. 3–24). Charlotte, NC: Information Age Publishing.

Cairney, T. H., and Ruge, J. (1998). *Community literacy practices and schooling: Towards effective support for students.* Final summary report to Federal Department of Education Training and Youth Affairs, Canberra, Australia. Retrieved from http://trevorcairney.com/wp-content/uploads/2012/11/cgi-lib.5818.1.CLP_.pdf.

Coppel, C. (2012). Chinese overseas: The particular and the general. *Journal of Chinese Overseas, 8*, 1–10.

Dawis, A. (2008). Chinese education in Indonesia: Developments in the post-1998 era. In L. Suryadinata (Ed.), *Ethnic Chinese in contemporary Indonesia* (pp. 75–96). Singapore: Institute of Southeast Asian Studies.

Duff, P., and Li, D. (2014). Rethinking heritage languages: Ideologies, identities, practices, and priorities in Canada and China. In P.P. Trifonas and T. Aravossitas (Eds.), *Rethinking heritage language education* (pp. 45–65). Cambridge, UK: Cambridge University Press.

Erickson, F. (1996). Ethnographic microanalysis. In S. McKay and N. Hornberger (Eds.), *Sociolinguistics and language teaching* (pp. 283–306). New York, NY: Cambridge University Press.

Gee, J. (1990). *Social linguistics and literacies: Ideology in discourses.* London, UK: The Falmer Press.

Giblin, S. (2003). Overcoming stereotypes? Chinese Indonesian civil society groups in post-Suharto Indonesia. *Asian Ethnicity, 4*(3), 353–368.

Hannon, P. (1995). *Literacy, home, and school: Research and practice in teaching literacy with parents.* London, UK: The Falmer Press.

Hoon, C.-Y. (2006). Assimilation, multiculturalism, hybridity: The dilemmas of the ethnic Chinese in post-Suharto Indonesia. *Asian Ethnicity, 7*(2), 149–166.

Hoon, C.-Y. (2008). *Chinese identity in post-Suharto Indonesia: Culture, politics, and media.* Brighton, UK: Sussex Academic Press.

Kuntjara, E. (2009). *Women and politeness: The hybrid language and culture of Chinese Indonesian women in Surabaya.* Saarbrücken, Germany: VDM Publishing.

Li, G. (2006). *Culturally contested pedagogy: Battles of literacy and schooling between mainstream teachers and Asian immigrant parents.* Albany, NY: State University of New York Press.

Mahfud, C. (2013). *Manifesto Politik Tionghoa di Indonesia* [Political Manifesto of the Chinese in Indonesia]. Yogyakarta, Indonesia: Pustaka Pelajar.

Mu, G. M. (2015). *Learning Chinese as a heritage language: An Australian perspective.* Bristol, UK: Multilingual Matters.

Norton, B. (2012). *Identity and language learning: Extending the conversation.* Bristol, UK: Multilingual Matters.

Oetomo, D. (1987). *The Chinese of Pasuruan: Their language and identity.* Department of Linguistics, Research School of Pacific Studies, the Australian National University.

Sai, S.-M. and Hoon, C.-Y. (2013). Introduction: A critical reassessment of Chinese Indonesian Studies. In S.-M. Sai and C.-Y. Hoon (Eds.), *Chinese Indonesians reassessed: History, religion and belonging* (pp. 1–26). London, UK: Routledge.

Wibowo, I. (1999). Introduction. In I. Wibowo (Ed.), *Retrospeksi dan rekontekstualisasi masalah Cina* [Retrospection and recontextualization of the Chinese problems] (pp. xv–xvi). Jakarta, Indonesia: PT Gramedia Pustaka Utama.

Appendix A

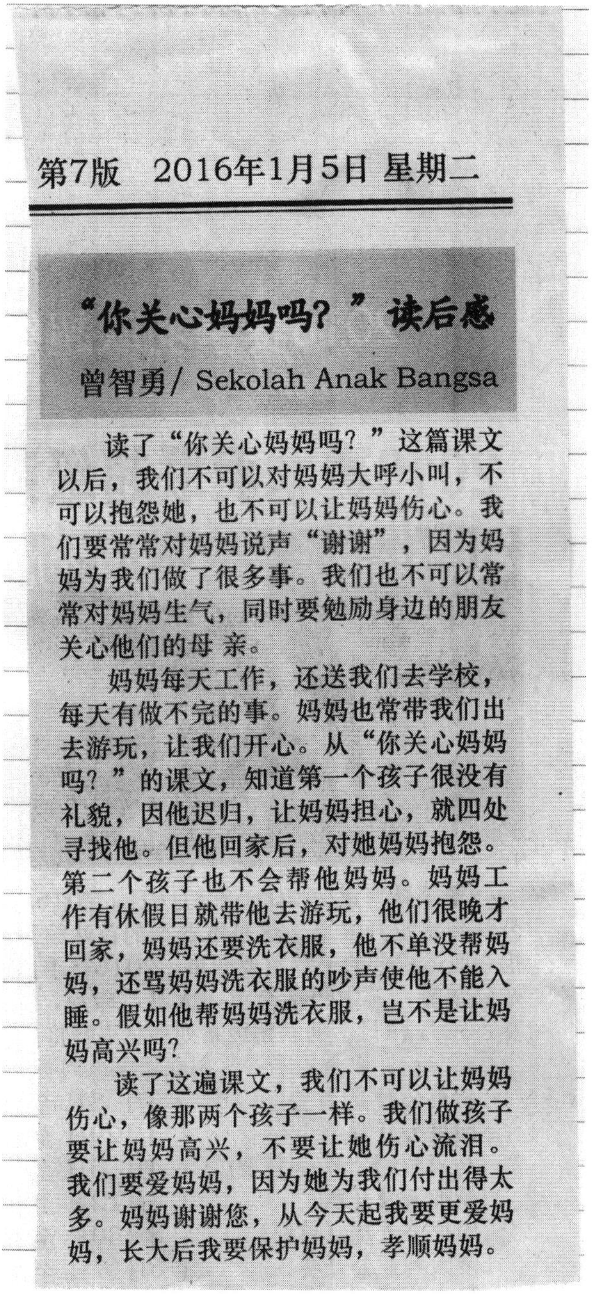

第7版　2016年1月5日 星期二

"你关心妈妈吗？"读后感

曾智勇／ Sekolah Anak Bangsa

读了"你关心妈妈吗？"这篇课文以后，我们不可以对妈妈大呼小叫，不可以抱怨她，也不可以让妈妈伤心。我们要常常对妈妈说声"谢谢"，因为妈妈为我们做了很多事。我们也不可以常常对妈妈生气，同时要勉励身边的朋友关心他们的母亲。

妈妈每天工作，还送我们去学校，每天有做不完的事。妈妈也常带我们出去游玩，让我们开心。从"你关心妈妈吗？"的课文，知道第一个孩子很没有礼貌，因他迟归，让妈妈担心，就四处寻找他。但他回家后，对她妈妈抱怨。第二个孩子也不会帮他妈妈。妈妈工作有休假日就带他去游玩，他们很晚才回家，妈妈还要洗衣服，他不单没帮妈妈，还骂妈妈洗衣服的吵声使他不能入睡。假如他帮妈妈洗衣服，岂不是让妈妈高兴吗？

读了这遍课文，我们不可以让妈妈伤心，像那两个孩子一样。我们做孩子要让妈妈高兴，不要让她伤心流泪。我们要爱妈妈，因为她为我们付出得太多。妈妈谢谢您，从今天起我要更爱妈妈，长大后我要保护妈妈，孝顺妈妈。

PHOTO 3.1 Zeth's published book review on *Caring for Mother*

64 Anita Lie

Appendix B

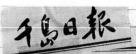

PHOTO 3.2 Lea's published report on her Singapore trip

Appendix C

Semi-Structured Interview Questions

For the participants:

Motivation and Investment

1. How important is Chinese proficiency in your life?
2. How important is English proficiency in your life?
3. How important is Indonesian proficiency in your life?
4. What do you think of young Indonesians who speak Chinese?
5. What do you think of young Indonesians who cannot speak Chinese?
6. Why is Chinese not important for you now?
7. Do you want your own children to speak Chinese in the future? Why? Who is going to teach them?

Literacy Practices and Challenges

1. Other than grandparents, who do you (would like to) speak Chinese to? When?
2. What are the challenges of learning Chinese?
3. What language(s) do you use to talk to your friends, cousins? Why?
4. Why do you prefer to use Indonesian or English with your cousins?

Psychological and Emotional Needs

1. How do you feel when speaking Chinese?
2. How do you feel when speaking English?
3. How do you feel when speaking Indonesian?
4. What is it like to be able to speak Chinese when you are among people who can speak the language?
5. What is it like to be able to speak Chinese when you are among your peers? When you speak Chinese, how do you feel (when your friends hear you speak Chinese)?
6. What do you like the most about being able to speak Chinese?

Language Use and Identity Formation

1. Do you see yourself as Chinese or Indonesian? Why?
2. Does that have anything to do with your ability to speak Chinese? Why? In what ways?
3. What do your friends see you? Why? Do you like that?

For Mother:

4. Why do you want your children to learn Chinese?
5. What are your expectations?
6. What are the challenges?
7. What efforts have you put into their learning of Chinese?
8. Are you happy with their progress?
9. Are you optimistic that they will meet your expectations?
10. What is your role in their Chinese learning?

For Grandparents:

11. What is your purpose of teaching them Chinese?
12. What are your expectations?
13. What are the challenges?
14. What outcomes do you see out of the Chinese lessons? Are you happy with their progress?
15. Are you optimistic that they will meet your expectations?

4

SPEAKING OR BEING CHINESE

The Case of South African-born Chinese[1]

Ke Yu and Elmé Vivier

Apartheid South Africa established race as the primary determinant of identity politically, economically, and socially. This racial identity in many cases reinforced ethnic groupings of those who share common ancestral experiences, homeland, cultural practices, and language, among other things. The Chinese in South Africa are no exception. Subject to discrimination and spatial segregation over the course of the twentieth century, the Chinese in the country exemplify an immigrant community's struggle to negotiate competing identities and demands for different language usage. In this chapter we trace the shifts in identity and language affiliations in the lived experiences of four South African-born Chinese (SABC).[2] The chapter draws on qualitative interview data from a study of Chinese communities in Pretoria, South Africa. Although the participants are all second-generation immigrants, their experiences extend over a lengthy historical period that includes the transformation of the South African apartheid context, and illuminate why Chinese identity and language ability may or may not have shifted during this time. We explore the relationship between language and identity through these shifts and their driving factors.

The chapter begins with a brief look at the literature on the relation between language and identity, followed by a historical review of the experiences of the earliest Chinese immigrants in South Africa. Thereafter we present the research methodology and a biographical summary of the four SABC. We then explore their perceptions around the meaning of identity and language practices through an analysis of four factors that shaped their environment: the context of reception; the organization of the Chinese community; socioeconomic needs; and family dynamics. We find great heterogeneity in their experiences of these four factors, resulting in varying degrees of affiliation with a Chinese identity. In the discussion section we elaborate on the implications of this for understanding the

68 Ke Yu and Elmé Vivier

language–identity link, and conclude that language is a flexible strategic resource for continuous identity construction as the individual interacts with dynamic situational forces.

The Language–Identity Nexus and the Immigrant Experience

Literature on the language and identity nexus is divided: one perspective denotes a strong link while the other takes a more situational view (although these should be seen to exist along a continuum). Some scholars consider the relationship between language and cultural identity to be interdependent and inseparable (Guardado, 2008; Fishman, 1991). Supporters of this view generally believe that language is more than a tool for communication and information exchange, being also a conditional marker of identity, closely linked with tradition and collective mythology (May, 2000). Every time one speaks a language, one is also organizing the sense of who one is and how one relates to the social world (Norton, 2000). In fact, the link between language and identity is believed to be so strong that language use alone is taken as sufficient to identify someone's membership in a given group (Kamwangamalu, 2007). This strong-link argument has also been used to advocate for the preservation of minority languages (May, 2000).

On the other hand, the situational view, as we will refer to it in this chapter, highlights the importance of examining particular historical and social contexts to understand identity and language use. Scholars taking this view claim that language and identity are not fixed and cannot be considered in isolation from social practices and membership (Miller, 2000; Phinney et al., 2001b). This perspective reverberates with the notion of social identity, taken up in disciplines from sociology to developmental and social psychology, which refers to "the idea that an individual's self-concept is derived, to some extent and in some sense, from the social relationships and social groups he or she participates in" (Brewer, 2001, p. 117). These groups (or identities) may be based on shared experiences, beliefs, traits, roles, interests and/or language, and are further subject to change over the course of a person's lifetime.

The complexity of the language–identity nexus especially comes to the fore in the context of immigrant and minority groups. On the one hand, language plays a central role in the process of culture and identity preservation among immigrants: mother tongue symbolizes origins, early memories, common ancestry, shared values, and beliefs. Thus, "retaining a native language is a crucial index of the preservation of cultural roots after immigration" (Sears et al., 2003, p. 427). On the other hand, linguistic adjustments are essential to the processes of adaptation and "fitting in" (Tannenbaum, 2005). For example, Tannenbaum (2005, p. 229) reports a positive relationship between host language proficiency and the immigrant's economic, academic, professional, and personal wellbeing. In this instance, language becomes a tool that provides the immigrant/minority individual with access to socioeconomic resources and additional social groups and roles. The situational view argues that these practically motivated shifts in language do not necessitate a shift in identity. Phinney (1998), for example, observes that many immigrants living in Europe often maintain a strong ethnic identity independent of language use.

At a macro-level, generational analyses of immigrant communities record a three-stage process that begins with increased pressure on immigrants to speak the language of the host country, followed by a period of bilingualism and concluding with the total replacement of their original language (May, 2000, p. 366). This three-stage pattern is similarly evident with regard to identity shifts (Edwards, 2004). This parallel shift in both identity and language over three generations seems to support the strong-link thesis where changes in one presuppose changes in the other. However, such macro-level analysis does not account for potential differences between individuals, or for other factors that may also be at play. In the rest of this chapter we examine this potential variation at the micro-level in the lived experiences of South African-born Chinese in Pretoria. We focus on the micro-level because it is through individual life stories that perceptions around the meanings of identities and language practices are revealed.

The Chinese in South Africa

The first Chinese in South Africa arrived in the late 1870s.[3] They came mainly from Guangzhou province and settled in the former Transvaal (what is today Gauteng Province) as well as in various coastal areas. While many Chinese were attracted to the country by the discovery of gold, anti-Chinese sentiment and racial discrimination prevented them from obtaining mining contracts. As a result, most became shopkeepers and general dealers (Accone, 2006). Key policies and legislation (e.g., Law 3 of 1885) determined where they could live, what they could do, and what they could own (South African History Online, 2014, hereafter referred to as SAHO). Almost all aspects of life were regulated: citizenship, travel, allowed profession, trade, area of residency, land/property purchasing rights, interracial marriage, etc. (Yap and Man, 1996). The formation of the South African Union in the early 1900s further disenfranchised all non-Europeans, and the 1913 Native Land Act formally divided the land between white and non-white people. The election of the National Party to government in 1948 also heightened the enforcement of segregationist policies in the already divided country. The Group Areas Act (1950) in particular began a process of "total segregation between the races," which in many cases involved so-called "forced removals" of some groups into areas designated for their race (SAHO, 2014). In addition to general race-based legislation, the Chinese during this time were further subjected to exclusively anti-Chinese policies.

Given this context, it should come as no surprise that many Chinese "continue[d] to look to mainland China as 'home'," finding a sense of comfort in "an increasingly distanced and mythologised China" (Park, 2008, p. 54). According to Park, this emotional attachment became an enduring point of belonging: "China, both political and cultural, the real and the imagined, provided the Chinese in South Africa with an identity 'refuge' and fulfilled their need to belong" (Park, 2008, p. 76). As early as the 1930s, the segregation of racial groups motivated the Chinese to organize themselves through social clubs, sports groups, and Chinese schools (Yap and Man, 1996), especially in the larger Chinese communities such as those in Johannesburg and Port Elizabeth. Alongside these efforts, they also tried to improve their situation through continual concession-seeking petitions and negotiations, often based on their distinct Chineseness (Park, 2006, p. 219). However, "the more they succeeded in becoming acceptable to white society [. . .] the less they needed their imagined China" (Park, 2008, p. 76). Many SABC interviewed by Park (2008, p. 112), for instance, "credited apartheid with keeping the community together" and thus "viewed their acceptance into white schools and white society . . . as the beginning of the end of Chinese culture."

Over the course of the twentieth century and into post-1994 democratic South Africa, the Chinese identity was challenged, strengthened, and diminished in various ways. In the next section we explore the extent to which various factors impacted on the language and identity shifts of the SABC.

Research Site and Methods

This chapter draws on a case study of the Chinese communities living in Pretoria, South Africa (Houston et al., 2013). The study explored the social roles of Chinese associations in the lives of three distinct Chinese communities, namely the SABC, the Taiwanese, and the recent immigrants from the People's Republic of China (PRC). Although the study did not directly examine the language–identity nexus, it was a strong undercurrent for many respondents in terms of their overall lived experiences. The affiliation with local Chinese associations also suggested an ongoing influence of a Chinese-oriented community on individual identities and practices.

Pretoria is the administrative capital of South Africa. Although just some 60 kilometers north of Johannesburg, it has historically been much less cosmopolitan, especially during apartheid. The Chinese community in Pretoria (including SABC, Taiwanese, and more recent PRC immigrants) is relatively small, forming less than 2% of the population (approximately 54,000) compared to almost 5% (approximately 216,500) in Johannesburg (IHS Global Insight, 2013). One of our interviewees estimated that there are roughly 200 SABC in Pretoria today.

A total of 26 in-depth interviews were conducted. A snowball sampling method was used where interviewees were identified through personal contacts, organizational websites, and desktop research, and further referrals were then requested. Interviews with the SABC were conducted in English. They were assured confidentiality and therefore only pseudonyms are used in this chapter. The recorded interviews were transcribed verbatim by a professional service provider and quality assured by the researchers. The data was analyzed in conjunction with available literature on immigrant communities and on the Chinese in South Africa.

For the purpose of this chapter we selected four SABC whose stories show the pronounced heterogeneity of individual language and identity profiles. Although they are all second-generation immigrants, they vary in age (and thus period of immigration), as well as in Chinese language ability. While the sample is small, the range of their experiences provides a glimpse of the complex, fluid, and multidimensional nature of identity and the perceived roles of language therein. The biographical sketches in the next section and Table 4.1 provide a general indication of each person's language abilities and affiliation with Chinese and South African identities.

Interviewee Biographies

Bill

Bill was born in 1944 in a black township near Pretoria. His grandfather moved to Johannesburg as a businessman around 1904, and although Bill's father was born in South Africa, he went to school in China. Bill attended the Pretoria Chinese School (PCS) for most of his primary schooling. As an adult he worked for a long time in so-called black areas, eventually opening up his own accounting firm in a predominantly white urban neighborhood. Bill has on occasion gone to China to visit extended family, and also keeps up with what goes on in China through English television. He participates in some Chinese associations in Pretoria and his social circle comprises mainly other SABC. He tries to instill what he believes is a Chinese work ethic (e.g., being productive) in his family and workplace, although he considers himself to be a South African.

Bill still speaks fluent Cantonese, usually with his family and other older SABC, but he speaks mostly English with his daughter. He is also proficient in Sesotho, one of the indigenous languages in South Africa, which he believes helps his interactions with black South Africans.

James

James was born in 1959 in Marabastad, a township near Pretoria. After attending a local Indian school and the PCS, James became one of the first Chinese in Pretoria to be granted admission to a private white high school established by a Catholic church.[4] After school he managed his father's hardware store. While he was not very active in the Chinese community due to family and professional commitments at the time, he still spent weekends and social time with Chinese friends at the Chinese school. Currently he is much more involved with the local

Chinese organizations. Although James insists that he will always be Chinese, he also describes South Africa as home: "because this is where I was born; my roots are here."

According to James, his experience in the English school taught him that language can be a barrier or enabler for social and business interactions. His poor English was often the subject of teasing and made it feel degrading to be Chinese. He therefore worked hard to improve his English while also retaining Cantonese. Today he speaks mostly English, although he is still fluent in Cantonese and uses it when interacting with older SABC.

Andrew

Andrew was born in 1971. His grandparents immigrated in the 1930s, and his mother was born in South Africa and his father in China. He attended the PCS before going to an English high school. Today his two children are also enrolled in the PCS. While he attends local Chinese functions and assists with fundraising for various Chinese associations, his social circle comprises his family as well as local South African friends. Andrew considers himself to be fully South African culturally and socially. He associates the Chinese identity and culture with that of Mainland China today, which he finds foreign to his own. As he explains: "I may just look like a Chinese outside, but I'm nothing like Chinese inside."

Despite this strong South African identity, Andrew can speak Cantonese and Mandarin relatively well, although he describes it as "kitchen Chinese" that he feels ashamed to speak among other Chinese. His Afrikaans (the language of the Afrikaners) is better than his Chinese, and he speaks mostly English at home and with friends. He learned Cantonese as a child as it was the only way to communicate with his grandparents, and learned Mandarin through the Chinese school and some Taiwanese friends. Today he uses this language skill mostly with his parents and as an informal translator during business trips to China.

Sarah

Sarah was born in 1990 in Hong Kong and brought to South Africa as a baby by her adopted parents. Growing up in Pretoria she attended private English schools. Most of her friends today, including her fiancé, are South African. While she sometimes attends functions organized by the Chinese community, this is mostly at her parents' request. Although she does not socialize in the local SABC community, she is still proud to be a "Chinese South African." Her sense of being Chinese remains distinct from China, however, which for her is simply the place of her birth and home of her ancestors. Instead, she describes how her parents have taught her aspects of Chinese culture through specific practices (e.g., the honoring ceremony, giving tea with two hands), which she plans to teach to her children as well.

TABLE 4.1 Interviewee biographies

Name	Chinese language abilities			Identity
	Listen	*Speak*	*Read/write*	
Bill	Fluent Cantonese Little Mandarin	Fluent Cantonese; with parents (100% of the time) and older SABCs (90%) No Mandarin	None	Claims to be South African, but socialises largely with other SABC. Chinese ethics very important to him.
James	Fluent Cantonese Little Mandarin	Fluent Cantonese; with older SABCs (65%) No Mandarin	None	Feels both South African and Chinese. Currently active in SABC community associations and affairs.
Andrew	Fluent Cantonese Little Mandarin	Fluent Cantonese (with grandparents 100%) Fluent Mandarin (for business in China)	None	Claims to be fully South African, but participates in local SABC associations and events and children go to Chinese school. Social circle comprises local South Africans.
Sarah	Little Cantonese	None	None	Feels half Chinese, half South African. Plans to instil Chinese culture in her children. Friends mostly local South Africans. Engaged to a South African.

74 Ke Yu and Elmé Vivier

Sarah does not speak any Chinese language, but has some minimal understanding of Cantonese. Her parents speak English and Cantonese with one another and used to speak Cantonese to her when she was younger. They also sent her to a Saturday Chinese language school for a while, but none of this succeeded in motivating her to learn the language. The small number of SABC in her generation, who mainly speak English, has also created little incentive for her to speak Chinese.

Table 4.1 provides a summary of the language abilities and generalized identity claims of the four SABC.

Factors Influencing Language and Identity

Factors that influence immigrant experiences provide a lens for examining identity and language shifts at the micro-level, as well as perceived meanings of identity and language usage. In the case of the SABC in Pretoria, we found four key factors influencing their experiences: the context of reception; the organization of the Chinese community; the need for social mobility and advancement; and family needs and efforts. These factors are by no means unique to the South African Chinese case and are, among a number of other factors,[5] relevant to immigrant experiences across the globe. As part of a larger narrative, the details of these individual life stories demonstrate how such factors are not uniformly "felt." They also do not impact the immigrant experience independently from one another but together influence perceptions and actions in multiple and complex ways.

Factor 1: The Context of Reception

One of the primary factors, at least for the older generation of SABC interviewees, has been the hostile context of reception created by apartheid. "Context of reception" refers to the general attitude of the host society towards an immigrant community, and is considered "an important factor for understanding the group's integration into, acceptance of, and success in a host society" (Doucet, 2003, p. 78). In instances of real or perceived hostility, "immigrants may downplay or reject their own ethnic identity," or they may "assert their pride in their cultural group and emphasise solidarity as a way of dealing with negative attitudes" (Phinney et al., 2001b, p. 494). Daha (2011, p. 563) finds, for instance, that negative stereotyping of Iranians by Americans strengthened the Iranians' loyalty to their ethnic identity, "even when many had not travelled to Iran and could not speak the language well."

In the case of the SABC, our interviewees' experiences reveal how the antagonistic context of South Africa reinforced their sense of Chineseness. Both Bill and James recall the impact of racial discrimination and segregation, such as having to ask permission to work and/or reside in white neighborhoods.

As with the Iranian example, this hostile environment actually kept the Chinese community closer together. Bill described the experience as follows:

> [B]ecause of the apartheid system, we were a very close knit company . . . I always say it's a consolation to live among our own people. You don't have to know everyone, but because of apartheid, it's always better to be among your group.

South Africa's transition to democracy since 1994 has, however, changed this environment, as well as the SABC's attachment to their community, as the two younger SABC (Andrew and Sarah) illustrate. Although Andrew has some memories of being one of the only Chinese in an English school, and of discrimination when his family bought a house in a white area in the 1980s, he admits never really being bothered by a sense of being different. This suggests that the influence of even a generally negative context of reception depends on how it is received by the individual.

Sarah feels the most distanced from this hostile past, which is understandable given her age. This was evident in her reflections on a 2008 Black Economic Empowerment (BEE) court case. The case was raised by the SABC community (through the Chinese Association of South Africa) against several national government departments in an attempt to challenge the exclusion of the Chinese from the new government's affirmative action policies. After nearly eight years of lobbying and legal efforts, the court confirmed that the Chinese are indeed also "previously disadvantaged" due to apartheid (Huynh et al., 2010). But Sarah distinguishes this from her experiences growing up:

> I'm very happy that they got it for their generation. But for my generation, I don't think we need it because we didn't grow up in the struggle that they had. We grew up in multiracial schools. We became friends with blacks, whites, Indians and everybody.

These four cases illustrate how the nature of the context of reception can reinforce an attachment to a particular identity, be it a heritage/ethnic identity or a more localized one. While we have not discussed the impact of the context of reception on language use and ability, this seems to occur through its influence on the next three factors.

Factor 2: Organization of the Chinese Community in Pretoria

Studies show that community organization often provides institutional and social support to immigrants or minorities (Lieber 2010; Zhou and Lin, 2006). Such organization is usually more feasible in large, concentrated communities where

76 Ke Yu and Elmé Vivier

individuals can join cultural organizations, share cultural practices and values, and form a cohesive "speech community" (Lai, 2012). In cities where the immigrant community is small and dispersed, however, cultural participation and exposure is limited, and thus learning and maintenance of home language may decline and sense of ethnic identity may weaken. As discussed earlier, in the large Chinese communities such as in Johannesburg, their crucial mass is said to have sustained such community associations, clubs, schools, and festivals (Park, 2008, p. 112). In Pretoria, however, the community was relatively small, although some key organizations were established as early as the 1930s.

Of particular importance to the Pretoria Chinese was the establishment of the PCS. Schools that teach the heritage language have been recognized as being "of the greatest importance in sustaining the language" (Edwards, 1985, p. 147). Beyond language retention, these schools often provide opportunities for social networks and transmission of culture through the observation of events and celebrations (Francis et al., 2009). This has also been the case with the PCS, which aimed at providing a quality education for Chinese children, as well as teaching Chinese language (originally Cantonese and switching to Mandarin in the 1970s due to teacher availability), and preserving Chinese culture and identity (Yap and Man, 1996, p. 283). The school quickly became the center of the SABC's social engagements, providing facilities for other local community associations, sports activities, religious meetings, and cultural celebrations. Drawing on his experience of discrimination in an English school, James speculates that many Chinese parents sent their children to the PCS during apartheid in order to avoid racist attitudes. In this sense, the school protected their ethnic identity.

Many SABC today, however, seem not to have a strong attachment to the Chinese organizations or Chinese community. This is apparent in the low Chinese enrolment rate at the school (10% of the total student population, including Taiwanese and PRC children). It is also evident in the lives of Sarah and Andrew. Sarah never attended the PCS and it could be argued that this is one of the reasons for her lack of Chinese language skills. Andrew on the other hand exhibits a paradoxical attitude towards Chinese language and culture. Although he placed his children in the Chinese school to expose them to Chinese culture, they do not observe any Chinese practices or speak any Chinese languages at home. He also plans to eventually move them to an English school because he believes it will be more "like the real world" and will provide more opportunities for them.

Factor 3: The Need for Socioeconomic Mobility and Advancement

The SABC's efforts to find their place in the South African community were also influenced by the desire and/or need for socioeconomic advancement, as the experience of James shows. Being one of the first to attend a private white school, James was among the early examples of the SABC's shift in interest from Chinese to English education because of the need for "upward economic mobility" (Park, 2008, p. 82). Park's observations seem to reverberate with those of John Edwards in his seminal work, *Language, Society and Identity* (1985). Edwards argues that security and freedom (or other pragmatic needs) often preoccupy minority groups much more than the concerns regarding culture or language, especially in the face of increasing urbanization, in-migration, and socioeconomic pressures. In this sense, maintaining one's heritage language may bar social access and mobility by the minority groups (Edwards, 1985, p. 96). The relatively low socioeconomic status of the early Chinese immigrants, alongside the oppressive apartheid state, could have meant that practical concerns were more pertinent in their approach to language and identity because they did not have the "psychological and economic capital" (Edwards, 1985, p. 94) for "luxury" concerns over identity.

Prizing the value of success over the value of language has been observed in several studies of overseas Chinese communities as well. For example, Zhang (2004, pp. 45–46) finds that Chinese immigrants often encourage their children to shift to English as soon as possible in order that they may achieve success academically and in their future careers. Similarly, Kim and Chao (2009) conclude that the transfer of Chinese values (often with an emphasis on success) among second-generation Chinese in Los Angeles was significant in maintaining a sense of ethnic identity despite language loss.

Factor 4: Family Needs and/or Parental Efforts

Parental efforts are another factor in retaining a sense of Chinese identity or Chinese language ability. Family dynamics and parents' efforts to transfer cultural awareness and values to their children are especially significant where there is little contact with the culture of origin (Suarez-Orozco, 2004). Parents who believe that their ethnicity is important are likely to engage in cultural behaviors, thus promoting this identity in their children (Phinney et al., 2001a, p. 138). Similarly for language, Shin (2010, p. 216) asserts that, "successful language learning and maintenance strategies usually . . . start with language transmission at the level of the family."

Sarah's sense of Chineseness as well as her lack of Chinese language ability may be attributed in large part to her parents' efforts to transmit values and cultural practices. However, despite her parents' efforts, she has not developed a desire to learn Chinese. While she still feels Chinese in some ways (and observes traditional practices at home), her friends and school experiences have influenced her attitude towards the Chinese language. Sarah's case therefore reflects the significance of the interplay of social environment and individual choices on language usage.

The need for family communication also sometimes drives the effort to retain the heritage language. James, for instance, maintained his Cantonese despite

78 Ke Yu and Elmé Vivier

attending English-speaking schools, which could be attributed to his parents' and grandparents' limited English. While in the example of Andrew, the passing of generations led to a decreased need to use Chinese as a communicative language. Similar experiences have been noted by Park in her study of SABC who, with the passing of older generations, "lost both the impetus and opportunity to practise the language" (Park, 2008, p. 109).

This review of SABC experiences illuminates some of the key factors that may impact on immigrants' retention and/or loss of their language and ethnic identity. It shows the complexity of being an immigrant (or minority) group in a changing environment, as well as the tensions accompanying individual identity claims and language practices. In the next section we discuss the fluidity of SABC identity affiliations and what it implies for the link between language and identity.

Discussion

The Heterogeneity and Fluidity of SABC Identities

The four case studies confirm a general weakening over time of both Chinese language proficiency and Chinese identity. However, they also show a fluid coexistence of Chinese and South African identity affiliations. What becomes especially apparent is the multiple degrees and expressions of Chineseness, and the complex variety of "markers" defining this identity, of which language is but one. Thus we see all four SABC describe themselves as South African,[6] aligning their culture with white South African culture and distinguishing it from that of contemporary Chinese. And yet, a sense of being Chinese also remains, although their perceptions of this identity and how they practice it vary widely. For instance, for Bill and James, their Chineseness is embedded in their experiences within a particular sociopolitical history and the social community with whom they share this history. It is lived out through continued social interactions of the SABC community and local SABC organizations, their continued use of Cantonese as the medium of conversation, and the public observation of particular Chinese holidays and events. Sarah's and Andrew's attachments to their Chineseness (or SABC identity) comprise different markers. For Sarah, being Chinese is predominantly cultural yet private. It is made possible by her parents' efforts to preserve and observe specific Chinese traditions and ceremonies at home. Language has little if any role in this identity. Andrew on the other hand insists that he is South African, yet he sends his children to the Pretoria Chinese School, attends local Chinese functions, and assists with fundraising for various Chinese associations. He therefore demonstrates continued affiliation with the local SABC community, although without a strong sense of belonging. His practical use of the Chinese language also, paradoxically, reflects his Chinese heritage yet reinforces for him the gap between himself and those whom he sees as "real Chinese."

The Role of Language in the Fluidity of Identities

The variety of ways that Chineseness (or identity in general) is perceived and expressed among these four interviewees confirms numerous identity theories that highlight the complex fluidity of continuous identity formation. These theories generally agree that identity is, at least in part, socially constructed. It is derived from one's lived experiences within particular historical, political, and social contexts, relationships, and roles. It is "negotiated, on-going, changing constantly across time and space" (Wenger, 1998, p. 163). Our study further confirms to an extent the social constructivist paradigm that emphasizes the reflective and productive role of the individual in the construction of his or her own identity (Ochs, 1993). In this sense, one can be strategic in choosing to display only a certain part of one's identity in a certain situation, or to prioritize identities as needed. This has been captured by Cohen (2000, p. 582) as follows: "One can be Muslim in the Mosque, Asian in the street, Asian British at political hustings and British when travelling abroad, all in a single day."

These strategic actions echo Jaspal and Coyle's (2009) proposal that identity coping strategies are complex and dynamic. This, we argue, is especially relevant with regard to the language and identity link. When identity is under threat, individuals may "seek to deprecate the importance of aspects which pose a threat to the positive evaluation of one's identity" (Breakwell, 1986, quoted in Jaspal, 2009, p. 19), including the "denigration of the language" (Jaspal and Coyle, 2009, p. 163). Thus one may downplay or embrace both heritage language and identity, or one may downplay only heritage language while maintaining one's heritage identity. Language thus becomes a "dynamic symbolic object that can be applied strategically in identity making" (Lauring, 2008, p. 344).

Due to the flexibility of language, one could also expect more strategic use of language (compared to other identity markers) in the presentation of particular identities. An individual may adopt a new language, combine different languages into a single linguistic system (Woolard, 1998), or select a particular vocabulary or accent to reflect a social/group identity or role (Jaspal, 2009). Furthermore, acquiring a new language may be desirable as it is usually positively received in the host environment as a demonstration of the willingness to adjust to the host culture, and also invokes less sense of betrayal and objection within the heritage community given the practical functions it serves.

Flexible coping strategies in the production of identity also illuminate the influence and interplay of various factors and how these are perceived and addressed at the individual level. Different strategies may be used in different circumstances, as is evident in the narratives of the four SABC. James learned English in order to fit in at school, yet still speaks Cantonese fluently when he is with other SABC. Learning English was therefore a strategy to protect rather than simply diminish his Chinese identity. Andrew on the other hand, as mentioned above, feels less Chinese whenever he speaks the Chinese language due to his "poor" ability. Each social actor therefore experiences various factors through their individual needs, motivations, and a multitude of identities, which further influences language and identity choices. For this reason, a language and cultural identity that is initially linked could at the same time be impacted differently and even in opposite directions. This challenges the expectation that language and identity shifts occur together as held by the strong link thesis. At the micro-level, individual experiences of historical and social contexts reveal how the link between language and identity, far from being deterministic and static, is rather multiple, complex, and contextually specific.

Conclusion

This micro-level study of four South African-born Chinese, although too small to make conclusive generalizations, has brought to light the dynamic and highly variable manner in which the meanings of identities and languages are perceived and expressed. Thus, even though there seems to be a general shift occurring away from a strong Chinese identity and Chinese language usage, each of the four individuals retained some degree of attachment to being Chinese and Chinese language abilities. However, they also define this Chineseness differently, appealing to shared sociopolitical experiences as Chinese during apartheid, specific cultural practices and traditions, and sometimes language. Their experiences illuminate how the interplay of environmental, social, and individual factors continually influence the place of different languages (alongside other identity markers) within one's self-concept. Language can therefore be a strategic yet flexible symbolic resource for managing tensions and shifts between varying identities.

Furthermore, the interplay of the sociohistorical context and individual needs and motivations emerges as a driving force behind identity and language choices and the link between the two. From the lens of only four contextual factors, we find, for example, a situation where a negative context of reception that emphasizes difference is reinforced by a positive family environment that protects that difference, while simultaneously a difficult school experience pushes an individual to strategically undermine that difference (as in the example of James). In this interplay of factors, the relationship between language and identity can strengthen or weaken as it is influenced by emotional and pragmatic needs and experiences. For instance, this relationship may remain strong as an individual retains his or her heritage language and culture in the face of an adverse environment (more likely with the support of an organized community and similar family efforts). It may also, however, remain closely linked while potentially decreasing in relevance overall as an individual adapts to the host society, either learning a new language or changing cultural practices.

Conversely, the link between heritage language and culture may weaken. First, a language shift may occur while other cultural markers and practices are retained.

The Case of South African-born Chinese **81**

From our case studies we see this occurring through the presence of a shared, organized community, or through a strong family influence. Each of these seems capable of retaining a heritage culture despite a language shift. Sarah's case further suggests that at the family level, and in the absence of a strong heritage culture and language community, cultural practices are more easily passed down than language. Second, heritage language may be maintained while identity changes. In the case of Andrew we see how heritage language becomes a functional tool with little deeper cultural value, which is a strong possibility for Chinese given the increased presence of China in the global economy that has increased the language's socioeconomic capital.

In conclusion, we propose that the argument for a strong link cannot account for the experiences of the individual, which is precisely where the relationship between language and identity is shaped and plays out. Instead, the situational view of the language–identity link (arguing for a weak relation) is better able to capture the heterogeneity evident at the micro-level as this perspective is able to explain cases of weak and strong language–identity links, as well as the varying degrees in between. The situational view allows that, while there may be a broader shift across a community, identities linger and transform in a continuous process of identity formation and expression. It is precisely this kind of pluralism that characterizes human experiences and practices.

Notes

1 Originally printed as "Speaking or being Chinese: The case of South African-born Chinese" by Ke Yu and Elmé Vivier (DOI: 10.1515/ijsl. 2015–0021). De Gruyter. Reprinted by permission of the publisher.
2 Some refer to themselves as South African Chinese, others as Chinese South Africans, each reflecting how they relate to South Africa and identify with being Chinese.
3 Scholarship on the Chinese in South Africa distinguish between this early group of settlers who are today considered SABC, Taiwanese who began arriving in large numbers from the 1970s onwards, and newer immigrants from the People's Republic of China (PRC) who began arriving since the late 1990s.
4 From the 1930s onwards, it became possible for non-whites to attend private white schools established by Catholic churches on the basis of their conversion to Christianity (Yap and Man, 1996, p. 303).
5 Other factors include demographic variables such as socioeconomic status, length of residency in the host country, age at the time of immigration, and gender. These are beyond the scope of this chapter.
6 An additional layer of complexity arises in the fact that South Africa, with 11 official languages, comprises a variety of cultural groups and languages.

References

Accone, D. (2006). "Ghost people": Localising the Chinese self in an African context. *Asian Studies Review, 30*, 257–272.
Brewer, M. B. (2001). The many faces of social identity: Implications for political psychology. *Political Psychology, 22*(1), 115–125.

Cohen, R. (2000). The incredible vagueness of being British/English. *International Affairs*, *76*, 575–582.

Daha, M. (2011). Contextual factors contributing to ethnic identity development of second-generation Iranian American adolescents. *Journal of Adolescent Research, 26*, 543–569.

Doucet, F. (2003). Identities and their complexities: A review essay of trends in ethnic identification among second-generation Haitian immigrants in New York City by Flore Zephir. *Race and Society, 6*, 75–82.

Edwards, J. (1985). *Language, society and identity*. Oxford, UK: Basil Blackwell.

Edwards, J. (2004). Bilingualism: Context, constraints, and identities. *Journal of Language and Social Psychology, 23*, 135–141.

Fishman, J. A. (1991). *Reversing language shift: Theory and practice of assistance to threatened languages*. Clevedon, UK: Multilingual Matters.

Francis, B., Archer, L., and Mau, A. (2009). Language as capital, or language as identity? Chinese complementary school pupils' perspectives on the purposes and benefits of complementary schools. *British Educational Research Journal, 35*(4), 519–538.

Guardado, M. (2008). Language, identity, and cultural awareness in Spanish-speaking families. *Canadian Ethnic Studies, 40*(3), 171–181.

Houston, G., Wentzel, M., Yu, K., and Vivier, E. (2013). *Bodies that divide and bind: Tracing the social roles of associations in Chinese communities in Pretoria, South Africa*. HSRC Project Report. Pretoria, South Africa: HSRC.

Huynh, T. T., Park, Y. J., and Chen, A. Y. (2010). Faces of China: New Chinese migrants in South Africa, 1980s to present. *African and Asian Studies, 9*, 286–306.

IHS Global Insight. (2013). Rex regional explorer database version 2.5n. Retrieved from www.ihsglobalinsight.co.za.

Jaspal, R. (2009). Language and social identity: A psychosocial approach. *Psychtalk, 64*, 17–20.

Jaspal, R., and Coyle, A. (2009). Language and perceptions of identity threat. *Psychology and Society, 2*(2), 150–167.

Kamwangamalu, N. W. (2007). One language, multi-layered identities: English in a society in transition, South Africa. *World Englishes, 26*(3), 263–275.

Kim, S. Y., and Chao, R. K. (2009). Heritage language fluency, ethnic identity, and school effort of immigrant Chinese and Mexican adolescents. *Cultural Diversity and Ethnic Minority Psychology, 15*, 27–37.

Lai, D. W.L. (2012). Ethnic identity of older Chinese in Canada. *Journal of Cross Cultural Gerontology, 27*, 103–117.

Lauring, J. (2008). Rethinking social identity theory in international encounters: Language use as a negotiated object for identity making. *International Journal of Cross Cultural Management, 8*(3), 343–361.

Lieber, M. (2010). Chinese migrants in Switzerland: From mutual assistance to promoting economic interests. *Journal of Chinese Overseas, 6*, 102–118.

May, S. (2000). Uncommon languages: The challenges and possibilities of minority language rights. *Journal of Multilingual and Multicultural Development, 21*(5), 366–385.

Miller, J. M. (2000). Language use, identity, and social interaction: Migrant students in Australia. *Research on Language and Social Interaction, 33*(1), 69–100.

Norton, B. (2000). *Identity and language learning: Gender, ethnicity and educational change*. London, UK: Longman/Pearson.

Ochs, E. (1993). Constructing social identity: A language socialisation perspective. *Research on Language and Social Interaction, 26*(3), 287–306.

Park, Y. J. (2006). Sojourners to settlers: Early constructions of Chinese identity in South Africa, 1879–1949. *African Studies, 65*(2), 201–231.

Park, Y. J. (2008). *A matter of honour: Being Chinese in South Africa.* Johannesburg, South Africa: Jacana Media.

Phinney, J. (1998). *Ethnic identity and acculturation.* Paper presented at the Conference on Acculturation, University of San Francisco, California, USA.

Phinney, J., Romero, I., Nava, M., and Huang, D. (2001a). The role of language, parents, and peers in ethnic identity among adolescents in immigrant families. *Journal of Youth and Adolescence, 30*(2), 135–153.

Phinney, J., Horenczyk, G., Liebkind, K., and Vedder, P. (2001b). Ethnic identity, immigration, and well-being: An interactional perspective. *Journal of Social Issues, 57*(3), 493–510.

Sears, D. O., Fu, M., Henry, P. J., and Bui, K. (2003). The origins and persistence of ethnic identity among the "new immigrant" groups. *Social Psychology Quarterly, 66*(4), 419–437.

Shin, S. J. (2010). "What about me? I'm not like Chinese but I'm not like American": Heritage language learning and identity of mixed heritage adults. *Journal of Language, Identity and Education, 9*(3), 203–219.

South African History Online (SAHO). (2014). South African history online: Towards a people's history. Retrieved from www.sahistory.org.za.

Suarez-Orozco, C. (2004). Formulating identity in a globalized world. In M. M. Suarez-Orozco and D. Qin-Hilliard (Eds.), *Globalization: Culture and education in the new millennium* (pp. 173–202). Oakland, CA: University of California Press and Ross Institute.

Tannenbaum, M. (2005). Viewing family relations through a linguistic lens: Symbolic aspects of language maintenance in immigrant families. *Journal of Family Communication, 5*(3), 229–252.

Wenger, E. (1998). *Communities of practice.* Cambridge, UK: Cambridge University Press.

Woolard, K. A. (1998). Simultaneity and bivalency as strategies in bilingualism. *Journal of Linguistic Anthropology, 8*(1), 3–29.

Yap, M., and Man, D. L. (1996). *Colour, confusion and concessions: The history of the Chinese in South Africa.* Hong Kong: Hong Kong University Press.

Zhang, D. (2004). Home language maintenance among second-generation Chinese American children. *Working Papers in Educational Linguistics, 19*(2), 33–54.

Zhou, M., and Lin, M. (2006). Community transformation and the formation of ethnic capital: Immigrant Chinese communities in the United States. *Journal of Chinese Overseas, 2*(2), 193–219.

5

IMPACT OF THE "HIDDEN CURRICULUM" ON THE UNDERSTANDING OF CHINESE INTERNATIONAL STUDENTS IN NEW ZEALAND

Xiudi Zhang

> Anyway, I was impressed by the environment of this country when I first came to New Zealand. Wow, the air is really good and the sun is different in its color—it is white but is yellow in China. On the first day, I felt the light of the sun to be harsh and uncomfortable. In the beginning, my accommodation was in an old train station for half a year, which I felt was like a jail because it was too small and the window was too high. Until I met Wayne (a Chinese friend). We decided to live together in the same apartment.
>
> (Xu, a doctoral student)

When I interviewed Xu over coffee and pizza, he had been studying in New Zealand for three years. Xu, it seems, had not involved himself much in the local culture, just casually talking with his colleagues and other foreign students from his faculty. Only once had he spent time with a non-Chinese friend; this was when they were hiking.

> I think it is very simple. People here are living a relaxed life with less pressure compared with Chinese people, as they have a relatively developed social welfare system so that Kiwis [New Zealanders] don't have wild ambitions for their career and they just enjoy their own life which is based on basic life conditions.
>
> (Xu, a doctoral student)

He had observed the above by walking around the city and seeing local people relaxing on the beaches, playing games in parks, hiking, and riding on bicycles with their family and friends.

86 Xiudi Zhang

> It is easy to observe; local people like sports and exercise, which is so different from China. For another example, local people would not study on weekends. Usually, we see people from Iran, India, China, or the Third World countries still working hard on weekends. It is OK if we Chinese international students have merely superficial associations with local people, but it would become difficult to talk once the conversation involves deep thinking because of different cultures and the language barriers.
>
> (Xu, a doctoral student)

The above excerpt is from one of the interviews I conducted with Chinese doctoral students who are studying in New Zealand. Students from China are often enticed to study abroad by the promises that they will broaden their vision of the world, and that they will be better prepared for future jobs because they will have the opportunity to acquire advanced knowledge. Consequently, from 1978 to the end of 2012, more than 2.6 million Chinese studied outside their country, funded by the government, employers, or at their own expense, making China the world's top source of overseas students (Xinhua, 2013). These students are committed to their studies while living in a new environment and speaking another language. However, studying abroad is not a simple process that merely presents the opportunity for experiencing a different lifestyle. As Brown University's Office of International Programs suggests, studying abroad promotes "the awareness of the values and the way of life of your own country, your own place in that country, and its place in the world" (Dolby, 2004, p. 150). In addition, it develops the idea that studying abroad is a way for students to encounter and learn more about themselves.

This chapter places Chinese international students in a different perspective: that of the hidden curriculum in China and New Zealand, by interviewing Chinese doctoral students who are studying in New Zealand. Before coming to New Zealand, these students immersed themselves not only in Chinese formal schooling but also in Chinese hidden-curriculum programs (Jackson, 1990). However, through their experiences in New Zealand they are immersed in a hidden curriculum different from that in China; this chapter will focus on what the hidden curriculum is for Chinese students and how it influences their overall experiences in New Zealand. Of particular interest is the way in which students' histories, including their personal and education experience, shape their attitudes, their means of interpreting the world, and how they view and understand themselves and their life via the perspective of a democratic community and nation.

Studying Abroad in a New Zealand Context

In New Zealand, Chinese students comprise the main source of international students, with around 20,000 students from China studying in New Zealand each year from 2006 to 2012 (see Table 5.1). Specifically, each year nearly 6,000 Chinese students enroll at university level in New Zealand (see Table 5.2). In general,

TABLE 5.1 Source countries of students in New Zealand since 2006 to 2012 (copyright 2013 by Ministry of Education, reprinted with permission)

Distribution of international fee-paying students by Country of Citizenship for major source countries for the period 1 January to 31 August (2006 to 2012)

Country of Citizenship	2006	2007	2008	2009	2010	2011	2012	% distribution 2012	% change 2011 to 2012
China (incl Hong Kong)	29,140	22,475	17,959	18,152	18,249	19,773	21,462	27.1	8.5%
India	2,222	3,104	5,004	7,476	9,107	10,429	9,364	11.8	−10.2%
South Korea	11,703	14,918	14,469	13,330	13,022	10,973	8,869	11.2	−19.2%
Japan	10,814	9,733	8,772	7,933	8,191	7,762	8,216	10.4	5.8%
Saudi Arabia	1,427	2,028	2,946	4,421	4,477	4,796	3,702	4.7	−22.8%
Germany	1,753	2,469	2,592	3,065	3,390	3,109	2,681	3.4	−13.8%
Thailand	2,269	2,603	2,296	2,653	3,033	2,694	2,549	3.2	−5.4%
Brazil	1,456	1,840	1,883	2,211	2,420	2,451	2,065	2.6	−15.7%
Vietnam	855	926	944	1,276	1,642	1,888	1,901	2.4	0.7%
USA	2,215	2,261	2,202	2,236	2,325	2,159	1,886	2.4	−12.6%

studying abroad for students is more than language acquisition, academic outcomes, and adaptation to a new environment. Indeed, for these students, "the primary encounter during the study-abroad experience is with themselves as national and global actors" (Dolby, 2004, p. 150).

Much research has paid attention to East Asian students in New Zealand (Campbell and Li, 2008; Ho et al., 2007; Holmes, 2008; Malcolm et al., 2004; Zhang and Brunton, 2007), especially to Chinese students as being the main component of international students in New Zealand. The issues of Chinese students in New Zealand relate to communicating with their New Zealand peers (Holmes, 2008), and adjusting to academic problems (Campbell and Li, 2008), and the reconstruction of their cognitive culture has attracted attention from central and local government, educators, and researchers. A large amount of research has also investigated "service quality" or "satisfaction of learning experience" to measure whether the host country's current educational products and services satisfy Chinese students (Campbell and Li, 2008; Henze and Zhu, 2012).

Overall, even though prior studies on cultural aspects are fewer in number than those studies related to critical self-reflection, they are more focused on improving the performance of export education through economics (Butcher, 2004). Dodds maintains it is evident that "a relative lack of a coherent frame of theory-building in international education research exists, particularly concerning study-abroad programs" (cited in Henze and Zhu, 2012, p. 92). Henze and Zhu's (2012) study corresponds with Dodds' view that current study-abroad programs merely present solutions to a practical problem universities face in reforming their teaching and research. I shall argue that current research only focuses on solutions for the problems of teaching, and that research on international Chinese student experience is insufficient. What is important is that we should understand why and how they are facing personal, social, and academic problems while overseas. Campbell and Li (2008) concede that international students need to deal with many challenges derived from cultural differences. In the process of meeting and overcoming those challenges, those students are also able to take advantage of, and benefit from, their prior educational experience that obligated them to embrace various different sets of cultural values and beliefs. Thus, their prior educational experience in China, including the Chinese hidden curriculum, influences how they view their study and life in New Zealand. Furthermore, in order to assess, more realistically, the effects the study-abroad experience is likely to have on attitudes towards the hidden curriculum they are experiencing, we need to think about the situation of Chinese international students more analytically. We need to take into account the fact that Chinese students themselves differ in many ways; that the experiences they have in New Zealand may vary widely; that New Zealand presents many different aspects about which Chinese students may gain impressions or make evaluations; and that, while their views about some aspects could be influenced by certain kinds of experiences, their views about other aspects may be untouched by any experiences they could have.

TABLE 5.2 Number of international fee-paying students by sector from the top five source countries for the period 1 January 2012 to August 2012 (copyright 2013 by Ministry of Education, reprinted with permission)

Country		School Sector							Total
		Primary	Secondary	Polytechnic	University	SDR PTEs	Non-funded PTEs	Subsidiary providers	
China	Number	143	3,200	3,181	6,473	2,518	4,969	978	21,462
	% across sectors	1%	15%	15%	30%	12%	23%	5%	100%
	% within sector	6%	26%	32%	37%	26%	21%	30%	27%
India	Number	9	46	2,485	953	2,921	2,945	5	9,364
	% across sectors	0%	0%	27%	10%	31%	31%	0%	100%
	% within sector	0%	0%	25%	6%	30%	12%	0%	12%
South Korea	Number	1,600	1,964	468	930	756	2,586	565	8,869
	% across sectors	18%	22%	5%	10%	9%	29%	6%	100%
	% within sector	67%	16%	5%	5%	8%	11%	17%	17%

90 Xiudi Zhang

Thus, this chapter, from a psycho-political perspective, rather than a cultural one, regards students as independent agents interweaving their personal, professional, and even national goals under the influence of a hidden curriculum, which is ignored by current research. The phrase "hidden curriculum" was coined by Philip W. Jackson (1990), who considered education as a socialization process. The curriculum that was "hidden" allowed the school to function and gave it meaning as a social institution, apart from the formal curriculum based on teaching and learning, which Jackson saw as secondary. The term has been used widely since the 1990s. The hidden curriculum consists of the unspoken, unpublished, or implicit academic, social, and cultural views in the student's mind. As we have seen from Xu's comments about his life in New Zealand at the beginning of this chapter, we might never know what he thinks of his conversations with local people in formal classes and his teacher might not teach him how to talk to or have deep conversations with locals in the university. Xu's observations and thoughts about life in New Zealand are the hidden curriculum.

How do we define the hidden curriculum for Chinese overseas students? The hidden curriculum is "taught by the school, not by any teacher, and it is something coming across to the students which may never be spoken in the lesson" (Meighan and Harber, 2007). In general, the hidden curriculum for Chinese students is what they see, think, and experience in New Zealand society, except that, at the same time, during their formal education at university, they are carrying with them the Chinese hidden curriculum that shaped who they are, in China.

However, it may be hard for me to interview the Chinese students as those students may be shy and unwilling to share their experiences, for certain political and cultural reasons. The method I employed in my research can address this problem.

Method

This is a case study. It is a case of Chinese students who have come to New Zealand with a set of values that have been built up through the years by the Chinese hidden curriculum. Research has not investigated whether Chinese students with certain kinds of values, strategies, and identities are likely to undergo changes in the field of New Zealand's hidden curriculum. Thus, considering that case study as a site (Stake, 1978) is to discover the meaning or lived experience of the investigated topic and to address the meaning individuals or groups ascribe to a social or human problem (Creswell, 2012), this study contributes to a greater comprehension of the cross-cultural and national observations and perceptions of Chinese overseas students' education, from a global perspective.

In this study, it is considered important to examine the knowledge, perceptions, and issues that Chinese students have prior to and after a study-overseas experience, in order to depict in how Chinese students relate to the new people, new groups, and new patterns of behavior they encounter in the New Zealand hidden curriculum. At the same time, it is important to know how they stumble in their attempt to reconcile their values and identities within the context of the new and different society of New Zealand.

Therefore, this study applied multiple-site methods such as café-style focus groups and interviews to collect data in order to provide a comprehensive examination of how Chinese students are shaped by their experiences in New Zealand.

Participant Selection

The participants in this study are Chinese students in New Zealand universities. Due to issues related to feasibility, a purposive sampling approach was adapted. In particular, this study focuses on Chinese students from Mainland China, excluding Hong Kong students on the grounds that Hong Kong's education system is different from Mainland China's (Fairbrother, 2003). One important criterion for selecting university students is that they have a background of formal education from within China, so may have a reasonable understanding of the educational contradiction in the new context. As they are going to enter into society as citizens as well as social protagonists, they should have the ability to think critically, to cooperate with others, to appreciate their perspective and experiences, and to tolerate other points of view. Overall, the criteria for selection of the participants included:

- Over 18 years old and enrolled as a student at a New Zealand university.
- Born and raised in, and attended secondary or high school in, Mainland China.

Research Question

This chapter is part of a larger study that explored the way in which Chinese students negotiate their Chinese identity in New Zealand and its education system, with the aim of gaining an increased understanding of the way in which those Chinese students construct meaning for themselves, particularly in the context of the discourse of an increasingly globalized world. This chapter presents the findings about the influence of hidden curriculum. This chapter addresses the following research question: In what way are Chinese students' perceptions of citizenship shaped by their study experiences in New Zealand?

Interviews

In this study, the interviews were unstructured so that the interviewees could freely express their own ideas. As I mentioned above, interviewing Chinese students in the field of hidden curriculum is not easy. For example, I remember

92 Xiudi Zhang

that one of my interviews was stalled when I asked the participant a question. I had presented a paper with the word *citizen* on it, to Song (a participant). A few seconds later, she reluctantly said, "Uh, citizen, that is, uh, if I have a problem, the country should be able to protect me, and I should fulfill my duty such as to pay taxes, and then that's all, I only thought of those." I tried to ask her to draw further on the relationship of citizen to society, on a piece of paper, but she pushed it back to me.

That is my failed interview experience. In fact, I did not know the right questions to ask Chinese students, and I just cared about the data, rather than the person I was interviewing. Eventually, I realized that to fully understand the conduct of respondents acting in the two contexts—China and New Zealand—understanding the person first is important, and second, I needed to do unstructured interviews rather than asking fixed questions.

In addition, I played the roles of both outsider and insider during data collection. As an international Chinese student, I was an insider. It was inevitable that I readily took the stories, with which I am familiar, for granted, and failed to ask further questions about them. As a result, I had to remind myself to act as an outsider to keep a distance from the interview participants.

Café-Style Focus Groups

In this study, 45-minute café-style semi-structured focus groups were utilized in order to trigger memories, thoughts, and ideas among the participants (Lichtman, 2012). My aim was to share some of the ideas and perceptions arising from the individual interviews and to generate second-order data. The second reason for choosing to use the café-style focus group with Chinese students was the consideration that those participants may be shy and unwilling to share their experiences for political and Chinese-cultural reasons. Therefore, I imitated Wood's (2011) café-style approach with Chinese students to create a safe space to explore their ideas. It enabled the students who have had similar study-overseas experiences to exchange their opinions, to adapt, to omit, or to insert responses to research questions.

Two focus groups were undertaken after the interviews. Both focus groups had five international students. In one group, students were invited from the 21 interviewed participants to negotiate the interview data. In the other group, students were completely new to the study. The aim of the two focus groups was to triangulate the interview data, to ensure the validity of their communication, and to reduce the likelihood of misinterpretation.

Results

The findings show that the New Zealand hidden curriculum mainly influences Chinese overseas students by changing their views of study, their lifestyle, life

Impact of the "Hidden Curriculum" **93**

values, and their personal relationship with China. These changes, it will be argued, result from students' critical responses to the disparities that exist between Chinese hidden curriculum and New Zealand hidden curriculum.

"Chinese Education Is Poisonous"

Li: I think our generation is poisoned by Chinese education . . . In high school, all I knew was studying and doing homework from morning to evening, seven days a week. Because of the demands of my six years' studying in high school, the result was that I was not able to keep up with a lot of other interesting stuff. I mean the way of teaching is extremely arduous for students.

Xia: Unfortunately, college examinations are a single-lane bridge. Too many students are competing for it so that you have no choice, you must work very hard.

Ma: I agree, that fierce situation will reverse with the decline in the number of students. In my case, 60 students in a class and only ten students are admitted to university.

Xu: Looking back, we had no extracurricular life, only reading books, from 7 a.m. to 11 p.m.; even so, it was a kind of fulfilling life.

These conversations reveal the daily life of students in China. This was also a reflection of Chinese hidden curriculum. For millions of diligent students, imperial college examinations offer a ladder from provincial village schools to the nation's best universities. Historically, in China, the university entrance system has been "an imperfect heir to its imperfect father—the imperial civil service examinations. But it does represent a continuing meritocratic trend in Chinese society with a history unparalleled elsewhere" (Crozier, 2002). To survive the college examinations, Chinese students have to study both day and night; as Li says, he gave up his hobbies for study. Study in New Zealand might be another scenario:

> I have confidence in the quality of China's primary schools. For example, students are good at doing some math questions—better than New Zealand students. New Zealand teaching methods focus on a child's life skills. However, it is impossible for China to copy Kiwi ways, as we have a large population. In China's circumstances, the kids must study hard otherwise they would struggle for survival in the future. Facing this fierce competitive environment, kids have no other choices. Chinese students must learn to work hard. In New Zealand, if you don't go to university and work, you still can live very well. China's social context is different from here. You can critique our education system, but you cannot think of a better education system.
>
> (Tian, a doctoral student)

Tian noted that "China's circumstances" is the key to the different education system between China and New Zealand. Study, it seems, is the only choice for Chinese to survive in society, but it is not the same for New Zealanders as they "can live very well if they don't go to university," according to Tian. Furthermore, examining the Chinese overseas students' life experience in New Zealand, participants reflected that they might miss out on something in their life by doing nothing except study.

> Our education does not teach us about love, because our education system places more and more emphasis on students gaining knowledge for their future. I don't think Chinese kids have the opportunity to feel peace and happiness on a daily basis. They are taught how to find a good job and they are told that you must have a postgraduate degree. They don't care so much about how those children feel inside. They seem to care more about teaching them about how they should behave and study. Even though my parents treat me very well, they continually taught me "you must be a good child" while they never touched my heart.
>
> (Judy, a doctoral student)

Judy pointed out that Chinese students might not know what the meaning of life is and may merely know they need to study as their parents and society expect. Parental authority might be a factor in persuading Chinese children to behave and study well, but it is criticized by the Chinese overseas students who experienced a different study life in New Zealand. Thogersen (2012) asserts that students studying abroad hope to make positive contributions to the national project of the party-state and, as well, try to reconcile their personal and family agenda in the process of the transformation of both the individual and their family. In other words, regardless of the way in which the political authorities hope to confine and control the changes it has called for, the hidden curriculum in New Zealand enables Chinese students to understand the educational-system differences from a critical perspective. While not every Chinese student criticized or reflected on their life regarding education, they mentioned other things as well, such as their national identity.

"A Love and Hate Relationship"

Chinese national identity and the Chinese political system may be a sensitive topic for overseas Chinese students. In an interview, Ming pointed to the question "Is democracy a good thing?" on the interview question lists. He winced, saying it was a sensitive question.

Interviewer: Why is it a sensitive question?
Ming: Er . . . you know.

Impact of the "Hidden Curriculum" 95

[Laughing]

Ming:	I saw it is a sensitive question at my first glance at this sheet. Are you sure what I am going to say is strictly confidential?
Interviewer:	Sure.
Ming:	I am very serious and earnest regarding this interview. Keep. It. Secret.

We might not have heard the conversation about their identity in the host country, in the formal curriculum, but it is inevitable and often occurs in daily life between Chinese international students and Western host-country members. The experience of studying abroad may cause Chinese students to more strongly identify with their home country—China—and some of them feel uncomfortable hearing host-country members criticize any aspect of China (Hail, 2015). Hail's analysis is from a social-identity theory point of view. However, while I assume that the theory of social identity may explain the reason in general, it cannot grasp the whole complexity of the picture, which is vivid and deep.

For example, on September 3, 2015, almost every person in China was involved in the victory day celebrations to mark the end of the People's War of Resistance against Japanese aggression. Almost everybody watched the vainglorious march-past on TV in China. Most Chinese TV channels broadcast how the Chinese Communist Party won the war. A passion of patriotism permeated everywhere as it considered wrong for Chinese people to not profess love for their country. A conversation between several Chinese students in the study reveals their feelings about this:

Interviewer:	Could anyone help me to make sense of the two conceptions: love of one's country and love for people. First, some people love China because they were awed by the strong power of the country. But that doesn't mean they say they are like their fellow man. Second, I sense that if anyone didn't say they loved their country in the QQ group [an instant messaging software service], he or she would be criticized. So can we say it is wrong if we don't love our country?
Yan:	Some people see the strengths and others see the shortcomings.
Han:	In America, I can visit the government and talk with the mayor! Can you visit the Chinese government? The mayor in America is just a common person. Can you find the mayor in China?

Han is a little agitated as he was attacked by other Chinese students before, in a group conversation, because he sometimes criticizes China.

LV:	I have a love/hate relationship towards the Chinese government and the Chinese people. It depends on the situation.

	Sometimes I have much more love and sometimes I have much more hate. Many times, I am not free to choose between the emotions of love or hate as there are many other limiting factors. My attitude is like a chameleon.
Yan:	Love and hate emotions may be true feelings.
LV:	I hate the country that doesn't respect its people. In the early times of China, some doctors used humans as experimental objects. That's why we later have human ethics. Some supervisors do not treat their students as humans. It is too ideal for the students to be treated as humans. This is my chameleon attitude: I am in the middle of being a human and a chess piece in a huge country. I hope this is helpful to your research.
Raine:	Interviewer, if you are interested in Tiananmen Square, you can talk with the people who immigrated to New Zealand years ago. Their attitude and how they thought of that part of history are not the same as Western media reports.
Qiang:	I agree with Raine!
Interviewer:	Thanks Raine. I don't want to argue with you guys about who is wrong and who is right about the Tiananmen Incident, otherwise we can easily become immersed in political issues.
Raine:	Love the people is right. But if our country doesn't exist, what is the meaning to the people?

These excerpts show a complicated picture of Chinese international students' feeling towards China: some felt uncomfortable, angry, or annoyed when discussing some negative aspect of China, like Raine and Qiang; some chose not to mention or talk about it, like Ming; some criticized China, according to their overseas experience, like Han; and some felt neither hate nor love towards China, but love/hate together, like LV and Yan.

The interviews revealed diverse opinions that Chinese overseas students held towards their home country. Those who chose to study in a democratic culture faced a change from their previous experience under the Communist Party culture, as Carlson and Widaman (1988) revealed. Students who had previously lived abroad showed a significantly smaller change in, and a more positive and critical attitude towards, political concerns, cross-cultural interests, and cultural cosmopolitanism compared with those who had not previously lived abroad. Han's voice might be a good example. His experience—the hidden curriculum in America—in which the American government was challenged by other students, seemed challenged by the Chinese hidden curriculum that if anyone didn't say they loved their country, he or she would be criticized.

In terms of LV's ambiguous attitude, "love or hate" reflects the process of thinking of changing and of sociological interaction in a new society. LV may be able to act independently to make her own free choices in New Zealand, opting for a Western culture-patterned arrangement, as a way of gaining meaning and scientific understanding of the society as conscious agents in a key dimension of a studying-abroad environment.

In New Zealand, international students from China have to learn to make decisions by themselves, with respect not only to their belonging and their identity, but also to their studies and other daily-life matters, and they have to take responsibility for what they have done. As a result, they find it is challenging to adapt to their overseas life, with so many free choices. Some of them felt that outside of China, life is like being "out of a zoo."

"Life Can Be Like This"

> As for me, I have been in NZ for half a year. Looking back to China, I thought I was locked in a bird cage or, say, a zoo. I lived in a big zoo but I did not realize it until I walked out of the zoo. Wow, I lived in a zoo! Now that I am out of the zoo I am changing my thinking about my previous life in China. For example, what is a good life? In China, it is very basic that everyone wants to make much more money. But here [NZ] is not like that. I can choose a different life, rather than making money. Oh, life can be lived like this—enjoying the sunshine beside the beach or being close to nature on weekends. The whole world is much broader and bigger than I imagined. So is my life value. As another example, parents in China have always advocated that their child acquire a quality educational background; the higher level of schooling, the better. Here, things are different.
>
> (Qi, a doctoral student)

Qi's eyes glowed with pleasure when he described the "new" world that he found in New Zealand in which he felt he was outside of a cage or a zoo. He realized that until he experienced a different lifestyle in New Zealand, his life had been about worshipping the making of money, with his parents or his friends telling him what kind of life he should have.

Qi seemed happy to be out of the zoo while in New Zealand, with a chance to find himself, and he was enlightened by experiencing "the sunshine beside the beach or being close to nature on weekends" rather than merely knowing how to make more money. Out of the zoo, a lifestyle was developing with people surrounding him who motivated all his wishes, efforts, dreams, and ambitions; he felt "the whole world is much broader and bigger." Then his declaration that "Oh, life can be lived like this" showed the freedom of an individual who knows what he is looking for in the rest of his life.

Holmes (2008) found that Chinese students are able to reconstruct and renegotiate their identity that is inevitably tied to the deep origin of the inculcated structure of their Chinese cultural beliefs. It should be noted that the hidden

98 Xiudi Zhang

curriculum in New Zealand can contradict their former hidden curriculum by revealing or criticizing what the Chinese hidden curriculum holds with regard to stated views and values, according to what students actually experience in their daily life. In Qi's case, he dismissed his previous lifestyle, which was shaped by the people or the society around him, and redefined the choice he thought he should have, to "choose a different life, rather than making money." This shows that the hidden curriculum in New Zealand means that students with prior experience in China redefine themselves as independent individuals and to interweave their personal, professional, and even national goals (Thogersen, 2012). This also reflects on changing their ways of thinking about study.

> In New Zealand, the most important thing that I learned was independent thinking. Chinese culture has weaknesses which hinder innovation, such as being afraid to criticize, being afraid to show personality, or think independently. In China, the supervisor would be too involved in your research. In New Zealand, the supervisor has a culture of non-intervention. My supervisor does not have too much understanding of what I am doing in my research area, so I need to explore the whole process by myself, including my creative research and facing up to solving study problems by myself, which is a common phenomenon here. Probably the main benefit of my supervisor is that he can help me revise my thesis, that's all. I don't approve of this training experience but I have no choice. On the contrary, I am more independent than before. Another thing, I felt I improved my communication skills with foreigners by confidently appearing in front of them at an international conference.
>
> (Lee, a doctoral student)

Changing to "independent thinking" is a positive aspect of studying abroad for Chinese students. One of the challenges of the Chinese hidden curriculum: "being afraid to criticize, being afraid to show personality or think independently," is conveyed in the transmission of norms, values, and beliefs in the classroom and the social environment. It is also an outcome of comparing two hidden curricula: "In China, the supervisor would be too involved in your research. In New Zealand, the supervisor has a culture of non-intervention." The independence not only removes limits on Chinese overseas students' study, learning skills, and thinking, but also on their attitudes towards life. As Qi says at the beginning: "Oh, life can be lived like this."

Discussion

We have seen from the above that the dynamics of the hidden curriculum are difficult to pin down, whether in China or in New Zealand. It is, after all, hidden. This is also because it is as complex as interactions between learning styles, national identities, languages, and cultures make it. Nevertheless, this chapter has emphasized how Chinese international students' values and identities are challenged by New Zealand hidden curriculum.

As indicated in the literature review, current research on Chinese students in the New Zealand context is mainly limited to solving academic problems. This study made a major breakthrough in reaching the respondents' private thoughts and feelings, as ones that they sometimes had not articulated even to themselves. The focus-group data revealed that students surprised themselves with how open and critical they could be.

Furthermore, my hidden curriculum approach locates whether and how Chinese students in New Zealand are being socialized in a way that makes them reflect critically on life back home—i.e., socialized into more independent thinking. The methodology is an important aspect of addressing this question. The data include more than one source, which allows access to all the complexity of subjective and intersubjective experience. The mix of individual interview and group discussion allows for some movement between subjective and intersubjective views.

It should be clear, nonetheless, that Chinese students have a background of formal Chinese education, including the formal school curriculum, and a Chinese hidden curriculum that somehow interconnects with school, state, and family, all of which teach the importance of respecting authority and living in a rule-bound society. In New Zealand, while engaging in formal study at university, the experience of doctoral study, and the relationship with supervisors, is part of a different hidden curriculum—also made up of these Chinese students' relationships with local people—through which they learn new freedoms and identities. At the same time, those international students experience an internal process of having to negotiate the divergence between these two hidden curricula. They reflect critically on China and on themselves, beyond following their formal goals in educational institutions: test scores, language and literacy, and other academic achievements and challenges.

Revealing features of the hidden curriculum, as my research aims to do, may help to see the hidden curriculum as an educational resource, one that provides opportunities for Chinese students to discover an intellectual autonomy that might be unexpected, and that provokes them to refashion their understanding of—and relationship to—China.

We see best the educational potential of such reflections in the discussion groups. As shown above, some Chinese students stated that the "Chinese education is *poisoned*," when compared with the local Western education system, and that both experiences reflected on their own lives. Others, such as Tian, did not agree with such a negative view of Chinese education and were more confident of the value of the Chinese education system. Changing or not changing their lives, education, and identity is challenging, not least because the messages are transmitted tacitly and received unconsciously. Often their processing of the information also occurs below conscious thought. My study speaks with a diversity of voices in relation to identities. Han clearly stated his view in terms of his relationship with the government while reacting to Raine and Qiang. We saw LV and Yan still standing indecisively in the middle—caught between hate and love. In these very discussions we saw a curriculum in operation, a self-questioning, and a process of learning. In this important sense, this is an *educational* methodology.

Part of that learning process can be seen in the data as students grapple with their response at an emotional level, interpreting their own educational history and prior experiences. At the same time, they are seeking to interpret the New Zealand hidden curriculum to redefine themselves as independent individuals in a globalized but still individualized world. Perhaps, above all analyses lies evidence of an emergence of a different sense of individualism being learned, with potentially wide-ranging social and political consequences. In China, those international students' personal, professional, and national goals are closely interwoven under the banner of "party-state-managed individualisation" (Yan, 2010, p. 495)—a fusion of person and people, of individual and collective. However, their Chinese way of life (personal), study (professional), and national identity (national goals) bear the brunt of learning through New Zealand's hidden curriculum, enabling these students to understand their own educational experience and prior life experiences in a critical light and with more room for individual development.

Perhaps the key message of this study is that a hidden-curriculum perspective is useful for evaluating the impact of overseas study on Chinese students. The particular approach to curriculum in this study takes the classroom as the critical, reflective space. The findings contribute to understanding of Chinese students' social interactions in overseas contexts bearing on the larger body of research on Chinese heritage. In fact, crossing from a communist society to a democratic one causes a huge shake-up of identity for the Chinese international students. It is essentially an axiological shift: foundational values are destabilized and questioned. This often discomforting process of reassessment is not well understood by Western academics who teach and supervise Chinese students. In light of globalization, the study plays a role as a trailblazer for future research on Chinese-heritage learners to consider the impact of hidden-curriculum factors in the research and to pay much more attention to the heritage learners' Chinese-cultural background.

Acknowledgments

This research was supported by the Chinese Scholarship Council. The author is grateful to Professor Saville Kushner for his critical and constructive comments on an earlier draft of this chapter.

References

Butcher, A. P. (2004). Educate, consolidate, and immigrate: Educational immigration in Auckland, New Zealand. *Asia Pacific Viewpoint*, *45*(2), 255–278.

Campbell, J., and Li, M. (2008). Asian students' voices: An empirical study of Asian students' learning experiences at a New Zealand university. *Journal of Studies in International Education*, *12*(4), 375–396.

Carlson, J. S., and Widaman, K. F. (1988). The effects of study abroad during college on attitudes toward other cultures. *International Journal of Intercultural Relations*, *12*(1), 1–17.

Creswell, J. W. (2012). *Qualitative inquiry and research design: Choosing among five approaches* (4th edn). Upper Saddle River, NJ: Pearson Education.

Crozier, J. (2002). *A unique experiment*. Retrieved from www.sacu.org/examinations.html.

Dolby, N. (2004). Encountering an American self: Study abroad and national identity. *Comparative Education Review*, *48*(2), 150–173.

Fairbrother, G. P. (2003). The influence of socialization and critical thinking on students' attitudes toward the nation. In G. P. Fairbrother (Ed.), *Toward a critical patriotism: Student resistance to political education in Hong Kong and China* (pp. 135–160). Hong Kong, China: Hong Kong University Press.

Hail, H. C. (2015). Patriotism abroad overseas Chinese students' encounters with criticisms of China. *Journal of Studies in International Education*, *19*(4), 311–326.

Henze, J., and Zhu, J. (2012). Current research on Chinese students studying abroad. *Research in Comparative and International Education*, *7*(1), 90–104.

Ho, E., Li, W., Cooper, J., and Holmes, P. (2007). *The experiences of Chinese international students in New Zealand*. Hamilton, New Zealand: University of Waikato.

Holmes, P. (2008). Foregrounding harmony: Chinese international student's voices in communication with their New Zealand peers. *China Media Report Overseas*, *5*(2), 73–83.

Jackson, P. W. (1990). *Life in classrooms*. New York, NY: Teachers College Press.

Lichtman, M. (2012). *Qualitative research in education: A user's guide* (3rd edn). Thousand Oaks, CA: Sage.

Malcolm, P., Ling, A., and Sherry, C. (2004). *Why do Chinese students study in New Zealand and how can they be helped to succeed?* Paper presented at the Higher Education Research and Development Society of Australasia Annual Conference, Miri, Malaysia.

Meighan, R., and Harber, C. (2007). *A sociology of educating* (5th edn). London, UK: Continuum.

Ministry of Education. (2013). *Students in regular higher education institutions*. Retrieved from www.moe.edu.cn/publicfiles/business/htmlfiles/moe/s7382/201305/152553.html.

Stake, R. E. (1978). The case study method in social inquiry. *Educational Researcher*, *7*(2), 5–8.

Thogersen, S. (2012). Chinese students' great expectations: Prospective pre-school teachers on the move. *Learning and Teaching*, *5*(3), 75–93.

Wood, B. E. (2011). *Citizenship in our place: Exploring New Zealand young people's everyday, place-based perspectives on participation in society*. Doctoral thesis. Retrieved from http://researcharchive.vuw.ac.nz/handle/10063/1671.

Xinhua. (2013). *China becomes largest source of overseas students*. Retrieved from http://english.people.com.cn/203691/8351461.html.

Yan, Y. (2010). The Chinese path to individualization. *The British Journal of Sociology*, *61*(3), 489–512.

Zhang, Z., and Brunton, M. (2007). Differences in living and learning: Chinese international students in New Zealand. *Journal of Studies in International Education*, *11*(2), 124–140.

PART II

Motivation, Challenges, and Adaptation of Chinese–Heritage Learners in and across Globalized Contexts

6

MAINLAND CHINESE UNDERGRADUATES' CHALLENGES AND STRATEGIC RESPONSES IN ADAPTING TO HONG KONG

Jian (Tracy) Tao and Xuesong Gao

One of the critical notions researchers studying Chinese-heritage language learners need to engage with is the diversity of language learners. The so-called "Chinese-heritage language (CHL) learners" are not homogenous in terms of cultural beliefs and practices. Instead, they display different values and practices in the language learning process because of different life experiences and ways of cultural socialization in different contexts. These differences may well constitute significant challenges for CHL learners from different backgrounds to be addressed when they are together (Li and Duff, 2008). To illustrate such challenges, this chapter draws on the second author's inquiry into Mainland Chinese undergraduates' language learning experiences in an English-medium university in Hong Kong. This chapter focuses on how these students responded to various sociocultural challenges when socializing with local students who share similar cultural heritage.

The perception that English proficiency helps individuals achieve social mobility fuels popular longing for English-medium (EM) education, particularly in tertiary sectors, across the globe (e.g., Gao, 2010a, 2010b; Nunan, 2003). Many Mainland Chinese students pursue tertiary studies in English medium abroad, assuming such education provides rich opportunities to improve their English and thus adds value to the academic credentials they acquire. Although Hong Kong has a comparatively small tertiary education sector, it has recently emerged as a popular destination for elite Mainland Chinese school graduates to pursue tertiary education because of the aforementioned appeal of EM tertiary education (e.g., Gao, 2010a, 2010b; Xu, 2014). EM universities in Hong Kong receive an overwhelming number of highly qualified applicants from Mainland China. For instance, the University of Hong Kong usually receives more than 10,000 applications and admits only 2% or 3% of these applicants (Gao, 2017). Despite its geographical proximity and cultural affinity, researchers have noted significant challenges that Mainland Chinese undergraduates need to address in the process of academic socialization and language learning (e.g. Gao, 2010a, 2010b; Xu, 2014). Like many cross-border students who are confronted by sociocultural challenges during adaptation to the host communities (e.g., Montgomery and MacDowell, 2009; Tran, 2011; Xu, 2014), Mainland Chinese undergraduates in Hong Kong are no exception although the host community has a similar cultural heritage.

The present inquiry started to explore Mainland Chinese undergraduates' educational experiences in Hong Kong with a focus on the linguistic challenges that these students might have in adapting themselves to EM academic studies. At the very start of the inquiry, it became apparent that these students face significant challenges when socializing with local Chinese students in Hong Kong, which profoundly mediated their efforts to learn and use both Cantonese and English. For this reason, this chapter is an attempt to answer the following questions:

1. What challenges did they encounter when socializing with local students?
2. What strategic efforts did they invest to engage with local students for academic socialization?

Social Networks for Academic Socialization and Mainland Chinese Undergraduates in Hong Kong

The inquiry was informed by research on language learning that contends that language learning should be conceptualized not only as a cognitive process to acquire linguistic forms but also as a process of struggling for participation and acquiring membership of the target speech community (Pavlenko and Lantolf, 2000; Norton, 2012; Lantolf et al., 2015). In the light of this theoretical perspective, successful language learning requires efforts for creating, maintaining, and developing supportive social learning networks that facilitate language learning efforts. According to Bourdieu (1986), a social network is "not given" but is born as a result of individuals' investment efforts that are sustained by continuous exchange of valuable resources (p. 249). These resources are derived from an individual's cultural capital, such as linguistic competence and educational credentials. It has been noted in research that individuals with similar lifestyles and socioeconomic characteristics are more likely to participate in social interactions and forge "closer and more supportive relationships" (Lin, 2001, p. 39), which in turn facilitate individual language learning efforts. In the meantime, individuals of different backgrounds need to spend "more efforts" to access social networks "because of resources differentials and lack of shared sentiments"

(p. 47), which may undermine their learning efforts. This issue can be particularly salient in many students' educational experiences, including those of Mainland Chinese undergraduates in Hong Kong, in the context of internationalization of higher education that embraces students of diversified backgrounds.

The presence of students having different cultural and social experiences has transformed many universities into "complex and overlapping communities in which variously positioned participants learn specific, local, historically constructed and changing practices" (Norton and Toohey, 2001, p. 312). Although these Chinese undergraduates share cultural and ethnic origins with their local counterparts, it is worth noting that these two groups of students do not have "a shared repertoire of stories, artefacts, tools, actions, historical events, discourses, concepts and styles" that bind them together into a cohesive community (Wenger, 1998, p. 4). Mainland Chinese students and their local counterparts may not have sufficient common topics to discuss with each other (Lam, 2006).

Hong Kong was a British colony for 150 years and has developed into a highly affluent metropolis while Mainland China experienced numerous setbacks in its development path before it became one of the leading economies in the world. Moreover, Hong Kong and Mainland China have quite different sociopolitical systems and sociolinguistic situations. In Mainland China, Putonghua is being promoted as the national spoken standard Chinese for use in all public arenas, including schools and government services, while the status of a variety of regional Chinese varieties spoken by many is diminishing. In contrast, Cantonese, one of the regional Chinese varieties, is the lingua franca for socialization in Hong Kong, although English is considered a highly prestigious language despite Putonghua rising as a significant competitor. Due to these sociolinguistic differences, the same thing can be referred to in different terms in Hong Kong and Mainland China. For this reason, Mainland Chinese undergraduates need to make strategic efforts continuously to acquire relevant resources to build supportive learning social networks, which can be crucial to participation in and adaptation to the host community in Hong Kong (e.g., Yu and Downing, 2012; Xu, 2014).

The shifting sociopolitical conditions in Hong Kong have also added complexities to Mainland Chinese students' adaptation to the host communities in universities. Since 2003, Hong Kong has relaxed visa regulations for Mainland Chinese visitors and students. The number of Mainland Chinese undergraduates in Hong Kong universities has been increasing steadily. According to the University Grants Committee (UGC), 4,638 Mainland Chinese undergraduates were studying in its funded universities in the academic year 2010/2011 and 1,591 more were admitted as undergraduates in July 2013 ("香港8所高校錄取約1590名內地新生," 2013). To encourage Mainland Chinese students passing out from local universities, the Hong Kong government implemented a new visa regime in 2008 that encourages them to stay and search for local employment upon graduation (Geng and Li, 2012). However, the increased presence of Mainland

Chinese undergraduates in Hong Kong universities does not diminish "physical boundaries" between the two groups of students; instead this has galvanized many into "us-against-them" posturing (Kim, 2006, pp. 283–284). Local opinion leaders have openly demanded answers to the question as to whether Hong Kong's universities should be for its own students or elite outsiders from across the border (Kan, 2011). There have been repeated public protests against Mainland Chinese visitors who are held responsible for causing congestion on the streets and other social problems in Hong Kong (Liu, 2012; BBC, 2015). Therefore, it is important to understand how Mainland Chinese undergraduates socialize with local students when adapting to new ways of life and academic studies in Hong Kong.

The Study

The data on Mainland Chinese undergraduates' experiential accounts in Hong Kong were collected by the second author, who intended to understand the linguistic and sociocultural challenges in academic socialization (see Gao, 2017). The second author has been following up Mainland Chinese students' experiences in a series of inquiries with particular focus on micro-political strategies they use when negotiating for opportunities to learn and use English (Gao, 2010a, 2010b, 2014, 2017). The first author has experienced and witnessed the rising anti-Mainland Chinese social atmosphere since arrival in Hong Kong as a doctoral student in 2013. By using part of the data from Gao (2017), this chapter problematizes the notion of Chinese-heritage speakers, often conceived as a homogeneous group, and argues for the existence of heterogeneity creating challenges for these migrants from one Chinese context to another.

The inquiry involved 26 Mainland Chinese students who had enrolled in undergraduate programs lasting no less than three years (Gao, 2017). At the time of data collection, the participants were all Year 2 or 3 students who had studied and lived in Hong Kong for at least two or three years. It is believed that the prospect of employment and continuation of stay in Hong Kong might motivate such students to overcome various challenges and participate in the local social network during their academic studies. Consequently, the participant recruitment was particularly oriented to students from business and social sciences faculties because these students were most likely to stay on in Hong Kong upon graduation (Huberman and Miles, 1994). We believe that they may find the linguistic and sociocultural challenges most pressing upon arrival in Hong Kong. All but two participants could not speak Cantonese before arrival in Hong Kong.

Data Collection

During the data collection period, the second author conducted in-depth narrative interviews with 26 participants, since narrative interviews encourage the participants to share experiences (e.g., Benson, 2005). In the interviews, the participants were asked to recall how they came to Hong Kong for studies, what specific challenges they had experienced upon arrival and how they had responded to these challenges during academic socialization. He also took the opportunity to ask them to reflect on the recent incidents associated with Mainland Chinese visitors and students covered in the mass media. He also shared some observations of participants interviewed earlier with those who were interviewed later. Such sharing may serve as a member checking strategy and it also helps the later interviews be more focused.

Data Analysis

To address the research questions, we analyzed the participants' experiential accounts of arriving and adapting to the English-medium (EM) university to identify how they overcame various challenges of creating and sustaining supportive social networks to facilitate language learning and use. We adopted a "paradigmatic and analytic" approach to data analysis, which was to identify and classify data extracts with shared themes through multiple rounds of reading. At first we read through all transcripts to gain a general impression of the data that may be used as part of the research background. By rereading each transcript, we teased out the reported experiences chronologically and wrote mini-biographies of all participants that served as the baseline data for this study. Then the narratives were compared across participants to generate four stages of the socialization process. The four stages cover how they sought access to the local social networks initially, what challenges they were confronted with, how they responded with alignment efforts and lastly what the engagements resulted in. After that, further rounds of readings were conducted to search for commonalities across participants in each stage to elicit major themes. The involvement of two authors in the analysis, supplemented with participants' confirmation of our preliminary interpretations, helped enhance the quality of analysis.

Findings

Analysis of the data helped reveal that most participants were aware of the necessity of learning Cantonese and improving English to better adapt themselves to the new educational context. Unfortunately, they also reported significant linguistic, sociocultural, and ideological differences that undermined their intentions to integrate into the students' community through socialization (Q1). These obstacles were found to have stemmed from lack of a shared repertoire of "stories, artefacts, tools, actions, historical events, discourses, concepts and styles" (Wenger, 1998, p. 4). The participants responded with a variety of strategic efforts to reduce the "resource differentials" (Lin, 2001, p. 47) so that they could access and sustain participation in local student communities (Q2). In many cases, such strategic investments yielded mixed results.

Linguistic, Sociocultural, and Ideological Barriers

As revealed by the participants' narratives, they needed to address a variety of differences between them and their local counterparts in the process of adaptation and in linguistic pursuits. Instead of English, a functional command of Cantonese is usually the most pressing linguistic challenge they needed to overcome. They also needed to deal with cultural differences that often tend to separate them from local students, resulting in the need to socialize more with other Mainland Chinese undergraduates. The ideological and political differences further discouraged them from engaging with local students in productive discussions that could potentially lead to better mutual understanding and enhanced language proficiency.

Echoing previous research on Mainland Chinese students' academic socialization, ability to communicate in Cantonese emerged as one of the most critical barriers upon arrival in Hong Kong. Although many were concerned whether they had sufficient English knowledge for academic studies and had some idea about the importance of Cantonese, many were probably unprepared for the fact that inability to communicate in Cantonese considerably undermined socialization with local students. This linguistic challenge was explicitly articulated by Han,[1] a Year 3 accounting and finance student, as follows:

Extract 1

Cantonese is a big issue even though they understand Putonghua and we understand a little bit of Cantonese. When we get together, they like to use Cantonese but we cannot follow their conversations. When they crack jokes and laugh together, we do not even know why they laugh.

(Gao, 2017, p. 370)

As can be seen in the extract above, Cantonese is the predominant medium for socialization with local students; it is used even in the presence of Mainland Chinese students although they "cannot follow their conversations." The language choice of local students in social interactions as described above can be utterly subconscious and natural, but it can be interpreted by many Mainland Chinese students as an indication of lack of intention to accommodate. The dominance of Cantonese in socialization excludes Mainland Chinese and other students who do not speak Cantonese even when they are physically present.

In tandem with linguistic challenges, many Mainland students believe cultural differences are another significant "cause for separation" from local students. Even though both Mainland and local Chinese students share similar cultural heritage, they have quite different approaches to life, study, and work because of their respective backgrounds and educational experiences. The different life and educational experiences are manifested in their "communication styles" and things "they are interested in" or "like to talk about," as reflected by Ming, another Year 3 accounting and finance student:

Extract 2

Researcher: Why do you think that Mainland and local Chinese students belong to two separate groups [. . .]?

Ming: [. . .] Cultural differences are the most important cause for this separation. We grew up in different circumstances. They received British education and were exposed to Hong Kong culture since they were young [. . .]. We have acquired different mindsets, languages and even communication styles. [. . .] We are not familiar with things that they are interested in. They do not know what we like to talk about. [. . .] We feel more secure among ourselves when working with other Mainland Chinese students on projects.

(Gao, 2017, p. 368)

The extract speaks for the "resource differentials" that undermine Mainland Chinese students' socialization with their local counterparts (Lin, 2001, p. 47). Consequently, this participant observed that many Mainland Chinese students choose not to work with local students, which reduces potential opportunities to use Cantonese and improve their understanding of local students. What happened is probably repeated in many other parts of the world where Mainland Chinese students spend more time socializing with each other—which isolates them from other students—because of the convenience of shared mindsets.

Apart from the differences in prior experiences, the participants perceived that they had priorities and objectives quite different from those of local students. Fudan, a Year 2 accounting and finance student, felt that local students wanted to "enjoy themselves" and "are not interested in studies." In contrast, Mainland Chinese students like him are highly committed to achieving academic excellence:

Extract 3

I feel that [. . .] [t]hose (students) who chose to study here, especially those who live in residential halls, come to university to enjoy themselves. They are not interested in studies. Therefore, it is difficult for us to integrate ourselves into this local students' community. Even if we do, this means that we will not have good academic results. [. . .] We do not really have any conflict with them but we live in two worlds that are wide apart. We just respect each other. This is most regrettable.

(Fudan, Year 2, accounting and finance;
in Gao, 2017, p. 371)

Given such different attitudes towards academic studies, the participants were concerned whether successful socialization with local students can be achieved only at the cost of academic studies; their future options upon graduation depend on

112 Jian Tao and Xuesong Gao

academic results, irrespective of whether they planned to stay in Hong Kong for employment or leave for academic studies or career options elsewhere (Gao, 2010a, 2014). Although many local students may also share similar objectives, the perceived differences apparently separate the two groups of students, as Mainland Chinese and local students hardly share activities. It seems that they live "in two worlds that are wide apart" despite sharing a similar cultural heritage, which undermines the initial desire to learn and use Cantonese and English through socialization.

Apart from the perceived differences in attitudes towards academic studies, different political stances and ideological persuasions also emerge as an increasingly salient challenge for Mainland Chinese students to overcome during academic socialization. For example, Jing, a Year 3 economics and finance student, found it difficult to understand her roommate's participation in "radical" political activities:

Extract 4

My first roommate is [. . .] a radical girl in Hong Kong. We have pictures on our room door showing she participated in public demonstrations and sit-ins. [. . .] At the beginning, I was curious about why she was so involved in these activities. We Mainland Chinese students are also interested in political affairs but we will not be that radical. [. . .] She thinks that demonstrations are much more important than her studies.

(Jing, Year 3, economics and finance; in Gao, 2017, p. 370)

Jing's inability to comprehend her roommate's enthusiasm for public demonstrations is suggestive of the difference between her agenda or objectives and those of her roommate with regard to university experiences. Fortunately, different political stances did not lead to breakdowns in communication between Jing and her roommate. However, different political stances can trigger local students' criticism and despising of Mainland Chinese students, which can be detrimental to their desire to socialize with local students. As the only Mainland Chinese student in a course, Yuan's friend was labeled as a member of "the 'fooled' generation" by the local classmates when discussing political issues in Mainland China.

Extract 5

Yuan: My friend took a course in which she is the only Mainland Chinese student. She was sometimes criticized for being one of the "fooled" generation and having no political freedom. We have quite different political views. [. . .]

Researcher: Maybe we have different political views here. I was wondering if you tried to understand some issues from

	their political perspectives or you just cannot accept their views?
Yuan:	I do not like to discuss politics with them. I feel that they behave like religious people. It is difficult to change their views. I am afraid that we will quarrel instead of discussing. It is not necessary for us to quarrel. It is not worth the effort.

(Gao, 2017, p. 370)

As she recalled her friend's experience, Yuan portrayed these local students as political fanatics and for this reason, she avoided discussing any sensitive issues with them. In the light of the rising tensions between Hong Kong and Mainland China, it is inevitable for these students to discuss some sensitive issues if they wish to deepen their engagement with each other through socialization. By treating these issues as a forbidden zone, Chinese Mainland students essentially reduce opportunities to exchange views with local students for mutual understanding. For these reasons, many participants found it difficult to sustain engagement with local students even though they had the desire to integrate themselves into local student communities upon arrival in Hong Kong. Since they can achieve only superficial rather than deep personally meaningful interactions with local students, they soon gave up socialization efforts like Yiqi, a Year 2 accounting and finance student said:

Extract 6

When I first came here, I really wanted to integrate into the local student community. I spent a lot of time and energy socializing with them. [. . .] then I realized that my efforts were not being rewarded. [. . .] I have no private life together with local students except for hall events. After one year, I started asking myself why it is like this. We are good friends with each other, aren't we? [. . .] Why have I never thought of inviting them for a meal or for something else? Why have they never invited me for some personal activities?

(Yiqi, Year 2, accounting and finance;
in Gao, 2017, pp. 372–373)

Even though Yiqi spent "a lot of time and energy socializing with them" initially, he still found that his engagement with local students was confined to events that all hall residents are eligible to participate in. He probably realized that there was a clear boundary between Mainland students and the local counterparts. Even though Mainland Chinese students like Yiqi had endeavored to interact with local students for mutual understanding, the social network he managed to establish with local students might have been fragile because he did not have the resources required to sustain continuous exchanges (Bourdieu, 1986). As mentioned earlier, the differential styles of academic lives separate the two groups of students having

Strategic Responses to Overcome Barriers

In order to overcome the above-mentioned barriers, the participants were found to have adopted different strategic efforts at different stages of adaptation, especially during the period immediately after arrival. Most of these efforts were undertaken to help them achieve linguistic and sociocultural alignment with local students (see also Gao, 2010a, 2010b).

The data indicate that almost all participants attempted to learn Cantonese so that they could have the linguistic tool for socialization with local students upon arrival. In many cases, their efforts to learn Cantonese were appreciated by their local counterparts and that did facilitate interactions. Nevertheless, adopting a shared linguistic practice did not always guarantee success in socialization with local students because the sociocultural differences are too deep for most of them to bridge. Even when they were using Cantonese for interacting with local students, participants like Wei, a Year 3 economics and finance student, felt that she had to speak with great caution:

Extract 7

Wei:	Every time I chatted with local students, I paid particular attention to my language use. That is partly because I need to think about how to say something in Cantonese. [. . .] I still need more time to process it. I am particularly cautious in using Cantonese because I do not want to create any misunderstanding. There are always some biased people, you know. For instance, when I speak with friends in Putonghua, I sometimes use foul language or some not-so-nice words. I will never use such words when talking to local students.
Researcher:	What kind of biased people are you worried about?
Wei:	These people always think that Mainland Chinese have no manners. [. . .]
Researcher:	Apart from the choice of language, what else are you cautious about? How about topics?
Wei:	I do not talk about myself. Of course, they do not ask questions about myself. It seems to be always like this. I talk about myself with others but I do not talk about myself with local students.

(Gao, 2017, p. 372)

As can be seen in the extract, Wei was quite aware of the negative stereotypical image of Mainland Chinese that many local students have. For this reason, she felt obliged to be extremely careful in language use and tried her best not to use any "foul language or no-so-nice words," which were often used by local students in conversations. She was quite concerned that her use of "foul language" may confirm her local counterparts' perception that Mainland Chinese "have no manners." Therefore, she invested efforts in building a positive self-image before local students by using "clean" Cantonese. Unfortunately, the desire to present herself positively meant at the same time that she did not wish to reveal too much of herself when socializing with local students. The lack of self-revelation and exclusion of personal topics may contribute to the maintenance of harmonious relationships on the one hand but on the other hand, they might limit the social interaction to the superficial level, as reported by Fudan (in Extract 3). Despite the strategic efforts that these participants made, they might have put themselves in a dilemma.

Besides attaching importance to the learning of Cantonese, participants committed themselves to fully participating in local students' activities. For instance, Qun, a Year 3 accounting and finance student, became a floor chief in his residential hall. By doing so, he established close relationships with local students and also developed outlooks similar to them in the socialization process.

Extract 8

I am the first non-local student floor chief in my hall. [. . .] I got to know my floor mates very well and have a good relationship with them. [. . .] They do not treat me as a typical Mainland Chinese student. They always say that I am not like those Mainland Chinese students we know of. [. . .] But I like to socialize with them and play with them. Many Mainland Chinese students are not willing to participate in local students' activities.
(Qun, Year 3, accounting and finance; in Gao, 2017, p. 373)

So far, this seems to be one of the most successful strategies for Mainland Chinese students to get integrated into local student communities. As can be seen in the quote, many of Qun's local friends did not regard him as a typical Mainland Chinese student, which Qun clearly considered a compliment and a consequence of his efforts. Indeed, what he did probably differentiated him from other Mainland Chinese students who had failed to successfully socialize with local students. Qun also felt that he might have distanced himself from "many Mainland Chinese students" who are known for their unwillingness to participate in local students' activities. As Qun immersed himself in the local student communities and assumed responsibilities expected of him, he was ushered into a process of acculturation, in which he did invest "more efforts" than many other Mainland Chinese students so that he could acquire shared "resources" and "sentiments" for successfully socializing with local students (Lin, 2001, p. 47).

116 Jian Tao and Xuesong Gao

Qun is probably one of the most successful Mainland Chinese students in the context of socialization with local students. Many others who undertook similar efforts to participate in local students' activities failed to achieve what they expected to achieve. These participants recalled that they had to endure considerable "pain" before they could have any "joys." Xinhan, a Year 2 accounting and finance student, was one of those who described her socialization experience as "a mixture of pains and joys." While she joined the executive committee of a student club to get involved in the local community, her experience of working with local students was not quite positive:

Extract 9

It is a mixture of pains and joys. [. . .] I do not really understand their views. Whenever we plan something, they will consider many many issues. [. . .] They keep changing the plans [in light of new emerging issues], which takes a lot of time. I feel extremely bored by the process.

(Xinhan, Year 2, accounting and finance; in Gao, 2017, p. 373)

Although Xinhan adapted herself to the local student community, she was still baffled by the ways local students manage such affairs. For instance, student clubs customarily have annual meetings of the executive team non-stop for three successive days. Xinhan participated in such meetings but could not understand or accept that meetings had to be that long. However, she still managed to forge close relationships with some local students.

In comparison with local students' society activities, participants like Yifan, a Year 2 surveying student, socialized with local students in off-campus settings. During internship, he worked with local students in a non-governmental organization (NGO):

Extract 10

When I was working as an intern at an NGO last summer, I worked with three local students. They were quite reliable. I had never worked with local students before on particular projects. They were much more reliable than I expected. However, my friend had a few local students as team members and they were very unreliable. It depends on individuals.

(Yifan, Year 2, surveying; in Gao, 2017, p. 373)

The experience of collaborating with local students changed Yifan's initial impressions about local students, who were considered unreliable by many Mainland Chinese students. This invited him to reflect on whether the so-called local students are a homogenous group with shared beliefs and practices. Zhiying, a Year 2 accounting and finance student, reported that he had developed a deep friendship with a local student and had also changed his perception of local students.

Extract 11

I know a Hong Kong student very well. He has been trying his best to find internship opportunities and lives under great pressure. He thinks about looking for a job, etc. [. . .] We came to know each other during exchanges. [. . .] We spent quite a lot of time going out [. . .] Mainland Chinese students are not inclined to talk about themselves willingly. My Hong Kong friend told me that he lives in Tin Shui Wai and what his parents are doing. I did not ask him about them. He shared these with me.

(Zhiying, Year 2, accounting and finance; in Gao, 2017, p. 373)

As Zhiying gained deep insights into local students' feelings and lives through socialization, he acquired an increasingly positive image of local students in general. At the same time, he seemed to distance himself from Mainland Chinese students who were reportedly reluctant to share much about themselves. These participants also began to be self-critical and attributed the gap between them and local students to their own obsession with academic studies as reflected by Chao, a Year 3 social sciences student.

Extract 12

I feel that many Mainland students here are particularly anxious about success. [. . .] It is very easy for them to feel anxious because of reasons such as low grades in a course. They really blame themselves seriously when they fail to achieve the most desirable academic results even though they are already excellent themselves.

(Chao, Year 3, social sciences; in Gao, 2017, p. 374)

Despite the prevalence of failures as reported by the participants, critical reflexivity displayed by Chao shows great potential for the two groups of students to reach mutual understanding. Together with sustained engagement with local students through self-revelations and critical reflection, Mainland Chinese students like Chao and Zhiying were able to acquire deep appreciation of local students and maintain a mutually understanding relationship with them.

Discussion

Although Mainland Chinese students share a similar cultural heritage with local Chinese students, the study reveals a variety of the challenges they had when socializing with local students and their strategic responses in light of the rising tensions between Hong Kong and Mainland China (e.g., Kan, 2011; Liu, 2012). Analysis of the relevant data revealed the lack of "repertoire" and "sentiments" between Mainland Chinese and local Chinese students remains the most important challenge. This echoes the result from previous research that has problematized the perception of Hong Kong's universities as cohesive communities with practices that facilitate Mainland Chinese students' pursuit of language and academic competencies (Gao, 2010a, 2010b). The arrival of Mainland Chinese students in Hong Kong's universities means that they enter "complex and overlapping communities in which variously positioned participants learn specific, local, historically constructed and changing practices" (Norton and Toohey, 2001, p. 312). Before they learn and use the languages (e.g., Cantonese or English) that they desired to learn and use in this EM university, Mainland Chinese students need to make considerable efforts to forge and maintain a mutually understanding relationship with local Chinese students.

Since "a shared repertoire of stories, artefacts, tools, actions, historical events, discourses, concepts and styles" (Wenger, 1998, p. 4) and "sentiments" (Lin, 2001, p. 47) are crucial for these students to establish and sustain supportive social networks with local students, it is not surprising to see that many participants had made strategic efforts to redress these differences. Consequently, they were active in learning Cantonese, the dominant linguistic medium for socialization with local students, at least at the beginning of their studies. Their efforts to learn Cantonese might reduce the time that they had for learning English, which was essential for their academic success, if they failed to manage the learning of the two languages in a balanced manner (e.g., Gao, 2010a, 2010b). They had also attempted to participate in local students' activities, although most of them withdrew since they felt that they could achieve what they desired by investing the same efforts in other pursuits. Apart from learning and using English for academic studies, these students spent more time using Putonghua with other Mainland Chinese students, a phenomenon widely observed in many other universities that attract a large number of Mainland Chinese students (Zhang, 2013; Lam, 2006). Nevertheless, six participants reported successful integration into the local student community. Their success confirms the necessity of spending "more effort" to reduce "resource differentials" (Lin, 2001, p. 47) when they have different life-styles and sociocultural backgrounds. It must also be noted that local students are not homogenous in terms of values and attitudes. The diversity in local students offers Mainland Chinese students opportunities to succeed in socializing with local students with whom they might have found it easier to have shared "repertoire" and "sentiments" as well as reduce the resource differentials. This finding suggests that integration with the local community is not impossible for Mainland Chinese students but it does reveal that it is highly challenging to identify whom they can easily forge bonds with in the host communities. Successes in establishing such supportive social networks could then open more opportunities for them to learn and use Cantonese or English (Gao, 2010a, 2010b).

It is worth noting that Chinese-heritage students other than those from Mainland China may experience similar sociolinguistic challenges upon entering universities in Hong Kong. For instance, even locally born Chinese-heritage students, who undergo transition from EM international schools to universities, are confronted with identity struggle as they cannot socialize in Mandarin or Cantonese even though they are perceived as native Chinese speakers (see Chapter 1 in this volume). In tandem with Chapter 1, the findings of this study illustrate the sociolinguistic adaptation when Chinese-heritage students experience transition from one Chinese community to another, and call for more attention to their academic socialization.

Conclusion

The inquiry examined Mainland Chinese undergraduates' experiences after arrival in a leading EM university in Hong Kong with foci on challenges they faced and strategic responses they adopted for academic socialization with local Chinese students. The findings problematize the concept of Chinese-heritage students as a homogenous group and highlight the challenges that many Chinese-heritage learners have to cope with in socialization in Chinese-dominated translingual spaces such as Hong Kong, Singapore (Dimmock and Leong, 2010), and Macau (Zhang, 2013). It must be noted that these findings need to be used with caution as the study is solely based on one-time and retrospective interview data. More longitudinal studies are needed to keep track of migrant students' adaptation process while (non-)participatory observations with self-reported data are used to explore the issue and gain more insights into the process of adaptation. Despite the limitations, the study contributes to the existing literature as it highlights the importance of social networks for cross-border students wanting to build a supportive academic community in adapting to host universities that they migrate to for academic studies (e.g., Montgomery and MacDowell, 2009; Tran, 2011; Xu, 2014). These supportive social networks also open up space for migrating students to learn and use languages they desired to learn in host communities (e.g., Gao, 2010a, 2010b). In the light of the six participants who forged supportive relationships with local students, we argue that migrant students should be encouraged to exercise critical self-reflection on their "mindset" and be open-minded about local students' learning and lifestyles, which may be different from theirs. On the other hand, local students also need to be educated to be inclusive and adopt diverse ways to study and live. In other words, reciprocal adaptation would be essential to transforming a university into a supportive academic community, in which teachers and university administrators should take more actions to facilitate social interactions and integration among students of different backgrounds. Teachers should provide more opportunities for students to do teamwork that requires them to know each other and engage in meaningful interactions. For example, having them discuss shared concerns, such as internships or job-seeking, has the potential to reduce the perceived differences and prompt information-sharing or collaborative work (Gao, 2017). In addition, education administrators need to create platforms for the two groups to get to know each other. More cultural tours or sharing social events should be organized to foster experiential learning of each other's "stories, artefacts, tools, actions, historical events, discourses, concepts and styles" (Wenger, 1998, p. 4) and "sentiments" (Lin, 2001, p. 47). Despite the shared cultural heritage that Mainland and local Chinese students have, considerable efforts might be required to help them utilize potential opportunities for language development and achieve better mutual understanding.

Note

1   All the interviewees' names here are pseudonyms.

References

BBC. (2015, February 16). In Pictures: Hong Kong's "Parallel Trade" Protests. *BBC News*. Retrieved from www.bbc.com/news/world-asia-china-31483476.

Benson, P. (2005). (Auto)biography and learner diversity. In P. Benson and D. Nunan (Eds.), *Learner's stories: Difference and diversity in language learning* (pp. 4–21). Cambridge, UK: Cambridge University Press.

Bourdieu, P. (1986). The forms of capital. In J. Richardson (Ed.), *Handbook of theory and research for the sociology of education* (pp. 241–258). New York, NY: Greenwood Press.

Dimmock, C., and Leong, J. O. S. (2010). Studying overseas: Mainland Chinese students in Singapore. *Compare: A Journal of Comparative and International Education*, *40*(1), 25–42

Gao, X. (2010a). *Strategic language learning: The roles of agency and context*. Bristol, UK: Multilingual Matters.

Gao, X. (2010b). To be or not to be "part of them": Micropolitical challenges in Mainland Chinese students' learning of English in a multilingual university. *TESOL Quarterly*, *44*(2), 274–294.

Gao, X. (2014). "Floating elites": Interpreting Mainland Chinese undergraduates' graduation plans in Hong Kong. *Asia Pacific Education Review*, *15*(2), 223–235.

Gao, X. (2017). Mainland Chinese undergraduates' academic socialisation in Hong Kong. *Journal of Further and Higher Education*, *41*(3), 364–378.

Geng, C., and Li, H. (2012). Hong Kong's immigration policy for Mainland students and young professionals: Effectiveness and challenges. *Journal of Youth Studies*, *15*(2), 52–62.

Huberman, A. M., and Miles, M. B. (1994). Data management and analysis methods. In K. Denzin and Y. Lincoln (Eds.), *Handbook of Qualitative Research* (pp. 428–444). Thousand Oaks, CA: Sage.

Kan, M. (2011, November 23). 香港高等教育為誰而設 [Whom should higher education institutions in Hong Kong serve?]. *ejinsight*. Retrieved from http://forum.hkej.com/node/76831.

Kim, Y. (2006). From ethnic to interethnic: The case for identity adaptation and transformation. *Journal of Language and Social Psychology*, *25*(3), 283–300.

Lam, C. M. (2006). Reciprocal adjustment by host and sojourning groups: Mainland Chinese students in Hong Kong. In M. Byram and A. Feng (Eds.), *Living and studying abroad: Research and practice* (pp. 91–107). Clevedon, London and Toronto: Multilingual Matters.

Lantolf, J. P., Thorne, S. L., and Poehner, M. E. (2015). Sociocultural theory and second language development. In B. VanPatten and J. Williams (Eds.), *Theories in second language acquisition: An introduction* (pp. 207–226). New York, NY: Routledge.

Li, D., and Duff, P. (2008). Issues in Chinese heritage language education and research at the postsecondary level. In A. W. He and Y. Xiao (Eds.), *Chinese as a heritage language: Fostering rooted world citizenry* (pp. 13–36). Honolulu, HI: University of Hawai'i Press.

Lin, N. (2001). *Social capital*. Port Chester, NY: Cambridge University Press.

Liu, J. (2012, February 8). Surge in anti-China sentiment in Hong Kong. *BBC News*. Retrieved from www.bbc.co.uk/news/world-asia-china-16941652.

Montgomery, C., and McDowell, L. (2009). Social networks and the international student experience: An international community of practice? *Journal of Studies in International Education*, *13*(4), 455–466.

Norton, B. (2012). Identity and second language acquisition. *The Encyclopaedia of Applied Linguistics*. DOI: 10.1002/9781405198431.wbeal0521.

Norton, B., and Toohey, K. (2001). Changing perspectives on good language learners. *TESOL Quarterly*, *35*(2), 307–322.

Nunan, D. (2003). The impact of English as a global language on educational policies and practices in the Asia–Pacific region. *TESOL Quarterly*, *37*(4), 589–613.

Pavlenko, A., and Lantolf, J. P. (2000). Second language learning as participation and the (re)construction of selves. In J. P. Lantolf (Ed.), *Sociocultural theory and second language learning* (pp. 155–178). Oxford, UK: Oxford University Press.

Tran, L. T. (2011). Committed, face-value, hybrid or mutual adaptation? The experiences of international students in Australian higher education. *Educational Review*, *63*(1), 79–94.

Wenger, E. (1998). *Communities of practice: Learning, meaning, and identity*. Cambridge, UK: Cambridge University Press.

Xu, C. L. (2014). Identity and cross-border student mobility: The Mainland China-Hong Kong experience. *European Education Research Journal*, *14*(1), 65–73.

Yu, B., and Downing, K. (2012). Determinants of international students' adaptation: Examining effects of integrative motivation, instrumental motivation and second language proficiency. *Educational Studies*, *38*(4), 457–471.

Zhang, K. (2013). Mainland Chinese students' English use in Macao. *English Today*, *29*(2), 54–59.

香港8所高校錄取約1590名內地新生 [Over 1,590 Mainland students were admitted by eight universities in Hong Kong as undergraduates in the forthcoming academic year]. (2013, July 24). *Da Kung Pao*. Retrieved from http://edu.takungpao.com.hk/ksjy/gk/q/2013/0724/1782922.html.

7

A SECOND-GENERATION CHINESE STUDENT'S EDUCATION IN SPAIN

Challenges and Opportunities

Iulia Mancila

The Chinese immigrant population in Spain has grown rapidly over the past three decades and continues to increase, although the current economic crisis has resulted in a significant decline in overall migration flows. According to the 2014 Spanish Census, there are 191,078 Chinese, who account for 3.88% of the population and are the sixth largest group of immigrants in Spain. Chinese-heritage students number 33,182, approximately 4% of the total student body (Ministerio de Educación, Cultura y Deporte, 2015). With the increase of Chinese-heritage students in the Spanish educational system, one might assume that researchers have examined ways in which second-generation Chinese learners have learned in and experienced Spanish schools. For example, how have they influenced and been influenced by the national educational systems? If social inclusion is a goal of the Spanish school system, as it is a goal in many other countries, to what extent have such learners been included? The large number of these Chinese-heritage students merits such investigation pertaining to social justice and inclusion. However, there are relatively few studies that have focused on Chinese-heritage students, and it is even more unusual to find research that captures the "voice", needs, and expectations of second-generation learners (see Aparicio and Portes, 2014; Beltrán Antolín and Sáiz, 2004; Nieto, 2007; Pérez Milans, 2011).

To address such a gap in research, this chapter explores the lived experiences of one second-generation Chinese young woman in Spain. The chapter begins by outlining a conceptual framework for immigrant children's learning and development in Spanish schools. This is followed by an account of the research methods used in the study, followed by the findings. Finally, the chapter concludes with a discussion about the implications of this research and, here, extends the discussion beyond Spain to a global context.

Theoretical Framework

The magnitude and pace of immigrant population increase in Spain over the past three decades have given rise to a substantial body of national research. Because of the relative novelty of the presence of these students in Spanish schools and social systems and also because of the urgent necessity to address cultural diversity, the main goal of such research has been to diagnose the situation of children from immigrant backgrounds. National educational research has tended to focus on broad issues such as:

1. statistical data on immigrant students' characteristics and school provisions;
2. educational policies and measures intended to welcome and support immigrant students;
3. teaching and learning Spanish as a second language;
4. family—school relationships; and
5. school success/dropout of immigrant students.

(for a detailed overview, see García Castaño et al., 2008)

While the socio-educational experiences of various other minority groups (e.g. Moroccans, Latin Americans, East Europeans) have been relatively well documented, scant attention has been paid to Chinese-heritage children in Spain (Beltrán Antolín and Sáiz, 2004; Pérez Milans, 2011; Yiu, 2013). They became the focus of attention only when there was poor attainment or challenging behaviors as obstacles to success. As Aparicio and Portes (2014) argued, compared with more traditional destination countries, such as the United States, Australia, and, more recently, Italy and the United Kingdom, Spain is a country in which the phenomenon of immigration in general and Chinese immigration in particular is relatively recent. This helps to explain why studies on second-generation Chinese learners born in Spain are scarce (Aparicio and Portes, 2014). Of the limited studies that do exist, there is often no distinction made between students born in Spain and those arriving as newcomers at an early age (Gualda Caballero, 2010).

Notable exceptions are Aparicio and Portes' (2014) two large survey studies of second-generation student populations and their "integration" in Madrid and Barcelona. Chinese students and their parents participated in these studies, along with Dominicans, Ecuadorians, Moroccans, and Romanians. The findings show that, compared with non-Chinese participants, a higher percentage (75%) of Chinese parents seemed to experience discrimination. Chinese students appeared to have significantly lower educational ambitions and expectations and they entered the labor market prematurely, although only 32% abandoned school entirely. Drawing on Aparicio and Portes' (2014) extensive data, Yiu (2013) analyzed the educational attainment of Chinese-heritage students in Spain and their perceived low academic achievement compared with participating peers from other nationalities. Her study is striking because it contradicts data from studies on

Chinese-heritage students in the USA and the UK in which Chinese students tend to feature as high achievers, models of academic excellence and upwardly social mobility. Borrowing Xie and Goyette's (2003) concept of "strategic adaptations," Yiu (2013) suggests a possible reason for these conflicting results could be Spain's inequitable and comparatively exclusionary school system. Proposing that Chinese-heritage students in Spain tend towards an ethnic business orientation in preference to the pursuit of an educational career, Yiu indicated that this orientation might represent a strategic response to structural barriers to social inclusion. Two additional factors could be responsible for the low educational expectations of Chinese-heritage students in Spain. First, the economic global recession has affected almost all sectors of the economy and young people in general no longer regard educational success as a guarantee of success in the mainstream job market. Second, the Chinese community in Spain, perhaps in a form of resistance to the global recession and economic downturns, had the wherewithal to form an active flourishing niche in the national labor market via their own ethnic economy. However, as Yiu (2013) suggested, one should be cautious about such explanations; more qualitative in-depth research is needed to better understand Chinese learners' school experiences. Such learners "deserve an accurate and fair exploration of their lives told by their own textured voices and experiences" (Oh and Cooc, 2011, p. 398) if we are to uncover the rich multiplicity of their experiences and reveal the challenges as well as the successes of these students.

To address both the gap in research and to respond to Oh and Cooc's (2011) call for an exploration of their lives, this chapter draws on an investigation of one Chinese-heritage student's experiences and perspectives. Viewing learners as active agents rather than passive recipients, this study explored both subjective and objective aspects of this student's educational experiences, ranging from kindergarten to high school. These conceptual lenses inform the present research, which aims to provide empirically based insights into the complex interplay of factors and relationships within and across a family and school, which have, in turn, affected the experience of a particular second-generation Chinese-heritage young woman.

Methods

Seeking a research method that allowed an in-depth exploration of the specificity of my participant's story in ways that could allow hitherto missing voices to be heard (see Merrill and West, 2009), my chosen approach was to use qualitative research methodologies, particularly life history and narrative inquiry. Such methods provide a valuable means of exploring experiences and locating those within particular historical, economic, and cultural contexts. Moreover, such approaches are well-suited to revealing and telling the stories behind the statistics (Cole and Knowles, 2001).

The main participant in the research was a Chinese-heritage young woman, Mei Ling (a pseudonym), living in the particular social context of the city of Malaga in southern Spain. Educated in the Spanish educational system, she was in her twenties at the start of the research and so I was able to build a picture of her trajectory through the entire education system as I explored the impact of her education on her identity development. Alongside her, "key informants" also included members of Mei Ling's family, her friends, teachers, and different stakeholders such as policymakers related to the Chinese community in Malaga and those working in local educational authorities. The "voices" of these participants appear in this chapter, if only briefly, in italicized verbatim extracts.

The information-gathering process included a range of instruments: thematically and biographically focused interviews with Mei Ling and secondary participants in order to gather complementary information; non-participant observation in various settings related to Mei Ling's life; the analysis of personal and official documents, and the use of a field diary and artefacts such as photos, videos, novels, films, documentaries, and mass-media texts. For the analysis and interpretation phase, a combination of two complementary strategies: "narrative analysis" and "thematic analysis" were used (see Kohler Riessman, 2008).

Results

Overall, the findings show that Mei Ling's educational trajectory is far from straightforward. Her narrative provides a vivid portrait of the most important factors that facilitated or hindered a meaningful education. Her lived experiences reveal how different school policies and practices, such as the curriculum, teaching and learning strategies, the attitudes of teachers, and peer relationships shaped her trajectory and impacted on her educational and social identity, and I explore these themes in the following sections.

Doing Well in School

Mei Ling comes from a family in which she is the second of five children, all born in Spain and educated in state schools. They speak Spanish among themselves and use a Wu dialect to communicate with their parents and the Chinese community. Her parents came from a small village of poor peasant families. After a short immigration process in Europe, they arrived in Spain in the 1980s and since then they have made their lives here. However, Mei Ling had a Chinese passport at the time of my study and so was not, legally, a Spanish citizen.

As a student, Mei Ling was considered to be a successful high achiever and she was completing an MA in a UK university. However, when she talked, her own voice revealed a much more complex reality. Since her early years, along with both of her sisters, Mei Ling had been deemed a good student, getting top grades, always ranking among the best in the school.

We were the first of the class, my sister and me. I remember how, during exams, teachers separated us, one in a corner and another in the other corner and we were always getting the same grade—A. Teachers praised us and we were very happy at that school.

Mei Ling and her siblings were aware of power issues and the impact on their life of mastering the Spanish language and gaining top grades and good recommendations from teachers. Mei Ling was driven *"to be the best"* partly from pressure from parents, teachers, and, not least, from her peers. She regarded academic success as a precondition for social acceptance in school. However, Mei Ling remarked, with a bitter tone:

Only when they realized they could get help from me in maths, physics, English, I became a desirable friend. In school I was seen as the girl who got the best grades, and if they had problems they came to me, but only because of that, not for anything else.

Also, to do well in school provided Mei Ling with protection and security.

I had controlled the most dangerous classmates, I knew who they were and I helped them with their homework and some exams, so I had my back covered. "If I'm good with you, you will also behave well with me."

However, apart from pressure and these circumstances, she emphasized that she always had a great desire to learn and study for herself; her good marks represented a reward for her efforts but also indicated her joy in learning.

From a very early age, Mei Ling's identity was formed in a culture of effort and hard work. Mei Ling worked seven days each week after school helping her parents with the family business, in addition to her school studies and after-school activities. This led to a work and study overload with little free time. Such rare free time or time for leisure led to difficulties socializing and very few friendships. As she recalled:

Usually my parents are like this: "Hey, Mei Ling, hello." "Come right now to the store, please." Then, people will not make plans according to my parents' rules. This is the way my parents are. You have to be working, or studying. I am all day long working or studying and the others see me as a kind of rare person, as I have no life of my own. It is complicated.

Nonetheless, Mei Ling was aware of her parents' hardships and the sacrifices they had made and similar findings are common for Chinese children in a variety of contexts (Louie, 2004; Li and Wang, 2008). Internalizing the high expectations

128 Iulia Mancila

of her parents, Mei Ling and her sisters felt the burden of pressure that, in turn, produced feelings of anxiety, stress, and responsibility. Their parents had immigrated for economic reasons, to offer a better life and a more promising future for their children. Mei Ling and her sisters were aware of their parents' aspirations and felt obliged to achieve academic success as a form of appreciation for and recognition of the sacrifices of their parents (see also Zhou et al., 2003).

Parental Perceptions of the Value of Education and Schooling

The parent–school relationship was almost nonexistent. Teachers reported that they had never seen Mei Ling's parents in school or met them. Some of them knew vaguely about Mei Ling's family circumstances from her own descriptions and some had been interested enough to ask her directly. The apparent lack of parental interest and participation led to a falsely negative perception by some of the teaching staff. Contrary to their perceptions, Mei Ling's parents valued school highly, regarding education as the only possible route to social mobility and inclusion. They saw school as the very best institution to educate their daughters and to ensure they learned the social and cultural values of Spanish society. They believed that through education their children would be protected from the difficulties they themselves had encountered while striving for a good life. School, Mei Ling's parents believed, would provide their children with the skills and capacities needed to develop and function in the best possible way and, importantly, good schooling would protect their children from possible discrimination.

Mei Ling's parents also appreciated the importance of learning other foreign languages, encouraging their daughters to learn not only Spanish but also English. Foreign languages, they believed, were necessary for good employment opportunities. Although they spoke a Wu dialect with their children, they also emphasized the benefits of learning Mandarin, not only for utilitarian purposes, but as an expression of the "*identity and culture*" of the Chinese not living in China. They made it clear that, although they no longer lived in China, they were proud to be Chinese and to be part of that "*great nation*". So, learning Mandarin was seen as fostering part of their identity. All of the Chinese students with whom I talked attended a complementary Chinese school at weekends (see Nieto, 2007, for similar findings). Mei Ling attended this school for seven years and, apart from the pragmatic benefits of learning Mandarin, she displayed ambivalent feelings towards its cultural identity message and ideology with which she did not completely identify. "*Textbooks were ideologically biased, I did not like it at all. I hate manipulated information. Besides, lots of stuff, like folk tales, different anniversaries were so distant from my reality, I did not find it interesting.*"

A Chinese Student's Education in Spain **129**

Experiences of Discrimination, Prejudices, and Assumptions

Mei Ling and her siblings suffered discrimination in the education system at various levels comparable with that revealed in research in the USA and UK (Archer and Francis, 2005; Li and Wang, 2008). Discrimination was structural, occurring in mainstream educational policies. It was pedagogic with regard to curriculum, teaching, and learning strategies, and cultural with respect to attitudes and behaviors. Throughout her schooling narratives, Mei Ling talked very frequently about her and her siblings having to struggle against all kinds of odds with discrimination, from both peers and teachers, resulting in tension, anxiety, and isolation.

Discriminatory Mainstream Educational Policies

When Mei Ling started school, the 1990 Law on the General Education System in Spain (LOGSE) was adopted. At that time, both teachers and students were immersed in learning via a new educational and social model with student diversity a new reality in all schools for two reasons. First, compulsory basic education was extended to the age of 16. Second, "mainstreaming," a new form of educating children with what were then termed "special educational needs," was introduced and those children were to be educated in mainstream schools (Essomba, 2014). The period of time between 1990 and 2000 therefore represented significant challenges for the state education system in Spain as it strived to be more democratic, inclusive, and respectful in approach. In the same year that Mei Ling joined the secondary school, a new education law, the 2002 Organic Law on Quality of Education, was approved and then replaced by the 2006 Organic Law of Education (LOE). Secondary schools were now providing education to a high percentage of immigrant students. From 1986, when Mei Ling's parents had arrived in Spain, until 2011, four immigration laws and five decrees directly affected them, as did the enactment of five national education laws. The high number of national legislative norms applicable to immigration have been explained as:

> a strategy of prevention against migrant populations, a philosophy of control and restriction of freedoms based on the representation of immigrants as bearers of danger; they constitute danger, not as specific individuals, but as belonging to a "at risk" subjects category: "the foreigners."
>
> (De Giorgi, 2005, p. 93)

In addition, there was an intensification and diversification of migratory flows in Spain. These population flows were reflected both in classrooms and in the laws and policies on immigration and education with their respective decrees, orders, and adjacent programs. There was a sense of urgency in the new reality and so a need to implement policies and programs to address the education of immigrant students. Intercultural education in Spain became associated with education *for* immigrant students but interculturalism tended to, and arguably still does, have a high profile only in schools with a high number of immigrant students.

Underlying these policy discourses is a hegemonic thinking that regards immigrant students as a threat to the schooling process of the entire student body (Essomba, 2014). This discourse has contributed to the social construction of the category of "immigrant students" as a social and educational problem and this construction permeates to the conceptions and work of many teachers. The policy message suggests that the school system should "compensate" for linguistic, cultural, and educational deficiencies in order that the students can "adapt" to and become "integrated" in Spain's educational and social systems. In his analysis of the failure of the education system as an institutional tool for social cohesion, Essomba (2014, p. 16) claims that "the mismatch between legal norms and society can be reflected in two opposing cohesion social dynamics: the duplication and the ghettoization of the system . . . and its subsequent disarticulation." Additionally, Torres Santomé (2008) points to clear differences between the ratios of immigrant students and type of school and the particularly low presence of Chinese students in post-compulsory secondary education. He suggests that such differences are at least partly due to the abuse of the regulations that leave open the possibility of interpreting the law in the interests of various actors and stakeholders, against the principles of equity with regard to the accessibility of education as stipulated in the Organic Law on Immigration 2 (2009). Contradictions between the main principles of cultural diversity recognition and inclusion and the everyday realities and practices in school are embedded in Mei Ling's school trajectory as I shall illustrate below.

Discriminatory Pedagogic Practices

Mei Ling frequently reported being bored in school. She saw little connection between her life outside and in school: school life felt unrelated to her home life. She described mismatches between her personal-social identity and school, noting disconnects in, for example, religious events such as the Catholic First Communion Ceremony or final year graduation trips. Mei Ling's parents did not give her permission to participate because she was not a Catholic or because they needed her to help with family business or, simply, because they did not see any educational value in these sort of activities.

In terms of pedagogy, the language of instruction was Spanish and all Mei Ling's classroom teachers followed a curriculum designed for "mainstream"; that is, for Spanish children. No reference was made to China and, indeed, there was no significant shift in the curriculum to reflect the different sociocultural lives of immigrant students. But, based on her good performance, Mei Ling, and her siblings too, were assumed by some teachers to have adjusted well to the educational system, not to have major challenges or specific needs and, hence, not to need any changes in teaching methodologies (see Lee, 1996, for similar findings).

However, some of Mei Ling's teachers compared her to her siblings: "*she is not as prepared as her sisters,*" "*she is not a serious student.*" In her narrative she describes how she felt about what she regarded as unfair comparisons.

> *They [teachers] were disappointed because my academic results were not always top, as my sisters' were. Compared to the rest of my peers, I had got very good grades and despite the efforts I had made these always passed unnoticed.*

Regrettably, this extract confirms how some teachers, perhaps unknowingly, embraced a dangerous stereotype of the "good student." The general impression conveyed by such teachers was that good students were respectful, hard-working, and focused on learning and obtaining high grades. Chinese girls, especially, were seen as "*quiet, docile, always with a smile.*" If Mei Ling or her sisters rebelled in any way, they were quickly punished; they had not conformed to the Chinese good student stereotype. As any such incidents are not likely to be regarded as direct discrimination or manifestations of racism. Teachers and schools may not acknowledge the consequences, the real damage they may cause to the students concerned. However, I argue that such attitudes and behaviors will likely and negatively affect the teacher–student relationship, the development of learning processes and the construction of a flourishing identity.

While only some of Mei Ling and her sisters' teachers displayed these prejudices and assumptions, most of the teaching staff did not know anything of their home lives or their parents' lives. For many teachers, the home and the personal life of their students is either of no interest or they do not regard it as their responsibility. Moreover, many teachers were not aware of any of the needs or challenges of Mei Ling or her siblings: they were "*non-problematic*" students. Perhaps the knowledge that they had been born in Spain led to their assumptions that Mei Ling and her sisters were well integrated socially, with "*normal friendships,*" "*they behaved exactly as their Spanish peers.*" However, Mei Ling was often referred to as "*the Chinese*" in their classes.

A very different perception was repeatedly expressed when teachers talked about Chinese newcomers, especially those older than ten, whose main difficulty was the language and the inability to connect and communicate. Although supplementary Spanish language classes were offered by education authorities or NGOs, most of these first-generation young Chinese students failed to learn Spanish well and many eventually abandoned school. Some teachers at Chinese schools referred to a number of their pupils in this situation and this was confirmed by Mei Ling. "*We are different from these Chinese kids, we are born here, we learned Spanish first, Spanish is our mother tongue, but they did not know it, so this*

132 Iulia Mancila

is their major problem. Besides, they do not feel like they need it, neither for their work nor to communicate with other Chinese."

Discriminatory Attitudes and Behaviors of Peers

In school, Mei Ling and her sisters encountered additional challenges reflecting a hegemonic Eurocentric environment. Mei Ling and her siblings realized that their ethnic difference was perceived by their peers as a *"problem"*: they were different from the *"normal"* majority Spanish children. Their distinctive physical features were associated with a distant country and an exotic culture. Noteworthy is the comment of one of Mei Ling's schoolmates: *"In my class we are 30 and a Chinese girl."* The clearly marked distinction between *"a Chinese girl"* and *"we,"* the rest of her Spanish classmates, seems to assume that Mei Ling is representative: she carries a culture and mentality different from—other than—the majority. A "Chinese girl," in effect an "Other" may be perceived as a threat to the collective life and identity of the majority and as a danger threatening the established order.

Throughout her schooling, Mei Ling and her sisters talk of their desire to feel *"integrated"* and to be *"a member of the group."* Despite struggling to belong, they revealed that they often felt alone and isolated. They frequently felt *"left out"* and they talked often of the challenges of making friends. This they described as one of their *"sorrows"* and it appears to have been a constant feature of their schooling with, I suggest, clear consequences for their self-esteem and wellbeing.

Mei Ling also talked of prejudice and verbal assault. Some incidents may seem trivial, such as pronouncing her name incorrectly. Other incidents she recalled were direct verbal attacks: *"Chinorra," "Go back to China," "You are so ugly."* She occasionally felt harassed and was even threatened with physical assault. During their early years of schooling, Mei Ling and her sisters recalled feeling relatively safe although, occasionally, they had to deal with curious peers staring or laughing at them and remarking on their eyes.

The worst period, recounted Mei Ling, was in high school, which she perceived as a violent environment. Groups among her teenage peers created tension; the affirmation or rejection of one group over another generated continuous stress. *"Sometimes it was unbearable the tension between the two main groups in the class: a continuous competition in all areas—academically, personally and so on,"* recalled Mei Ling in one of the interviews. The violent clashes between groups and individuals were not apparently generated for any obvious reason but, importantly for Mei Ling, *"different"* students were often the preferred targets. Mei Ling talked at length about experiences that included her smaller brother and sisters being beaten, bullied, hit on the head, pushed and kicked, both inside and outside school, in the city, on the bus, in the bus station, and on the street. As she recalled it: *"The truth is that we all had problems at school. We knew we were different and we tried very hard to fit in. Back then, we all wanted to be integrated, to be as the others were."*

A Chinese Student's Education in Spain **133**

Mei Ling also talked of being bullied in school for *"getting good grades," "being too smart,"* and that bullying was from both Spanish and other immigrant students. This peer discrimination revealed subtler non-verbal forms of treatment. Mei Ling was socially avoided or ignored and this, she explained, affected her more deeply than any other form of discrimination. All told, such circumstances contributed to a gradual process of distrust of, and disaffiliation from, school, her peers, and her teachers.

Engagement and Disaffiliation towards Schooling

Mei Ling's trajectory at school was punctuated by varying levels of engagement, from total engagement to indifference. Describing her preschool days and early years in primary school as a positive experience, she *"was happy, felt good, felt like home, had fun"* and also, most importantly, she learned. This early experience of schooling provided a good learning environment: a protected setting that established a positive attitude and high expectations for school and learning.

However, because Mei Ling's family moved to another city, she had to change school when she was eight. Here she started to feel disengaged and disaffected: *"it was of no use for me that year as I did not learn anything new."* She was bored in class, she felt frustrated and became angry with the teacher and her teaching style. She openly argued with her teacher because she was obliged to do schoolwork such as teaching a group of classmates multiplication tables, giving dictations, and helping with revision during class time and breaks. While peer learning can, of course, be a beneficial strategy, Mei Ling resented being asked to play the role of an authoritarian teacher. Perhaps it is of no surprise that Mei Ling struggled in this new school to establish any friendships with her peers and she felt increasingly isolated.

Eventually, Mei Ling persuaded her parents to find another school for her and she began another school year in a new environment. These final two primary years were, she said, *"so so."* She described positive relations with some teachers, including one she admired for making learning a pleasurable process and who, she thought, cared about all of his pupils. With her classmates she developed mutually helpful relationships. She said, *"Still it was difficult to establish friendships,"* but she felt, at least, that it was not as bad as her previous school.

With regard to secondary school, Mei Ling described the educational policies and practices intended to deal with difficult behavior and conflict situations as inefficient and ineffectual: *"ten faults meant one excluded day, so what?"* Teacher–student and peer relationships varied from year to year and mentoring, especially necessary at that age, was almost nonexistent. Teachers continued to teach their subjects in the time allocated for mentoring or behavior disruption and conflict mediation activities. However, at this point, Mei Ling was actively and positively engaged in her own learning: she learned how to be the agent of her academic success. She was reading a great deal. If she did not know how to

134 Iulia Mancila

solve a math problem, she did not look for help from the teacher but tried to solve it herself. She was determined to move ahead, against the odds. She loved math, sciences, English, history, literature, but she was not happy with some of her teachers. Mei Ling did not conform to the pre-established norms and made the decision to fight against all barriers and constraints by looking for alternatives, for allies, and by planning and seeking to solve any problems she encountered autonomously. She regarded challenges as learning opportunities that would enable her to further develop as the following extract demonstrates. *"I have not lost anything, there always is a winning. Moreover, I learned the picaresque, when and how to act, when to be careful and when to be just there."*

Mei Ling also tried to renegotiate what she perceived to be a symbolic confinement to a single role, a role that would restrict her autonomy and sense of identity based on her sense of being "Other." *"We knew we were different, but we were not worse, we were better, you know,"* she asserted. Articulating a fine critical analysis of various elements of the system, Mei Ling spoke of positive as well as negative elements of her schooling with the latter including, as noted above, a happy early education and friendly teachers and pupils in her first school. Extracurricular activities that fostered some friendships were of fundamental importance for her self-image and helped meet her desire to feel valued and recognized. She talked of a math teacher in her secondary school who, she thought, knew how to combine an interest in and passion for math with caring pedagogical tact and a teaching approach that sought to reach all of his students, especially those who needed him the most. Moreover, although discrimination was experienced through the whole educational trajectory, it was not, insisted Mei Ling, continual. Ultimately, Mei Ling spoke of her schooling, in spite of some negative prevailing circumstances, as a *"very good thing."*

Discussion

This narrative account has attempted to give a voice to Mei Ling and to shed light on some of the experiences that she and her family encountered in schools and society. On reflection, I am very aware that while my study focuses on just one individual, Mei Ling is part of a family, a community, and so should not be seen as an isolated individual. Her family's history, language, occupation, needs, aspirations, and practices represent multiple and intersecting dimensions of life that affected Mei Ling's school trajectory and experiences. These findings allow us to further reflect on the structurally, institutionally, and culturally strong assimilative views that persist in the Spanish educational system with respect to immigrant students' schooling.

In particular, I would like to refer to the concept of a "good student," which carries a dual and potentially perilous connotation. Mei Ling faced many difficulties and problems, including anxiety, isolation, and strong pressure, exerted upon her by her parents, peers, and teachers. As indicated earlier, the "good student" label affected her self-image and relationships with her peers with academic success perceived to be a precondition for social acceptance in school.

Furthermore, the chapter highlights the need to both unveil and to combat prejudice through better understanding the experiences and challenges pertaining to Chinese-heritage students like Mei Ling. Direct or indirect discrimination and prejudices are risk factors that contribute to an increasing vulnerability and may result in eventual distrust and disaffiliation towards school, for any individual. Mei Ling never felt a complete sense of belonging to the school, she did not fit in and often she felt the pedagogies and the official curriculum did not reach her in a meaningful way. Nevertheless, and despite indicating varying levels of engagement, from total commitment to indifference, she was clear that she regarded education as crucial. Despite their lack of interaction with the school or teachers, her parents, contrary to, again, a rather unthinking assumption by Mei Ling's teachers, valued education and school. They considered education to be the key to open the doors of social mobility, economic stability, and recognition of the status that they had not achieved. They also regarded education as a strategy to prevention and protect against discrimination and racism. Of course, it can only be thus if educators are willing to understand what is going on in the lives of students such as Mei Ling.

Implications for Educators

Schools as institutions with a significant role in the socialization of all students must surely be alert to and combat any discrimination that may occur during the schooling process. The role of teachers is fundamental in transforming schools into non-violent spaces, spaces in which socializing and learning is based on respect, solidarity, and recognition of and respect for cultural difference as a value in itself. This suggests that we may need a greater focus, in teachers' education programs, on preparing teachers to educate diverse learners in ways that ensure they can create a safe and positive learning environment for all students. I suggest that learning activities in school might usefully take into account the dynamic and changing nature of culture, language, and identity. Such activities would start with and focus on the stories and voices of all students and so help to move teachers and all learners away from stereotypical images and assumptions. Indeed, such activities would analyze and interrogate sociocultural meanings and their implications (see Clandinin and Connelly, 1994). A close reading of the narratives, of the nested webs of the personal life stories of children in our schools, could help to transform classrooms into living learning communities. Focusing on students' own stories could help to break the vicious cycle of dangerous assumptions regarding the "Other", in this case Chinese-heritage students such as Mei Ling. As Schwab, Westbury, and Wilkof (1978, p. 322) have argued, "theories of curriculum and of teaching and learning cannot alone tell us what and how to teach, because questions of what and how to teach arise

136 Iulia Mancila

in concrete situations loaded with concrete particulars of time, place, person, and circumstances."

When studying a specific case, of course one must always use caution in generalizations. However, the study reported here could be potentially relevant for schools and teachers well beyond Malaga and Spain. It has implications for our current knowledge and understandings of schooling processes. It challenges stereotypes and prejudices related to Chinese-heritage students and it seeks to persuade educators that they could benefit from a deeper understanding of the strengths and needs these, and all, students bring to school, the community, and society. This would mean a shift in approaches to cultural diversity. It would require a shift from a deficit perspective towards a more socially justice-oriented, inclusive intercultural perspective (see Nieto, 2000; Enslin and Hedge, 2010). This, in turn, would require a shift from seeing the student as "a problem" to looking hard at the socio-educational context and how that might better respond to the specific needs or expectations of each student.

To conclude, the findings from this research resonate with those from previous national studies on Chinese students in Spain (Aparicio and Portes, 2014; Yiu, 2013) in terms of the perceived discrimination in school and the barrier such discrimination creates for a successful education and social inclusion. Research such as this adds new evidence indicating that educational trajectories are rarely straight-forward. This research focused on one particular Chinese-heritage student, but more similar studies, including practitioner enquiries in teachers' classrooms with, rather than "on," their own students, could help to significantly extend our understanding of their schooling and socialization experiences. Accordingly, this study could be a starting point to reflect on several key issues such as the following:

1. Mei Ling's experiences of schooling suggest that Chinese-heritage students born in Spain have specific developmental, educational, and social needs that are different from those who arrive as new students from China. Language and literacy may be the main obstacle for newcomers, but the traditional assimilative and homogeneous cultural pedagogical discourses and actions that continue to pervade the everyday life of school could be a great challenge to all of them. This may well be an important focus for consideration internationally as it seems unlikely that Spain is alone with respect to tensions between its prevailing discourses and realities and the need to meet the specific needs of both newly arrived and second-generation students from other countries.

2. The data in this study reflect the challenges and complexities of the learning and maintenance of a heritage language and culture, as has been pointed out by international researchers elsewhere (Francis et al., 2009). Even though Mei Ling acknowledged the benefits of learning the heritage language, she also displayed a counter-narrative around the Chinese identity and culture as fixed, essentialized notions.

3. Related to academic attainment, Mei Ling and her siblings were high achievers. Despite all kinds of odds, they succeeded in their schooling and, to date, they have fulfilled their aspirations. This study opens a space for debate regarding the school achievement of Chinese students, as previous studies showed that Chinese students in Spain, compared with peers from other nationalities, appeared to have significantly lower educational ambitions and expectations and they entered the labor market prematurely (Aparicio and Portes, 2014).

Additional future research might usefully address these issues, both theoretically and empirically, by comparing Chinese-heritage students in Spain with Spanish peers and those from other nationalities. In other international contexts, comparable studies might usefully extend our understanding while giving "voice" to the learners concerned.

This study has offered but a glimpse into the complex socio-educative realities of one student and much further research is needed in order to advance understanding as a foundation to defy discrimination, stereotypes, and myths in education and in society (see Griffiths and Troyna, 1995). Contributing to this emerging field of socio-educational research and its international literature is surely a prerequisite to the ultimate goal to provide high-quality learning, teaching, and appropriate learning support for all learners. Understanding the relationships between globalization, transcultural migration, citizenship, and their effects on the education of Chinese-heritage students in Spain, but globally too, is surely important if we are to offer them the educational experience to which they, and all other students, are entitled. Moreover, just as this study has revealed to me the ways in which Mei Ling's sense of belonging, affiliation, and inclusion were shaped by these factors, it has also revealed the complexities of schooling. Those complexities will surely pertain to all if we are to include and engage all students in the processes of schooling alongside their peers from Spain, China, or anywhere else in the world.

Acknowledgments

The author gratefully acknowledges the Formación de Doctores en Centros de Investigación y Universidades Andaluzas Scholarship Program (Junta de Andalucía, Spain), which funded this study. Of course, I also thank "Mei Ling" and all other participants. Special thanks are extended to Professor Nicki Hedge for her invaluable support in editing and revising this chapter.

References

Aparicio, R., and Portes, A. (2014). *Crecer en España. La integración de los hijos de inmigrantes.* Barcelona, Spain: La Caixa.

Archer, L., and Francis, B. (2005). "They never go off the rails like other ethnic groups": Teachers' constructions of British-Chinese pupils' gender identities and approaches to learning. *British Journal of Sociology of Education, 26*(2), 165–182.

Beltrán Antolín, J., and Sáiz, A. (2004). La inmigración china y la educación: entre la excelencia y la instrumentalidad. En Carrasco, S. (Coord.), *Inmigración, contexto familiar y educación. Procesos y experiencias de la población marroquí, ecuatoriana, china y senegambiana* (pp. 169–202). Barcelona, Spain: Institut de Ciències de l'Educació, Universitat Autònoma de Barcelona.

Clandinin, D. J., and Connelly, F. M. (1994). Personal experience methods. In N. K. Denzin and Y. S. Lincoln (Eds.), *Handbook of qualitative research* (pp. 413–427). Thousand Oaks, CA: Sage.

Cole, A. L., and Knowles, J. G. (2001). *Lives in context: The art of life history research.* Walnut Creek, CA: AltaMira Press.

De Giorgi, A. (2005) *Tolerancia cero. Estrategias y prácticas de la sociedad de control.* Barcelona, Spain: Virus Editorial.

Enslin, P., and Hedge, N. (2010). Inclusion and diversity. In R. Bailey, R. Barrow, D. Carr, and C. McCarthy (Eds.), *The Sage handbook of philosophy of education* (pp. 385–400). London, UK: Sage.

Essomba, M. A. (2014). Políticas de escolarización del alumnado de origen extranjero en el estado español hoy. Análisis y propuestas. *Revista Electrónica Interuniversitaria de Formación del Profesorado, 17*(2), 13–27.

Francis, B., Archer, L. and Mau, A. (2009) Language as capital, or language as identity? Chinese complementary school pupils' perspectives on the purposes and benefits of complementary schools. *British Educational Research Journal, 35*(4), 519–538.

García Castaño, F. J., Rubio Gómez, M., and Bouachra, O. (2008). Población inmigrante y escuela en España: un balance de investigación. *Revista de Educación, 345*, 23–60.

Griffiths, M., and Troyna, B. (Eds.) (1995). *Antiracism, culture and social justice in education.* Stroke-on-Trent, UK: Trentham.

Gualda Caballero, E. (2010). *La segunda generación de inmigrantes en Huelva: Estudio HIJAI.* Valencia, Spain: Junta de Andalucía.

Kohler Riessman, C. (2008). *Narrative methods for the human sciences.* Thousand Oaks, CA: Sage.

Lee, S. J. (1996). *Unravelling the model stereotype: Listening to Asian American Youth.* New York, NY: Teachers College Press.

Li, G., and Wang, L. (Eds.) (2008). *Model minority myths revisited: An interdisciplinary approach to demystifying Asian American education experiences.* Greenwich, CT: Information Age Publishing.

Louie, V. (2004). *Compelled to excel: Immigration, education, and opportunity among Chinese Americans.* Palo Alto, CA: Stanford University Press.

Merrill, B., and West, L. (2009). *Using biographical methods in social research.* London, UK: Sage.

Ministerio de Educación, Cultura y Deporte (2015, June 30). *Estadística de las Enseñanzas no universitarias. Datos Avance 2014–2015.* Press release. Retrieved from www.mecd.gob.es/dms/mecd/servicios-al-ciudadano-mecd/estadisticas/educacion/no-universitaria/alumnado/matriculado/2014–2015/Nota.pdf.

Nieto, S. (2000). *Affirming diversity: The socio-political context of multicultural education* (3rd edn). New York, NY: Longman.

Nieto, G. (2007). *La inmigración china en España. Una comunidad ligada a su nación*. Madrid, Spain: Libros de la Catarata.

Observatorio Permanente Andaluz de Migraciones. (2014). *Padrón de Habitantes. Explotación para España y CC.AA*. Retrieved from www.juntadeandalucia.es/justiciaeinterior/opam/es/pebHistorico?peb=90.

Oh, S. S., and Cooc, N. (2011). Special issue: Immigration, youth, and education—editors' introduction. *Harvard Educational Review, 81*(3), 397–407.

Pérez Milans, M. (2011). Being a Chinese newcomer in Madrid compulsory education: Ideological constructions in language education practice. *Journal of Pragmatics, 4*, 1005–1022.

Schwab, J. J., Westbury, I., and Wilkof, N. J. (1978). *Science, Curriculum, and Liberal Education: Selected Essays*. Chicago, IL: Chicago Press University.

Torres Santomé, J. (2008). Diversidad cultural y contenidos escolares. *Revista de Educación, 345*, 83–110.

Xie, Y., and Goyette, K. (2003). Social mobility and the educational choices of Asian Americans. *Social Science Research, 32*(3), 467–498.

Yiu, J. (2013). Calibrated ambitions: low educational ambition as a form of strategic adaptation among Chinese youths in Spain. *International Migration Review, 47*(3), 573–611.

Zhou, Z., Peverly, S. T., Xin, T., Huang, A. S., and Wang, W. (2003). School adjustment of first generation Chinese-American adolescents. *Psychology in the Schools, 40*(1), 71–84.

8

CHINESE-BACKGROUND AUSTRALIAN STUDENTS' ACADEMIC SELF-CONCEPT, MOTIVATIONAL GOALS, AND ACHIEVEMENTS IN MATH AND ENGLISH

Alexander Seeshing Yeung and Feifei Han

Students' self-concept and motivation are widely acknowledged as two important psychological constructs that have prominent influence on students' academic performance (Yeung, 2011; Yeung et al., 2016). However, research on how gender roles may affect students' academic self-concept and motivation often produces inconsistent results. What further complicates the issue is that gender often interacts with other factors, such as students' cultural backgrounds. For students from the same society but with diverse cultural backgrounds, self-concept and motivation may be affected by the cultural values formed in a particular cultural group. Hence these psychosocial constructs may vary among students from different cultures even though they are educated within the same educational system. Australia is well-known for its well-blended multicultural society, in which Western cultures meet Eastern cultures. While Western cultures tend to value people's innate competence, Eastern cultures—especially Chinese culture under the influence of Confucianism—merits effort and diligence in education (Yeung and Yeung, 2008; Yeung et al., 2016). According to Mak and Chan (1995), Chinese immigrant families in Australia, in general, retain many of their original cultural beliefs, irrespective of their socioeconomic status. Whether students from a Chinese or Anglo culture in Australia differ in terms of academic self-concept, and achievement goal motivation, is the focus of the current investigation.

More specifically, the current chapter studies gender and cultural background effects on students' self-concept, achievement goal motivation, and academic achievement in math and English, the two most important subjects for Australian high school students. Using Australian high school as the research context is meaningful because this allows us to examine whether students' cultural backgrounds rather than different educational systems influence their motivational beliefs; and whether similarities and differences between cultural groups are further affected by students' gender.

Theoretical Framework

Academic Self-Concept and Its Impact

Self-concept—"a person's perception of himself ... formed through his experience with his environment ... and influenced especially by environmental reinforcements and significant others" (Shavelson et al., 1976, p. 411)—has been positively described as "making things happen," and "enabling human potential to its full extent" (Marsh and Craven, 2006). Academic self-concept, which is defined as students' self-perception and self-appraised capabilities and enjoyment in academic domains, is a significant contributing factor to various desirable educational outcomes (Craven and Yeung, 2015).

The structure of self-concept has been empirically demonstrated as multidimensional and domain-specific (Arens et al., 2011). Marsh (1990), for example, found distinct self-concepts in a number of school subjects, including verbal, math, physical, art, music, and religion, with a general academic self-concept as an overarching construct. Following the domain specificity principles (Arens et al., 2011; Swann et al., 2007), in our study, we focused on the two most important school subjects for Australian high school students: math and English.

In recent years, academic self-concept has been differentiated into cognitive and affective components, known as the competence–affect distinction (e.g., Arens et al., 2011; Pinxten et al., 2014). While the competence part surveys whether students perceive themselves as being good at academic work, the affect part asks whether students consider themselves as liking schoolwork (Pinxten et al., 2014). The distinction of competence and affect is important. Confidence about one's ability in academic endeavor is likely to be associated with short-term educational outcomes, such as test performance and academic results; whereas liking of school and enjoyment in doing school activities tend to be linked with long-term educational benefits, like academic retention and future academic aspirations (Yeung, 2011). We only considered the competence component in this study, as we only examined short-term educational outcomes—achievement scores.

The relationship between academic self-concept and achievement is found to be reciprocal, dynamic, and mutually reinforcing (Marsh and Craven, 2006). This means that students' prior positive academic self-concept is able to lead to enhanced academic performance in the subsequent year, and their previous achievement also has positive effects on their later competence beliefs in schoolwork (Möller et al., 2011). Numerous researchers have emphasized the importance of nurturing students' self-beliefs of competence in academic work, because a high self-perception of competence is often found to be a stronger predictor of performance than students' actual ability in specific tasks (Pajares and Schunk, 2002).

Achievement Goals and Their Impact

In the past couple of decades, motivation research has advanced enormously and a number of theories have been generated. Among these different perspectives, achievement goal theory has remained popular in educational psychology (Hulleman et al., 2010). Achievement goal theory was established in order to understand "students' adaptive and maladaptive responses to achievement challenges" (Senko et al., 2011, p. 27). The goals are referred to as cognitive representations of students' purposes in different achievement scenarios (Pintrich, 2000). The goals set by students can provide them with meaningful learning purposes and help them understand learning situations (Seifert, 2004).

Among different types of goals held by students, two primary goals have been the focus of research, namely mastery and performance goals (Wolters, 2004). A mastery goal is defined as "desire to learn, improve, and develop competence" (Urdan and Mestas, 2006, p. 354). Students who hold a mastery goal orientation are said to pay attention to the process of acquiring and developing their capabilities, mastering and completing the tasks, improving their competence over time, and self-developing in relation to self-referenced criteria. On the contrary, students who pursue a performance goal predominantly focus on demonstrating and comparing their competence through social comparison processes and obtaining positive evaluations (Elliot, 2005; King et al., 2012). The two goals are not two dichotomous aspects of learning motivation; they can exist simultaneously within an individual (Daniels et al., 2008). While a student may focus on learning, at the same time he or she may also be competition-conscious (Pintrich, 2000).

In terms of whether the achievement goals should be conceptualized as domain-general or domain-specific, there is no conclusive evidence (Magson et al., 2014; Paulick et al., 2013). In this study, we used domain-specific measures of achievement goals for two reasons. First, domain-specific achievement goals would be consistent with domain specificity of self-concept used in the study. Second, as we measured math and English achievement separately, matching the achievement goals in math and English to the respective academic achievements would yield more useful information for practical applications.

Gender Issues

Research has revealed that there may be a gender stereotype on academic self-beliefs, motivation, and achievement (Meece et al., 2006; Yeung et al., 2012). Although boys and girls may have similar levels of self-belief and academic motivation to begin with, gender differences tend to become observable from early elementary school and the gap will continue in high schools (Usher and Pajares, 2008). Past self-concept research that focused primarily on competence perceptions has indicated that, in general, boys tend to have higher competence beliefs than girls (Midgley et al., 2001), as boys are more likely to overestimate their competence; whereas girls tend to underestimate their abilities (Metallidou and Vlachou, 2007). Furthermore, male and female students may have different competence beliefs in different curriculum areas. Research has consistently reported that male students tend to have higher perceptions of competence in math, science-related subjects, and sports and exercise (Klapp Lekholm and Cliffordson, 2009), whereas female students tend to have higher self-concepts in language and verbal-related subjects, as well as music (Kurtz-Costes et al., 2008).

The gender role effect has also been reported in some motivational constructs. Midgley et al. (2001) found that girls tended to have a higher level of mastery goal than boys. Adopting a domain-specific approach to motivation, Trautwein and Lüdtke (2009) showed that male students were more motivated and more compliant in some specific school subjects, such as math and physics, whereas their female peers tended to display avoidance or withdrawal in these subjects. These results suggest that similar to self-concept, gender may also play a role in achievement goals relevant to curriculum areas.

Cultural Issues

Cultural backgrounds may exert influences on students' academic self-beliefs and motivation (Yeung et al., 2012, 2016). This is because students from different cultural backgrounds hold specific values that are consistent with those within the societies they come from (Luo et al., 2014). They may therefore have different understandings of the goals of learning and processes of learning, which in turn may shape the beliefs and motivation they hold for learning (Dekker and Fischer, 2008). Under the influence of cultures, people in Western and non-Western societies have different educational theories towards learning (Yeung and Yeung, 2008; Yeung et al., 2016). Li (2002) maintained that "heart and mind for wanting to learn" is a typical thought among people in some Eastern cultures, such as Chinese. She found that Chinese students set up knowledge-seeking as a long-term goal to pursue from early years. Thus, Chinese students perceive learning process as a way to add meaning to their lives and to gain positive self-perceptions through acquiring knowledge. In her study, Li reported that Chinese students had more positive beliefs than their American peers, whereas American students placed an emphasis on learning style and intelligence. Other studies also highlighted differences in terms of self-beliefs in education between Western and Eastern cultures. While Western tradition merits students' innate competence, Chinese culture has a long historical tradition of valuing nurtured characteristics through hard work and effort, which is inherited from Confucius' thoughts dated back around 500 BCE (Hau and Salili, 1991; Yeung et al., 2016). These findings all point to the emphasis of a mastery goal in Chinese learners.

Interaction between Gender and Culture

The interaction between gender and culture was also found for self-concept and academic performance (e.g., Chiu and Klassen, 2010; Dai, 2001; Lai, 2010). For instance, Dai (2001) observed a reversed pattern in terms of gender differences on competence beliefs. For gifted American and European adolescents, males self-rated higher on general academic self-concept than females. In contrast, among gifted Chinese students, it was female students who self-perceived being more capable. Chiu and Klassen (2010) found that for students from wealthier countries and from a culture that tolerates more uncertainty, math self-concept had a stronger relationship with math achievement among boys than girls. Lai (2010) showed that Chinese girls performed better than boys in both primary and secondary schools, but for American students, this pattern was not consistent. American girls achieved better than boys in elementary school, but boys gradually caught up in math and science subjects in middle school.

The Present Investigation

The present study examines gender and cultural effects on self-concepts, two most important achievement goals (i.e., mastery and performance goals), as well as academic achievements in math and English among Australian high school students who are from a Chinese background and an Anglo background by adopting a multiple-indicator-multiple-indicator-cause (MIMIC) approach to structural equation modeling (SEM). Three research questions the study explored are:

1. What is the effect of gender on Australian high school students' academic self-concepts, achievement goals, and academic performance in math and English?
2. What is the effect of culture on Australian high school students' academic self-concepts, achievement goals, and academic performance in math and English?
3. What is the effect of gender and culture interaction on Australian high school students' academic self-concepts, achievement goals, and academic performance in math and English?

Method

Research Design

The research methodology we used is quantitative through a structural equation modeling (SEM) approach, which allows simultaneous analysis of all the variables in one model and controls for measurement error so that errors are not aggregated in a residual error term (Nachtigall et al., 2003). This is deemed suitable as it enables us to examine gender, culture, and their interaction on self-concepts and achievement goals in a single model.

The Participants

The study was conducted in eight high schools in Sydney, New South Wales, Australia. Altogether 2,362 students participated (males: 1,110, 47%; females: 1,250, 52.9%; two missing gender information). The students were in grades 7–10 with ages ranging from 11 to 17 years (M = 13.71, SD = 1.16). In this study, cultural background was operationalized as Chinese-background learners and Anglo-background learners. The Chinese category learners reported mainly speaking Chinese (Mandarin or Cantonese) at home. This sample of students included 461 Chinese learners (19.5%). The remaining 1,901 students (90.5%) were Anglo students who reported mainly speaking English at home.

Materials

The materials used for data collection were a questionnaire and the achievement test scores in math and English. The survey started with a section on demographic information including sex, age, grade, and cultural backgrounds. The main survey had two parts: one was on students' academic self-concepts in math and English, and the other was on achievement goals in the two subjects.

Academic Self-Concepts

To measure students' academic self-concepts in math and English, Marsh's (1990) Academic Self-Description Questionnaire II was adapted, as this questionnaire is the most widely used instrument for measuring academic self-concept of students from diverse cultures (Worrell et al., 2008). There were six items for each subject, and all of them reflected an individual's perception of competence in the subjects. The items were scored on a six-point Likert scale with 1 indicating "strongly disagree" and 6 representing "strongly agree." One negatively worded item was reverse-coded so that a higher score was reflective of higher self-concept. Both the math and English self-concept scales had high reliability (math: α = 0.91 and English: α = 0.94).

Achievement Goals

To measure students' achievement goals in math and English, we used the School Motivation Questionnaire (Marsh et al., 2003). There were two reasons for adopting this scale. First, this scale was shown to be reliable, valid, and invariant over time. Second, we considered the caution that is repeatedly mentioned by achievement goal researchers that the construct validity of instruments needs to be appropriate for the participants from the cultural groups to be studied (e.g., King et al., 2012). As Marsh et al. (2003) had validated the scale with Australian students, the instrument was deemed to be appropriate for our sample.

Mastery goal was measured using the intrinsic orientation scale (reflective of a mastery goal orientation), which consisted of six items on a six-point scale with 1 representing "strongly disagree" and 6 indicating "strongly agree." Performance goal was measured using the competition orientation scale (reflective of a performance goal orientation), which also contained six items on a six-point scale. The original items were for general schooling, so we made changes to reflect math and English respectively. The scales all showed high reliability (math mastery: 0.94, math performance: 0.96, English mastery: 0.94, and English performance: 0.92).

Math and English Achievement Scores

We used the 40 mathematics items of the Wide Ranging Achievement Test 4 (WRAT 4, Wilkinson and Robertson, 2006), which measures mathematical computational skills. We used 42 spelling items and 41 sentence comprehension items from WRAT 4 to measure students' English achievement. The WRAT 4 has been used widely to gauge academic achievements and the tests have been reported to be reliable and valid (Wilkinson and Robertson, 2006). A correct answer scored one point, thus the highest maximum scores were 40 and 83 for math and English achievement tests respectively.

Data Collection

The data collection strictly followed the requirements prescribed by the university ethics committee. The consent from the participants and their parents to participation on a voluntary basis was obtained. Every effort was made to ensure the anonymity of the participants. Students completed the questionnaires before completing the math and English achievement tests.

Statistical Analysis

As all the scales used in the study are well-established, we started with our analysis by checking the Cronbach's alpha reliability of scales. Then confirmatory factor analysis (CFA) of a model was conducted with two self-concept scales, four achievement goal scales, and two achievement scores. Because the achievement scores were single-item indicators, the measurement error of scores were fixed to 0 SD (equivalent to a perfect reliability estimate).

148 Alexander Seeshing Yeung and Feifei Han

The CFAs were conducted using Mplus software version 7. Following Jöreskog and Sörbom (2005), to evaluate the CFA models, we considered three fit statistics as primary indicators of model fit—the Tucker–Lewis Index (TLI, Tucker and Lewis, 1973), the Comparative Fit Index (CFI, Bentler, 1990), and the root mean square error of approximation (RMSEA, Browne and Cudeck, 1993). According to Bentler (1990), the values of TLI and CFI higher than 0.90 are generally considered an acceptable fit to the data. For the value of RMSEA, Browne and Cudeck (1993) suggest that RMSEA values below 0.06 are indicative of a good fit.

Support for the CFA model also requires:

1. acceptable reliability for each scale (i.e., $\alpha = 0.70$ or above);
2. acceptable factor loadings for the items loading on the respective scales (i.e., factor loadings above 0.30); and
3. appropriate correlations among the latent factors to ensure that they would be distinguishable from each other (*r*s below 0.90).

When the CFA model was established, we then conducted a series of tests to examine whether the model was factorial invariant by gender and cultural backgrounds. Evidence of invariance would enable us to compare gender and cultural groups using a MIMIC approach to SEM. In the current study, the MIMIC model examined the effects of three discrete grouping variables: gender (1 = male, 2 = female); culture (1 = Chinese, 2 = Anglo); and gender and cultural backgrounds interaction (i.e., gender x culture) on the eight variables established in CFA.

Results

Reliability and CFA

Each a priori scale was reliable (α above 0.90). The CFA model (model 1), which included six factors and math and English achievement scores, fitted the data: $\chi^2(639) = 4362.03$, TLI = 0.95, CFI = 0.95, RMSEA = 0.05. All the factor loadings were above 0.64, and the factor correlations were all below 0.7, supporting the CFA model.

Factorial Invariance across Groups

Invariance across Gender Groups

The baseline model (model 2A) wherein the parameters were allowed to be freely estimated resulted in a good fit ($\chi^2(1278) = 5274.89$, TLI = 0.95, CFI = 0.94, RMSEA = 0.05). Model 2B, which imposed that all the factor loadings were equal across males and females, produced similar fit ($\chi^2(1308)$ = 5328.58, TLI = 0.95, CFI = 0.94, RMSEA = 0.05), even though TLI was slightly reduced. Likewise, when the invariance constraints were imposed on both factor loadings and factor variances across groups in model 3C, a good fit was also attained ($\chi^2(1338)$ = 5485.94, TLI = 0.95, CFI = 0.95, RMSEA = 0.05). According to Cheung and Rensvold (2002), the negligible drops of our CFI in model 2B supported the factorial invariance by gender.

Invariance across Cultural Groups

The baseline model (model 3A) yielded a reasonable fit ($\chi^2(1278)$ = 5164.64, TLI = 0.95, CFI = 0.95, RMSEA = 0.05). Model 4B with factor loadings equal across groups also had a good fit ($\chi^2(1308)$ = 5224.74, TLI = 0.95, CFI = 0.95, RMSEA = 0.05). Model 3C, which specified invariance on both the factor loadings and factor variances, had a comparable fit to model 4B ($\chi^2(1338)$ = 5379.98, TLI = 0.95, CFI = 0.95, RMSEA = 0.05). These fit statistics provided us with a strong basis for group comparisons.

MIMIC Model

The MIMIC model displayed a good fit to the data, ($\chi^2(729)$ = 4581.70, TLI = 0.95, CFI = 0.95, RMSEA = 0.05). The factor correlations of model 4 are displayed in Table 8.1. The factor loadings and paths are presented in Table 8.2. The correlations from Table 8.1 showed us that mastery goal ($r = 0.46$, $p < 0.01$) and performance goals ($r = 0.70$, $p < 0.01$) in the two subjects were strongly related to each other than self-concepts in the two subjects ($r = 0.13$, $p < 0.01$).

TABLE 8.1 Factor correlations of model 4

Variables	1	2	3	4	5	6	7	8
1 Math self-concept	—							
2 Math mastery	0.57**	—						
3 Math performance	0.48**	0.39**	—					
4 English self-concept	0.13**	0.09**	0.10**	—				
5 English mastery	0.09**	0.46**	0.16**	0.56**	—			
6 English performance	0.21**	0.17**	0.70**	0.41**	0.37**	—		
7 Math achievement	0.49**	0.20**	0.26**	−0.03	−0.04	0.11**	—	
8 English achievement	0.17**	−0.03	0.04	0.18**	−0.01	0.04*	0.59**	—

Note: ** $p < 0.01$; * $p < 0.05$.

TABLE 8.2 Solution for model 4

Variable	Math SC	Math Mas	Math Per	English SC	English Mas	English Per	Math Ach	English Ach
Factor loadings								
item 1	0.84**	0.81**	0.85**	0.83**	0.88**	0.84**	1.00	1.00
item 2	0.81**	0.88**	0.91**	0.84**	0.84**	0.89**	—	—
item 3	0.74**	0.87**	0.91**	0.78**	0.83**	0.92**	—	—
item 4	0.73**	0.87**	0.90**	0.65**	0.75**	0.90**	—	—
item 5	0.86**	0.86**	0.91**	0.85**	0.85**	0.87**	—	—
item 6	0.79**	0.84**	0.87**	0.81**	0.81**	0.72**	—	—
Uniqueness								
item 1	0.30**	0.34**	0.28**	0.31**	0.23**	0.30**	0.00	0.00
item 2	0.35**	0.22**	0.18**	0.30**	0.30**	0.22**	—	—
item 3	0.45**	0.24**	0.17**	0.40**	0.32**	0.15**	—	—
item 4	0.47**	0.24**	0.19**	0.58**	0.44**	0.21**	—	—
item 5	0.26**	0.26**	0.18**	0.27**	0.28**	0.24**	—	—
item 6	0.38**	0.30**	0.24**	0.35**	0.34**	0.48**	—	—
Paths								
Gender	−0.03	−0.17	−0.20*	0.16	−0.15	−0.09	0.11	0.10
Culture	−0.06	−0.16*	−0.21**	0.20**	−0.15*	−0.09	−0.36**	−0.18**
Interaction	−0.17	−0.10	0.08	−0.05	0.36**	0.06	−0.18	−0.02

Note: ** $p < 0.01$; * $p < 0.05$. SC = self-concept scale, Mas = mastery orientation scale;

Per = performance orientation scale; Ach = schievement.

These results suggest that self-concepts are more domain-specific than achievement goals.

The relations between self-concept and achievement goals within one subject (from 0.37 to 0.48) were stronger than respective relations across the two subjects (from 0.10 to 0.21). The math and English achievement scores showed a positive and moderate correlation ($r = 0.59$, $p < 0.01$). The correlations of achievement scores with the self-concept ($r = 0.49$, $p < 0.01$) and achievement goals in math ($r = 0.20$, $p < 0.01$ with math mastery goal; $r = 0.26$, $p < 0.01$ with math performance goal) were higher than those in English. English scores and English self-concept ($r = 0.18$, $p < 0.01$), English scores and English mastery goal ($r = -0.01$, $p = 0.65$), and English scores and English performance goals ($r = 0.04$, $p < 0.05$) showed relatively lower correlations. Within each subject, achievement scores had higher correlation with the self-concept in that subject than achievement goals in that subject. Across the two subjects, we found that math achievement scores only weakly correlated with English performance goal ($r =$

Chinese-Background Students' Self-Concept **151**

0.11, $p < 0.01$), and that English achievement scores only weakly associated with math self-concept ($r = 0.17$, $p < 0.01$). These results supported the notion of domain specificity and the specificity matching principle (Arens et al., 2011).

Effect of Gender

From Table 8.2, we can see that the main effect of gender was only significant for math performance goal. Specifically, a significantly negative path was found from gender to math performance goal ($\beta = -0.20$, $p < 0.05$), suggesting that female students had lower ratings on their math performance goal. However, the path from gender to math achievement was not statistically significant ($\beta = 0.11$, $p = 0.21$), indicating that female students in fact did not perform poorly in math compared to male students. These results were in line with the notion of gender role stereotypes in motivation-related beliefs in the domain of math (Meece et al., 2006) but not necessarily in actual math performance (Klapp Lekholm and Cliffordson, 2009).

Effect of Culture

The main effect of culture was found for six variables out of ten examined, and among these significant paths, almost all were negative except for English self-concept ($\beta = 0.20$, $p < 0.01$). The positive path from culture to English self-concept suggested that Anglo-background students had significantly higher English self-concept compared to Chinese-background students. This might be because English was the first or the only language spoken by Anglo-background students, and this might boost Anglo-background students' beliefs in their English ability. However, we found a significantly negative path from culture to English achievement, suggesting that in reality it was the Chinese-background students who performed better in the English test even though their self-ratings of ability were lower than the Anglo-background students. The other significant and negative paths from culture were on math mastery goal ($\beta = -0.16$, $p < 0.05$), math performance goal ($\beta = -0.21$, $p < 0.01$), English mastery goal ($\beta = -0.15$, $p < 0.05$), and math achievement ($\beta = -0.36$, $p < 0.01$). The descriptive statistics are shown in Table 8.3.

Interaction Effect

A statistically significant interaction effect between gender and culture was found only on English mastery goal ($\beta = 0.36$, $p < 0.01$). From Table 8.3, we can see that female Anglo-background students had the highest English mastery goal ($M = 4.15$), followed by female Chinese-background students ($M = 3.88$) and male Chinese-background students ($M = 3.85$). The male Anglo-background students had the lowest ratings on their English mastery goal ($M = 3.77$).

152 Alexander Seeshing Yeung and Feifei Han

TABLE 8.3 Descriptive statistics of the variables by groups

Variables	Males M (SD)		Females M (SD)	
	Chinese(248)	Anglo(853)	Chinese (210)	Anglo(1032)
Math self-concept	4.82 (0.86)	4.52 (0.95)	4.60 (0.86)	4.18 (1.01)
Math mastery	4.30 (1.28)	3.92 (1.27)	3.99 (1.27)	3.74 (1.27)
Math performance	4.52 (1.21)	3.94 (1.27)	4.32 (1.23)	3.76 (1.28)
English self-concept	3.81 (1.07)	4.24 (1.00)	4.06 (0.97)	4.47 (0.94)
English mastery	3.85 (1.09)	3.77 (1.20)	3.88 (1.08)	4.15 (1.10)
English performance	4.03 (1.17)	3.89 (1.15)	3.93(1.04)	3.82 (1.16)
Math achievement	34.42 (5.02)	27.42 (6.30)	34.79 (4.26)	26.75 (6.07)
English achievement	60.34 (15.20)	53.66 (13.29)	62.54 (14.31)	55.78 (12.44)

Discussion

The present study investigated gender and cultural effects on Australian high school students' self-concepts, achievement goals, and academic achievements in math and English. We found that cultural background had more impact on these variables than gender or the interaction between the two.

Gender Difference

The MIMIC model showed that the only noteworthy gender difference was on math performance goal. The negative effect suggested that male students tended to set performance goals higher, such as being better than their peers, in math subjects more than their female counterparts, even though math performance was equivalent between male and female students. This result is consistent with the current literature on gender stereotypes in different curriculum areas. Male students, in general, have been shown to have higher competence beliefs in math and science-related subjects (Meece et al., 2006; Midgley et al., 2001). The result also aligns with previous findings that male students tend to overestimate their math ability, whereas female students tend to underestimate theirs (Klapp Lekholm and Cliffordson, 2009). In educational practice, teachers may need to make some efforts in boosting female students' beliefs of their competence in math and science-related subjects. Based on the known reciprocal effects between self-concept and achievement (Marsh and Craven, 2006), students may further increase their academic performance in these subjects through interventions that focus on boosting their competence beliefs (Craven and Yeung, 2015).

Cultural Differences

The majority of the significant paths generated from our MIMIC model were from cultural background, which reflected that cultural backgrounds indeed made a difference on students' academic self-concepts, the achievement goals they set, as well as their levels of academic performance. We found that even though Chinese students outperformed Anglo students in both math and English achievements, they did not perceive their competence in the two subjects as higher than as perceived by the Anglo students. That is, the Chinese students' actual performance and their respective self-concepts were not commensurate with each other.

Interestingly, the positive path from culture to English self-concept indicated that the Anglo students were more confident about their English competence, even though their performance was inferior to that of the Chinese students. For Anglo students, English is the main, and probably the only, language they use. For the Chinese students in our sample, they reported that they mainly used either Mandarin or Cantonese at home. They may perceive English as their second language, or a language for school and social activities to interact with their peers. These could be reasons for them to underestimate their English competence.

However, we also observed a similar pattern in the math subject, showing that relatively, Chinese students seemed to underestimate their competence whereas Anglo students overestimated their math competence. Even though the two groups of students did not differ in their math competence beliefs, Chinese students were superior to their Anglo peers in the math test. These results seem to suggest that language may not be the reason that explains the Chinese students' lower self-concept in English; culture may be more important and suitable to explain the differences in self-concepts in both the English and math subjects. Chinese students' lower levels of self-concepts may have been affected by the values and educational beliefs they have held from Chinese culture. Chinese culture, values, and beliefs, heavily influenced by traditional thoughts and Confucianism, emphasizes strongly that the human's fulfilment needs to be nurtured through effort and diligence, rather than through their "innate ability" (Hau and Salili, 1991; Yeung and Yeung, 2008; Yeung et al., 2016). By identifying themselves as Chinese, the students from a Chinese cultural background are likely to hold such values and beliefs as part of their identity (Luo et al., 2014).

These cultural beliefs may also explain why Chinese-background students had higher performance goals (although not for English performance goal), because they believed that they should work harder and be competitive to be better in the school subjects. Apart from higher performance goals, we observed that Chinese students were higher in mastery goal in math. As far as English mastery goal is concerned, we found that while the Anglo female and Anglo male students had the highest and the lowest English mastery goal respectively, the Chinese female and male students were in the middle. This means that for English, a verbal related subject, gender stereotyping tended to be strong among Anglo students. For the Chinese students, such a gender stereotype was much weaker. As mentioned earlier, Chinese culture sees knowledge-seeking as a way to fulfil the meaning of life, and therefore Chinese students tend to set knowledge acquiring as their long-term goal to keep them motivated to learn (Li, 2002). This important belief may equally influence Chinese male and female students and offset some of the effects from gender stereotyping.

The results from our study add an extra piece of information regarding cultural effects on students' psychological factors in academic learning. It is important to note that even though our students migrated to an Australian society where Western cultures are predominant, and even though the Chinese-background students attended the same schools as the Anglo-background students, Chinese heritage seemed to have enduring effects on the Chinese students' academic beliefs and motivation. Hence, although these students are educated under the same educational system, the culture that the Chinese-background students have inherited from their family could have maintained the values and beliefs of their ancestors. However, whereas high levels of motivation may be a pleasing finding for the Chinese-background students, their relatively lower competence beliefs could be worrisome. Given the known mutually reinforcing effects between academic self-concept and achievement, the Chinese students' relatively lower self-concepts may reflect limitations in their potential of achieving optimal performance.

Implications for Educating Chinese-Heritage Students

Our research findings showed that in a multilingual and multicultural society like Australia, a subculture, such as Chinese culture, is able to exert significant impact on learners with a Chinese heritage. It appears that Chinese students are motivated to learn and set knowledge-acquiring as their long-term goal because of the Chinese belief of "nurture." However, Chinese students tended to underestimate their competence and had lower self-concept about their capabilities. This may reduce Chinese students' confidence. With a lower level of confidence, Chinese students may lose opportunities in the highly competitive modern society. Thus, to better educate Chinese students in a multicultural society, educators and practitioners should be alerted about and should acknowledge the subculture embedded in the mainstream culture. They should know about Chinese culture and should try to help students evaluate their abilities and competence more appropriately and to encourage Chinese learners to become more confident. As past research consistently suggests that self-concept of competence and achievement are reciprocal and mutually enhancing each other (Marsh and Craven, 2006), with an improved self-concept, Chinese learners may obtain better academic achievement. Our findings call for self-concept enhancement interventions for Chinese-background students to maximize their potential. For instance, teachers may adopt intervention that emphasizes appropriate praise and/or positive feedback, as meta-analysis showed that this type of strategy yielded the highest improvements in self-concept and it was relatively easy to implement, in order to enhance students' sense of self-worth (O'Mara et al., 2006). Other intervention strategies, such as skills training and using decision-making exercises, also yielded positive results.

Strengths and Limitations

The current study adds to the literature on Chinese-heritage learners' self-beliefs and motivation in a Western context. It explicates gender and culture patterns between Chinese- and Anglo-background learners within the same educational system, so that the similarities and differences observed could be attributed to culture rather than the educational system per se. Despite the interesting findings and the strength of the MIMIC approach, the study did have some limitations, which may be addressed in future research. As our sample included only high school students, we could not generalize the findings to Chinese learners of other age spans. It would be interesting to examine these variables among primary and secondary school students to see if Chinese- and Anglo-background learners at different educational levels differ. This way, we may obtain useful information about whether culture has profound effects from an early age and continues through maturity.

Furthermore, our research was limited to an Australian schooling context. As Chinese-heritage learners are spread over the world, it would be interesting to compare the self-concept and achievement goals of Chinese-heritage learners from Eastern and Western countries to reflect nuanced influences by culture.

Conclusion

The current study compared two important academic psychological constructs— self-concept and achievement goals—and academic achievement in math and English among 461 Chinese-background and 1,901 Anglo-background high school students in Australia using a MIMIC approach to SEM. For these high school students, we found that gender did not have much significant effect whereas culture exerted influences not only on their academic performance, but also on self-concept and motivation. Even though Chinese students outperformed their Anglo peers in both math and English subjects, and were more motivated to learn, they had significantly lower levels of self-concept about their competence and capabilities, especially in English. It appeared that students with a Chinese background tended to underestimate their academic competence. These results were consistent with previous findings that students from Confusion heritage culture (e.g., Chen et al., 1996; Sue and Okazaki, 1990). Underestimation of one's abilities may undermine students' confidence in schools, hence Chinese students may suffer from psychological dissatisfaction at school and may lose opportunities to participate in school activities. For teachers who teach in a multicultural society, they need to acknowledge the influence of subcultures to students' psychological wellbeing. When teaching students from a Chinese background, teachers should especially pay attention to whether students have appropriate evaluation of their academic abilities and encourage these learners to be more confident about their academic capabilities and achievement in order to boost their self-concept.

References

Arens, A. K., Yeung, A. S., Craven, R. G., and Hasselhorn, M. (2011). The twofold multidimensionality of academic self-concept: Domain specificity and separation between competence and affect components. *Journal of Educational Psychology*, *103*, 970–981.

Bentler, P. M. (1990). Comparative fit indexes in structural models. *Psychological Bulletin*, *107*, 238–246.

Browne, M. W., and Cudeck, R. (1993). Alternative ways of assessing model fit. In K. A. Bollen and J. S. Long (Eds.), *Testing structural equation models* (pp. 136–162). Beverly Hills, CA: Sage.

Chen, C. S., Lee, S. Y., and Stevenson, H. W. (1996). Academic achievement and motivation of Chinese students: A cross-national perspective. In S. Lau (Ed), *Growing up the Chinese way: Chinese child and adolescent development* (pp. 357–374). Hong Kong, China: The Chinese University Press.

Cheung, G. W., and Rensvold, R. B. (2002). Evaluating goodness-of-fit indexes for testing measurement invariance. *Structural Equation Modeling*, *9*(2), 233–255.

Chiu, M. M., and Klassen, R. M. (2010). Relations of mathematics self-concept and its calibration with mathematics achievement: Cultural differences among fifteen year olds in 34 countries. *Learning and Motivation*, *20*, 2–17.

Craven, R. G., and Yeung, A. S. (2015). Motivation in Australian Aboriginal populations. In J. D. Wright (Ed.), *International encyclopedia of the social & behavioral sciences* (2nd edn, vol. 15, pp. 899–906). Oxford, UK: Elsevier.

Dai, D. Y. (2001). A comparison of gender differences in academic self-concept and motivation between high-ability and average Chinese adolescents. *Journal of Secondary Gifted Education*, *13*, 22–32.

Daniels, L. M., Haynes, T. L., Stupnisky, R. H., Perry, R. P., Newall, N. E., and Pekrun, R. (2008). Individual differences in achievement goals: A longitudinal study of cognitive, emotional, and achievement outcomes. *Contemporary Educational Psychology*, *33*, 584–608.

Dekker, S., and Fischer, R. (2008). Cultural differences in academic motivation goals: A meta-analysis across 13 societies. *The Journal of Educational Research*, *102*, 99–110.

Elliot, A. J. (2005). A conceptual history of the achievement goal construct. In A. J. Elliot and C. S. Dweck (Eds.), *Handbook of competence and motivation* (pp. 52–72). New York, NY: Guilford Press.

Hau, K.T., and Salili, F. (1991). Structure and semantic differential placement of specific cases: Academic causal attributions by Chinese students in Hong Kong. *International Journal of Psychology*, *26*, 175–193.

Hulleman, C. S., Schrager, S. M., Bodmann, S. M., and Harackiewicz, J. M. (2010). A meta-analytic review of achievement goal measures: Different labels for the same constructs or different constructs with similar labels. *Psychological Bulletin*, *136*, 422–449.

Jöreskog, K. G., and Sörbom, D. (2005). *LISREL 8.72: Structural equation modelling with SIMPLIS command language.* Chicago, IL: Scientific Software International.

King, R. B., Ganotice, F. A., and Watkins, D. A. (2012). Cross-cultural validation of the Inventory of School Motivation (ISM) in the Asian setting: Hong Kong and the Philippines. *Child Indicators Research, 5,* 135–153.

Klapp Lekholm, A., and Cliffordson, C. (2009). Effects of student characteristics on grades in compulsory school. *Educational Research and Evaluation, 15,* 1–23.

Kurtz-Costes, B., Rowley, S., Harris-Britt, A., and Woods, T. A. (2008). Gender stereotypes about mathematics and science and self-perceptions of ability in late childhood and early adolescence. *Merrill-Palmer Quarterly, 54,* 386–409.

Lai, F. (2010). Are boys left behind? The evolution of the gender achievement gap in Beijing's middle schools. *Economics of Education Review, 29,* 383–399.

Li, J. (2002). Models of learning in different cultures. In J. Bempechat and J. G. Elliott (Eds.), *New directions in child and adolescent development, no. 96: Achievement motivation in culture and context: Understanding children's learning experiences.* San Francisco, CA: Jossey-Bass.

Luo, W., Hogan, D. J., Yeung, A. S., Sheng, Y. Z., and Aye, K. M. (2014). Attributional beliefs of Singapore students: Relations to self-construal, competence and achievement goals. *Educational Psychology, 34*(2), 154–170.

Magson, N. R., Craven, R. G., Nelson, G. F., Yeung, A. S., Bodkin-Andrews, G. H., and McInerney, D. M. (2014). Motivation matters: Profiling indigenous and non-indigenous students' motivational goals. *The Australian Journal of Indigenous Education, 43*(2), 1–17.

Mak, A. S., and Chan, H. (1995). Families and cultural diversity in Australia. Retrieved from https://aifs.gov.au/publications/families-and-cultural-diversity-australia/4-chinese-family-values-australia.

Marsh, H. W. (1990). The structure of academic self-concept: The Marsh/Shavelson model. *Journal of Educational Psychology, 82,* 623–636.

Marsh, H. W., and Craven, R. G. (2006). Reciprocal effects of self-concept and performance from a multidimensional perspective: Beyond seductive pleasure and unidimensional perspective. *Perspectives on Psychological Science, 1,* 133–163.

Marsh, H. W., Craven, R. G., Hinkley, J. W., and Debus, R. L. (2003). Evaluation of the Big-Two-Factor Theory of academic motivation orientations: An evaluation of jingle-jangle fallacies. *Multivariate Behavioral Research, 38,* 189–224.

Meece, J. L., Glienke, B. B., and Burg, S. (2006). Gender and motivation. *Journal of School Psychology, 44,* 351–373.

Metallidou, P., and Vlachou, A. (2007). Motivational beliefs, cognitive engagement, and achievement in language and mathematics in elementary school children. *International Journal of Psychology, 42,* 2–15.

Midgley, C., Kaplan, A., and Middleton, M. (2001). Performance-approach goals: Good for what, for whom, under what circumstances, and at what cost? *Journal of Educational Psychology, 93,* 77–86.

Möller, J., Retelsdorf, J., Köller, O., and Marsh, H. W. (2011). The Reciprocal Internal/External Frame of Reference Model: An integration of models of relations between academic achievement and self-concept. *American Educational Research Journal, 48,* 1316–1346.

Nachtigall, C., Kroehne, U., Funke, F., and Steyer, R. (2003). (Why) Should we use SEM? Pros and cons of structural equation modeling. *Method Psychology Research Online, 8,* 1–22.

O'Mara, A. J., Marsh H. W., Craven, R. G., and Debus, R. (2006). Do self-concept interventions make a difference? A synergistic blend of construct validation and meta-analysis. *Educational Psychologist, 41*, 181–206.

Pajares, F., and Schunk, D. H. (2002). Self and self-belief in psychology and education: A historical perspective. In J. Aronson (Ed.), *Improving academic achievement: Impact of psychological factors on education* (pp. 3–21). San Diego, CA: Academic Press.

Paulick, I., Watermann, R., and Nückles, M. (2013). Achievement goals and school achievement: The transition to different school tracks in secondary school. *Contemporary Educational Psychology, 38*, 75–86.

Pintrich, P. R. (2000). An achievement goal theory perspective on issues in motivation terminology, theory, and research. *Contemporary Educational Psychology, 25*, 92–104.

Pinxten, M., Marsh, H. W., De Fraine, B., Van Den Noortgate, W., and Van Damme, J. (2014). Enjoying mathematics or feeling competent in mathematics? Reciprocal effects on mathematics achievement and perceived math effort expenditure. *British Journal of Educational Psychology, 84*, 152–174.

Seifert, T. L. (2004). Understanding student motivation. *Educational Research, 46*, 137–149.

Senko, C., Hulleman, C. S., and Harackiewicz, J. M. (2011). Achievement goal theory at the crossroads: Old controversies, current challenges, and new directions. *Educational Psychologist, 46*, 26–47.

Shavelson, R. J., Hubner, J. J., and Stanton, G. C. (1976). Self-concept: Validation of construct interpretations. *Review of Educational Research, 46*, 407–441.

Sue, S. and Okazaki, S. (1990). Asian-American educational achievements: A phenomenon in search of an explanation. *American Psychologist, 45*, 913–920.

Swann, W. B., Jr., Chang-Schneider, C., and Larsen McClarty, K. (2007). Do people's self-views matter? Self-concept and self-esteem in everyday life. *American Psychologist, 62*, 84–94.

Trautwein, U., and Lüdtke, O. (2009). Predicting homework motivation and homework effort in six school subjects: The role of person and family characteristics, classroom factors, and school track. *Learning and Instruction, 19*, 243–258.

Tucker, L. R., and Lewis, C. (1973). A reliability coefficient for maximum likelihood factor analysis. *Psychometrika, 38*, 1–10.

Urdan, T., and Mestas, M. (2006). The goals behind performance goals. *Journal of Educational Psychology, 98*, 354–365.

Usher, E. L., and Pajares, F. (2008). Self-efficacy for self-regulated learning: A validation study. *Educational and Psychological Measurement, 68*, 443–463.

Wilkinson, G. S., and Robertson, G. J. (2006). *WRAT4: Wide Range Achievement Test [Standardized Achievement Test]*. Lutz, FL: Psychological Assessment Resources.

Wolters, C. A. (2004). Advancing achievement goal theory: using goal structures and goal orientations to predict students' motivation, cognition, and achievement. *Journal of Educational Psychology, 96*, 236–250.

Worrell, F. C., Watkins, M. W., and Hall, T. E. (2008). Reliability and validity of self-concept scores in secondary school students in Trinidad and Tobago. *School Psychology International, 29*, 466–480.

Yeung, A. S. (2011). Student self-concept and effort: Gender and grade differences. *Educational Psychology, 31*, 749–772.

Yeung, A. S., and Yeung, A. (2008). Ability vs. effort: Perceptions of students from the east and from the west. In O. S. Tan, D. M. McInerney, A. D. Liem, and A. G. Tan (Eds.), *Research on multicultural education and international perspectives. Vol. 7:*

What the West can learn from the East: Asian perspectives on the psychology of learning and motivation (pp. 77–99). Greenwich, CT: Information Age.

Yeung, A. S., Craven, R. G., and Kaur, G. (2012). Gender differences in achievement motivation: Grade and cultural considerations. In S. McGeown (Ed.), *Psychology of gender differences* (pp. 59–79). New York, NY: Nova Science Publishers.

Yeung, A. S., Han, F., and Lee, F. L. M. (2016). Development of Chinese students' ability and effort beliefs influencing achievement. In R. B. King and A. B. I. Bernardo (Eds.), *The psychology of Asian learners: A festschrift in honor of David Watkins* (pp. 319–336). Singapore: Springer.

9

UNDERSTANDING UNDERGRADUATES OF CHINESE HERITAGE IN THE UK

Motivations and Challenges

Jiayi Wang

The British Council (2013) has unambiguously identified Chinese as one of the top five languages that the UK will need the most in the next 20 years. This conclusion was based on a range of economic and non-economic factors, including the current language deficit in the country. Among European countries, Britain has one of the largest populations of people of Chinese origin. According to the 2011 UK census, British Chinese numbered approximately 433,150, accounting for 0.7% of the UK population. The percentage was 0.4% in the 2001 census and 0.3% in the 1991 census, which was the first to include a question on ethnicity (Sillitoe and White, 1992). Primarily because of continuing immigration, over the past decade, the Chinese have become the fastest-growing ethnic minority in Britain (Jivraj and Simpson, 2015).

With no clear pattern in their geographical distribution, in contrast to North America, the Chinese are more decentralized and widespread than other ethnic minorities in the UK. However, the Chinese form no more than 3% of the population in any single electoral area (Office for National Statistics, 2009). It is perhaps because of such decentralization that Britain has not yet developed well-established institutional structures, such as publicly funded bilingual schools like those found in Canada (Comanaru and Noels, 2009), to support the cultural and linguistic vitality of the Chinese communities. The first English-Mandarin bilingual free school in the UK did not open until 2014 and it opened to promote bilingual education rather than to support the British-Chinese communities (Gurney-Read, 2013).

A growing number of British universities are offering degree programs in Chinese language. While Chinese-heritage language (CHL) learners have been a continuing source of students studying for a degree in Chinese at British universities, they remain an uncharted terrain of research. The goal of this study is to address this lacuna. In anticipation of the ability to take better advantage of the potential of CHL learners to meet the urgent language need, this study draws on an analysis of open-ended questionnaire responses and follow-up interviews to explore the motivations behind the CHL learners' degree choices and the specific challenges that they face during their studies.

Theoretical Framework

Robert Gardner and Wallace Lambert, both Canadian social psychologists, published their seminal work in 1972, through which they established language learning motivation as a research area. Based on the finding that the effect of motivation on learning another language was independent of the learner's aptitude or ability, they proposed two kinds of motivation: integrative motivation, which reflects "a sincere and personal interest in the people and culture represented by the other group," and instrumental motivation, which shows "the practical value and advantages of learning a new language" (Gardner and Lambert, 1972, p. 132). Gardner's (1985, 2001) widely cited socio-educational model, which spawned a wealth of research in a range of contexts, further elaborated these theoretical concepts.

While Gardner's model continues to serve as an important theoretical foundation in second/foreign language motivation research, scholars (e.g., Lu and Li, 2008; Ushioda and Dörnyei, 2012) have raised questions about the conceptual distinction between instrumental and integrative motivation. Moving beyond the social psychological perspectives on the analysis of motivation, Dörnyei (1994) expanded Gardner's framework into three levels: the language level (integrative and instrumental motivational subsystems), the learner level (individual need for achievement and self-confidence, including language use anxiety), and the learning situation level (course-, teacher-, and group-specific motivational components). The present study cuts across the different levels.

While motivational change during the process of second/foreign language learning became an area of research focus around the turn of the century (Dörnyei and Ottó, 1998), traditional research on the motivation to engage in learning (e.g., choices, reasons, and decisions) continued to dominate the discussion (Ushioda and Dörnyei, 2012). During the past 16 years, a shift toward more qualitative investigations provided rich insights into language teaching and learning (Dörnyei and Schmitt, 2001; Li and Duff, 2008; Ushioda and Dörnyei, 2012).

Nonetheless, it is noteworthy that, to date, second/foreign language learning motivation research has focused predominantly on the motivation to learn another language in non-language degree contexts. For example, Zhang (2013) investigated the attitudes of CHL learners studying Chinese as an elective module at a British university. Lu and Li (2008) conducted a comprehensive comparative analysis of the effect of integrative, instrumental, and situational motivation on Chinese learning of heritage and non-heritage college students enrolled in Chinese language classes in mixed classrooms in the United States. These authors (Lu and Li, 2008) made a finer distinction between non-heritage Asian students (e.g., Korean learners of Chinese language) and non-heritage non-Asian students: their results demonstrated the diversity within both the heritage and the non-heritage learner subgroups.

As with the above-mentioned studies, previous motivation research on CHL learners offered valuable insights into this group of students as well as Chinese language teaching in general. Nonetheless, research regarding CHL learners as degree students of Chinese remains scarce. Because choosing to study Chinese as a university degree entails a significantly greater commitment than learning the language as a study module, the stakes are generally higher for these students.

Regarding degree choices, although there is a substantial body of research on minority ethnic access to higher education, there is "much less work done on minority ethnic students' experiences of higher education and almost none" on these students' choices in higher education (Ball et al., 2002, p. 333).

The aim of the study is, therefore, to address this gap of understanding by launching a qualitative investigation into both CHL learners' motivation for choosing to pursue a degree in Chinese and the specific challenges that they face.

Method

This study takes a data-driven approach that uses open-ended questionnaires and interviews to explore why Chinese-heritage undergraduates decide to pursue a degree in Chinese, and what specific challenges they face during their course of study. Although these learners are a minority group in the UK's Chinese-degree student population, considering the ongoing Chinese language deficit in British society and the enormous benefits that heritage language speakers can bring, the lack of information about CHL students pursuing a degree in Chinese is rendered significantly more serious. This study attempts to explore this previously unexplored group of British university students.

The study participants included 20 CHL learners who graduated with a degree in Chinese within the past four years or who were final-year students enrolled in Chinese degree courses at two British universities. The two groups were chosen for three reasons. First, the final-year students have had a relatively complete experience of studying for a degree in Chinese, which included a year abroad in China. These students and the recent graduates are both likely to have a more holistic perspective of the subject than first- or second-year students. Second, many CHL learners have unambiguously stated that the final year was the most difficult for them. Therefore, it is crucial to consider this fact in the investigation of the difficulties that they faced. Third, although it is always difficult to contact students after they have graduated, in this study, they are a critical group

164 Jiayi Wang

of participants since they appear to be both more open to criticizing the staff and university and more willing to discuss sensitive issues than the current students are.

The questionnaire consisted of open-ended questions about participants' reasons for learning Chinese at the university degree level and the difficulties that they encountered in doing so. Questionnaires were sent via email to 25 Chinese-heritage graduates and final-year students of Chinese. In the email, they were informed about the confidential and voluntary nature of the study. Twenty recipients returned the completed questionnaire. It included questions about their ethnicity, place of birth, native languages and dialects (as well as those spoken by their parents and siblings), factors that they think most influenced their decision to study Chinese at the university level, and the difficulties and advantages that they believe they had in learning Chinese.

After the responses were thematically analyzed using NVivo, qualitative research software, all of the participants were invited to a follow-up interview. Although five agreed to be interviewed, one withdrew for personal reasons in the middle of the study. The interview transcripts and the survey responses were further analyzed around the common themes of motivations and challenges.

In addition to speaking English as their mother tongue, all 20 participants were characterized by the ability to speak a variety of Chinese dialects (e.g., Cantonese, Hakka, or Mandarin). They all indicated that both parents were native speakers of a variety of Chinese dialects and they all claimed a Chinese background as their ethnic heritage. All of the participants were British citizens. Pseudonyms were assigned to the participants who took part in the follow-up interviews. To anonymize their identity, other participants were referred to by their identified native Chinese language/dialect.

Results

Motivations for Pursuing a Degree in Chinese

All 20 participants were second-generation Chinese born in England. Among the varieties of Chinese, 14 participants identified only Cantonese as their mother tongue, four identified only Hakka, and two identified both Cantonese and Mandarin. They all learned Mandarin in their Chinese degree programs. In fact, only Mandarin courses were offered in their major course of study; the participants were fully aware of this fact when they chose the degree program. Consequently, it was particularly interesting to examine the main factors that affected their decisions to major in Chinese at the university level.

As noted earlier, one of the two central aims of this qualitative study is to fill the gap in the understanding of why CHL students choose to pursue a degree in Chinese. Overall, their answers to the open-ended question, "What factors do you think most influenced your decision to study Chinese as a degree at university?" indicated that they generally had *multiple* motivations for their choice of major and the instrumental and integrative orientations were not dichotomous.

Five distinct, albeit interrelated, categories emerged from a grounded thematic analysis of the data: getting back to ethnic/cultural roots (ten mentions, 50% of the respondents), better job prospects (nine mentions, 45%), a passion for Chinese popular culture (seven mentions, 35%), ease of learning (three mentions, 15%), and parental recommendation (two mentions, 10%). It is noteworthy that many participants identified more than one category of the factors.

First, although they were all native speakers of Cantonese or Hakka, half of the respondents (ten) mentioned connecting with ethnic/cultural roots as one of their main reasons for deciding to pursue a Mandarin-oriented degree in Chinese. Even though they were not native speakers of Mandarin, they still regarded learning Mandarin as a way to connect with their ethnic and cultural roots. In the follow-up interviews, the participants pointed to the status of Mandarin as a national and standard language of China and the fact that it is the closest to their own language and culture, which echoes the findings regarding university-level CHL learners in the United States (Lee, 2005).

Second, nearly half of the participants (nine) claimed better job prospects as one of the factors that most influenced their decision. Sophie elaborated that "Chinese has become a new popular language as China's economy is growing, resulting in better job prospects" (Interview #4). Other interviewees talked about global companies desperate for Mandarin speakers and that Chinese companies were expanding globally and were thus in need of bilingual employees as well. This is consistent with prior research findings about CHL learners' instrumental motivation for attending Chinese language classes in general (e.g., Comanaru and Noels, 2009; Mu, 2016).

Interestingly, 35% of the participants (seven out of 20) cited a passion for Chinese popular culture as one of their main reasons for choosing to pursue a degree in Chinese. Five indicated that, despite being British citizens, they were surrounded by Chinese popular culture. Three further specified familiarity with Mandarin popular culture, such as Chinese programs produced on the Chinese Mainland and in Taiwan. George explained that "[m]any Mandarin drama and TV shows are increasingly popular and more engaging than Cantonese shows" and then he gave examples of Mandarin variety talk shows and game shows that can be watched for free online (Interview #3).

Two participants extended the scope from Chinese to Southeast Asian popular culture. Both touched upon Korean TV shows. As Maria expounded in her follow-up interview, "my passion in Southeast Asian culture. I really enjoyed watching Korean television and films, which were dubbed in Chinese, and listening to Chinese songs [online]" (Interview #1). The comments reflect the interconnectedness of cultures in Southeast Asia and the global spread of pop culture, facilitated by the internet and unencumbered by time and space. While the influence of pop culture has been explored among English-as-a-foreign-language learners (Cheung,

2001), its study is rare within the CHL context, and it may be seen as an emerging trend. The discussion section below addresses this point.

Fourth, three participants (15%) claimed ease of learning as one of the main motivations for their degree choices. All three were native speakers of Cantonese. When probed in his follow-up interview, George elaborated that he could master Mandarin quickly because of his knowledge of Cantonese, and he really wanted to "learn it well and use it in [his] future" (Interview #3). Describing how hard he worked for his degree and how much culture shock he experienced during his year abroad in China, he went on to stress that it was not because he wanted to earn an easy A (Interview #3). While his elaboration indicates a connection between the motivation regarding ease of learning and the motivation related to future career opportunities, it may also lend support to previous observations that CHL learners tend to be "simply dismissed as 'native speakers' who do not need any instruction or are viewed derisively . . . as people seeking inflated grades" (Li and Duff, 2008, p. 15). This seems to overshadow the genuinely positive motivations for learning on the part of these students.

Fifth, two participants cited parental recommendation as one of the factors that most influenced their decision to pursue a degree in Chinese. The mother tongue of one was Hakka and the other's was Cantonese. The Hakka speaker referred to his parents' background in international trade and their belief that Mandarin skills would enable him to realize his dream of running his own business. Lisa, the Cantonese speaker, articulated her parents' thoughts about what jobs would suit her: "My parents thought that I was best suited to be a translator or interpreter in the future, so they encouraged me to further my Chinese studies" (Interview #2). Clearly, parental recommendations centered on their children's future career plans, which were also linked to the second motivation regarding job prospects. However, the perceived weight of parental involvement in the decision-making process seems to distinguish the two motivations. Although it is common to have parental involvement in students' choices regarding higher education (Reay et al., 2005), its overriding impact on how the candidates chose their majors is what stands out here.

Challenges of University-Level Language Learners of Chinese Heritage

In the open-ended questionnaire, the participants were asked to answer two questions regarding the challenges that CHL learners face when studying at the university level:

1. Compared with non-heritage learners, what difficulties did you have as a Chinese-heritage learner in studying for a degree in Chinese at university?
2. What difficulties do you think Chinese-heritage learners can have in general? Why?

The participants' answers focused on the following aspects: greater pressure, success taken for granted, marginalization and neglect by teachers, and the distancing attitudes of fellow students.

Higher Expectations, Greater Pressure: "You Look Like a Native Speaker"

The majority of the participants reported feeling extra academic pressure as compared with non-heritage learners. They described feeling pressure from teachers, peers, and numerous others as well. For example, a native speaker of Hakka mentioned that people expected her to speak and understand at a certain level of Mandarin simply because she is Chinese and even though she had very little knowledge of Mandarin before she started her university studies.

Sophie illustrated this point by recounting a personal experience. She had been strolling around with her friends during the Chinese New Year celebration in the China Town of a British city. The streets were swarming with people, many of whom were not Chinese. They had all gathered there for the Chinese New Year parade and to learn about Chinese culture. A white family—two middle-aged parents with a child—was standing next to Sophie and her friends. The father asked her about the meaning of a Chinese poster on the wall in front of them. After Sophie explained to the family that she could not understand the meaning of the words either, the father said, "Sorry, but you look like a native speaker." Sophie felt too embarrassed to explain that even though she was indeed a native speaker of a variety of Chinese dialects, she was actually studying for a degree in Chinese. As she explained, people may not be aware that "It is natural that you don't know everything about Chinese" (Interview #4).

This experience demonstrates that simply because an individual looks Chinese, people tend to expect him or her to be a native speaker of Chinese and to know everything about the language, thus placing higher, sometimes unrealistic, expectations upon the individual. In a similar vein, most participants also reported feeling the pressures of failing to live up to the expectations of teachers and peers and/or self-imposed pressures that they should succeed as heritage learners. For example, "There can be a dependency of non-heritage learners expecting Chinese-heritage Chinese students to be more competent with the language, therefore extra pressure to succeed" (a Hakka native speaker, questionnaire answer). These findings support prior research on CHL learners generally feeling more pressure than non-heritage learners regarding their Chinese language skills (Comanaru and Noels, 2009; Lee, 2005).

Success Taken for Granted: "Hard Work Overshadowed by Views that You Have an Unfair Advantage"

The second major challenge that emerged from the findings was that others took the success of the CHL students for granted. This is somewhat related to the first

168 Jiayi Wang

challenge of feeling extra pressure. According to most participants, teachers and non-heritage peers generally thought that they "ought to succeed" (a Mandarin and Cantonese speaker, questionnaire answer) and they "failed to appreciate [their] efforts appropriately" (a Cantonese speaker, questionnaire answer). For example, when probed about her questionnaire answer, "Your hard work tends to be overshadowed by views that you have an unfair advantage," recent graduate Maria offered an example of the issues that she and many other Cantonese speakers had with Mandarin pronunciation:

> I worked so hard to avoid my Cantonese accent popping up. But my teachers and classmates didn't notice my efforts at all . . . When my non-heritage classmates got one sound right in a very difficult four-character idiom, they were highly praised by my teachers. But even though I got all four sounds right because I had spent much more time after class to learn a lot of idioms and practice myself, my teachers didn't praise me.
>
> (Interview #1)

Mandarin has four tones (some say five, if the neutral tone is considered a tone); in comparison, many other Chinese dialects have more than that. Cantonese, for example, has six tones (nine, if the checked tones are included). It is noteworthy that the Chinese degree programs offered in this study in the UK did not have dual tracks in Cantonese and Mandarin, as is the emerging trend in heritage language education in North America (Kondo-Brown, 2010; Lee, 2005; Lu and Li, 2008). One of the reasons for this might be the relatively small number of heritage learners in Chinese program student populations.

In addition to tones, Maria mentioned other examples as well. For instance, she thought that her prior knowledge of very informal registers of Chinese actually became an additional difficulty with which she had to grapple when she learned formal registers at a more advanced level. Although she spent significantly more time addressing it than her non-heritage classmates, her extra efforts were neither appreciated nor acknowledged by her teachers, once again implying that her success was taken for granted.

One participant, native Cantonese-speaking Lisa, held a view that was opposite that of the other participants:

> I think Chinese-heritage learners won't be as hard-working as non-heritage learners because they think they already know it. However, sometimes things are taught which even the Chinese-heritage learners don't understand (e.g., idioms) and because they may not be as eager to learn as the non-heritage learners, then it may take them longer to fully grasp it.
>
> (Interview #2)

Unlike the other participants, Lisa had a relatively good knowledge of Mandarin before she began her studies. Her heritage background, including her family's history of migration and settlement, is examined in the case study section. Her perspective on this issue was idiosyncratic in the data. Because their hard work was not valued appropriately and their success was expected, the CHL students tended to feel frustrated during their studies.

Marginalization and Neglect by Teachers

The third specific challenge that the CHL students faced was marginalization and neglect by teachers. Although less than half of the participants (seven out of 20) mentioned the issue, it appeared to be a serious problem, as shown by Maria's comments below:

> Some teachers would *discriminate* [against] us [as compared to] . . . non-Chinese-heritage learners, which is rather discouraging. Since they believe we have an unfair advantage, they tend to neglect us in the classroom. For example, when going around the class to answer questions, they would naturally skip our turn every single time. Whilst studying year 2 material, I was once told to reduce the quality of our paired role-play work.
>
> (Interview #1, emphasis added)

This extract vividly depicts what the participants found particularly challenging during their studies. While the others did not use the word "discriminate," they reported feeling upset and frustrated at being neglected and marginalized by some of their teachers. Several mentioned being asked to reduce the quality of their paired work and were told that they should do so because their non-heritage partners could not compete with them at the same level. However, the CHL students seemed to view it in a different way. They thought that when working in pairs of mixed ability, they could "push their partners to achieve better scores" (George, Interview #3).

All seven of these participants reported that some of their teachers behaved differently toward heritage versus non-heritage students in classroom interactions and this seriously affected the students' motivation to learn the language. For example, many of the teachers deliberately shunned the heritage students in class and these students found it "very difficult to bring up the problem to the teachers" (Maria, Interview #1). This is a significant issue because they did not want to be regarded as troublemakers or seen as "not respecting teachers" (George, Interview #3), which is extremely important in traditional Chinese culture.

Distancing Attitudes of Fellow Students

The fourth main challenge identified by the CHL students was their non-heritage classmates' *distancing* attitudes in the use of the Chinese language as the medium of communication. Although the participants all got along with their non-heritage peers very well, they reported that their non-heritage classmates

170 Jiayi Wang

continuously avoided talking to them in Chinese since they were usually "not very confident with their Chinese language skills" in front of their heritage classmates (a Cantonese speaker, questionnaire answer). Lisa thought, "they felt a bit intimidated" (Interview #2). Because of their perceptions of their classmates' distancing attitudes in this regard, the heritage learners did not speak frequently in Chinese to their non-heritage classmates. Maria described this vividly and offered a few examples of when she did speak Chinese:

> I rarely speak Chinese with my classmates, but when I do, it is usually rather brief. It would never be a full-on conversation like the one we would have in English. For example, we would call each other's Chinese names, 你好！怎么了？你在哪儿？ etc. The response would also be brief, or even just in English.
>
> (Interview #1)

The extract above shows that the communication in Chinese between heritage and non-heritage students tended to be very simple and brief, such as "Hello!", "What happened?", "Where are you?" Whether explicit or implicit, the unwillingness of non-heritage peers to use Chinese with the heritage learners also seemed to have an adverse impact on the heritage learners. They found this difficult to deal with, since their non-heritage peers might be more likely to talk to each other among themselves in Chinese, which was "discouraging," since they "were all Chinese learners" (a Cantonese speaker, questionnaire answer).

Further Background of the Participants: Four Cases

The follow-up interviews with four out of the 20 participants allowed me to delve further into the questionnaire answers and engage the participants in their "personal stories of migration and settlement," which is vital in studying heritage learners (Comanaru and Noels, 2009, p. 154). The aim of this section is to allow the reader to gain a fuller picture of the diversity of this student population and to explore the genesis of their views and motivations.

Case One: Maria

Maria graduated with a First Class Honors degree in Chinese in 2014. Born and raised in Buckinghamshire, she identified herself as a native speaker of English first, followed by Cantonese. Her mother spoke Cantonese, Vietnamese, Mandarin, and English while her father spoke Cantonese, Hakka, and English. English and Cantonese were spoken at home among her family members. Both of her parents were ethnically Chinese.

Maria's father came to the UK from Hong Kong to join his family in 1978. He opened his own restaurant and sold it upon retirement in 2012. On her mother's side of the family, Maria's uncle had fled as a refugee to the UK from Vietnam. After settling down, he acted as a guarantor for her mother and the rest of their family to migrate to the UK. Her mother and father have been working together ever since.

Maria regretted that her Cantonese was not very fluent. Her parents were very busy with work as she and her brother were growing up. Since her family did not enforce a Chinese-only policy, she and her brother used English much more at home.

Case Two: Lisa

A recipient of a First Class Honors degree in 2015, Lisa was born in south England and grew up with her grandmother and mother, who did not speak any English. Her first language was Cantonese, as it was the main language they spoke at home. On starting primary school, she had a Cantonese-English interpreter to help her for about two years. Since she spent a significant amount of time at school and around English-speaking children, she soon became fluent in speaking English.

Her father came to England with his family at the age of 11. He studied in the UK at a college and polytechnic institute. Her grandmother worked at fast-food restaurants and grew bean sprouts to sell to support her father's education. After earning a degree in engineering, her father worked for British Airways for a couple of years. Later, he moved to the Sony Company and started making numerous business trips to China. Perhaps because he did not learn Mandarin until he started traveling on business to China, from the start, he took Lisa's Chinese language education very seriously.

Lisa was the only participant who had a good knowledge of Mandarin before she started her undergraduate studies: as proof, she had a General Certificate of Secondary Education (GCSE) in Chinese. She was the only participant who thought that heritage learners were not as hard-working as non-heritage learners were. Her main reason for choosing to pursue a degree in Chinese was her parents' recommendation: they thought that a job as a translator/interpreter would suit her best. Both of her parents were native speakers of Cantonese.

Case Three: George

Born and raised in London, George graduated with an Upper Second Class Honors degree in Chinese in 2015. Both of his parents were Vietnamese Chinese, speaking Vietnamese, Guangxi Cantonese (a variety of Cantonese spoken in part of the Guangxi Province), Mandarin, and English. They emigrated from Vietnam to the UK over 30 years ago and worked in textiles and catering. Earlier still, George's great-grandfather, on his father's side, had emigrated from Southern China to Vietnam. George identified English and Cantonese as his native languages.

172 Jiayi Wang

In addition to speaking those languages with his parents at home, George identified "watching Chinese programs" as one of the factors that he thought most influenced the way in which he spoke Cantonese and Mandarin. As the description in the previous section demonstrated, he also claimed Chinese popular culture as one of the main reasons for his degree choice.

Case Four: Sophie

Unlike the previous three interviewees who had already graduated, Sophie was a final-year student of Chinese. She was born and raised in Liverpool, where the Chinese community was relatively large. Her native languages were English and Hakka. Her parents came to the UK to get married and work 28 years earlier. Her mother spoke Hakka, Mandarin, Cantonese, and English. Her father spoke Hakka, Vietnamese, Cantonese, and English. Her parents raised her and her sister to speak Hakka at home, while they learned and spoke English at school. Attending weekend school was critical to improving her Cantonese fluency when she was younger.

Sophie also found it challenging that although she "already had knowledge of speaking Hakka and mild Cantonese, the different dialects could be confusing and easy to mix up at times" (Interview #4).

In summary, these four case studies illustrate the individual differences between heritage learners. I will address this point in more depth in the discussion below.

Discussion

Regarding the CHL students' motivation to pursue a degree in Chinese, the findings of the present study are generally consistent with the results of prior research regarding CHL learners not pursuing a degree (Lu and Li, 2008). Instrumental (e.g., better job prospects) and integrative motivation (connecting with cultural roots and interest in Chinese popular culture) are not mutually exclusive (Ushioda and Dörnyei, 2012) and can co-exist in the learners' degree choices. To connect with their ethnic/cultural roots supports the findings of previous studies regarding ethnic-related choices in higher education, in that, for some, the choice was "in part, about sustaining aspects of their ethnic identity or having this identity valued and defended" (Ball et al., 2002, p. 348).

A new finding is that, for some CHL students, their interest in popular culture was one of the main motivating factors that drove them to pursue a degree in Chinese. While almost none of them had visited China before beginning their studies, their engagement with current Chinese popular culture, such as Mandarin dramas and TV shows, was made possible by the internet. This finding demonstrates that not only the past, or tradition, but also the current popular culture connects heritage learners with their cultural roots, which in turn facilitates the learning of their heritage language and culture.

Familial influence was less evident in the heritage learners' degree choices, which is consistent with prior research on young people's higher education choices in general (Brooks, 2003). However, this study concurs with that of Reay and colleagues (2001, 2005) in that social class can play a significant role in the decision-making process. Although the case studies may provide some indications of the diversity of the participants' class background, this aspect requires further investigation.

The results of this study generally concur with the findings of prior research on CHL students' non-degree Chinese learning regarding the specific challenges that CHL students face while studying for their degree in Chinese (Lee, 2005; Comanaru and Noels, 2009). They experienced more pressure to succeed than non-heritage learners did and their academic success tended to be taken for granted.

Although the distancing attitudes of non-heritage students toward heritage students in mixed groups received significantly less attention in the previous literature, the findings of this study reveal that the two groups of learners indeed influenced each other's motivation in learning and using the language (Lu and Li, 2008, p. 90). The non-heritage learners seemed to be intimidated when speaking Chinese at length with heritage students and the heritage students were likewise reluctant to engage in longer conversations with their non-heritage peers.

As for teacher influence on the students' motivation to learn in mixed classrooms, very little is known about teachers' marginalization and neglect of heritage learners. As Lu and Li (2008) pointed out, learners' continued interest, including that of heritage learners, is "highly dependent on how well the teacher motivates them to want to learn more about the language and culture" (p. 101). The behaviors of some instructors, including such things as skipping the heritage learners' turns, as mentioned by the participants, seemed to be extremely discouraging.

From the perspective of the teachers, it is increasingly difficult to deal with students with mixed levels and abilities in the same classroom. This is probably why programs of study in Chinese in both Canada and the United Sates have begun to provide dual tracks, such as "Chinese for Chinese" (Lee, 2005; Lu and Li, 2008). However, these dual-track programs have not yet been established for degree study in the UK, perhaps due to the smaller demand for the study of Chinese.[1]

Pedagogical Implications

The findings of the present study have three main implications for educating Chinese-heritage students in a university context. First, the results show that some teachers tend to marginalize or neglect heritage learners in mixed groups, consciously or unconsciously. For effective teaching, one group of learners should not be preferred over another and there should be equal opportunities for all. The idea of creating cooperative, inclusive learning environments (Lage et al., 2000) is also relevant to educating heritage learners in mixed group settings.

The second implication is the influence of current popular culture on heritage learners. The findings suggest that heritage learners are increasingly engaged with current Chinese popular culture, due partially to its spread over the internet. It is, therefore, beneficial to consider expanding the curriculum (Kondo-Brown, 2010) to include a wider range of perceptions, products, and practices of the target culture. Learners may be informed about the current popular culture landscape, which may further motivate them to find out more about the language and culture that they are learning.

Finally, the findings have implications for the structuring of Chinese degree programs. In a British context, heritage learners and foreign language students are frequently merged into a single-track language degree program. The results of this study lend support to the call that originated in North America (Lu and Li, 2008; Lee, 2005) to offer dual or multiple tracks for language programs. It may be helpful to consider grouping learners with similar backgrounds and levels of ability in a similar track, in part because of the differences between heritage and non-heritage learners, but also because of the diversity within the heritage language learner subgroups (Kondo-Brown, 2005), which is also illustrated by the case studies in this research.

Directions for Future Research

In this chapter, the motivations for choosing a degree in Chinese and the specific challenges of students of ethnic Chinese backgrounds in the UK were examined. In addition to demonstrating the coexistence of both instrumental and integrative motivation, the findings highlight the influence of current popular culture on the degree program choice of heritage learners. As for challenges, analysis of the data reveals the distancing attitudes of non-heritage fellow students, the teachers' marginalization and neglect, and the fact that there is greater pressure to succeed while success is simultaneously taken for granted.

Although heritage language education is a new and emerging field (Trifonas and Aravossitas, 2014), heritage students studying for a degree in their heritage language remain an uncharted area of research. Preliminary insights into their choice of degree program and difficulties during study were obtained from analyzing their questionnaire answers and follow-up interviews. Clearly, more research is needed. This chapter concludes with a list of three potentially fruitful areas for future research.

- What are the heritage students' experiences during their year abroad in their heritage "motherland"? How do they navigate their identities between feeling "at home" and "abroad"?
- In longitudinal terms, what is the impact of the changing relational dynamics between heritage learners and non-heritage learners on teaching and learning in mixed groups? It would be beneficial to follow cohorts throughout the entirety of their course of study.

- What is the effect of dual/multiple track programs on language learning? How does it compare to single-track programs? How can we address the needs of different groups and develop appropriate and consistent curriculums?

Note

1   One exception is the School of Oriental and African Studies (SOAS) at the University of London. Its Chinese degree cohorts are usually larger than those of other British universities. It clearly states that its "BA Chinese also caters to the needs of non-beginners and/or heritage students, who are partly taught in special groups during the first year" (SOAS, n.d., p. 6). In the case of this university, dual track appears to be implemented at the basic level of language instruction.

References

Ball, S. J., Reay, D., and David, M. (2002). "Ethnic choosing": Minority ethnic students, social class and higher education choice. *Race, Ethnicity and Education, 5*(4), 333–357.

British Council (2013). *Languages for the future: Which languages the UK needs most and why.* London, UK: British Council.

Brooks, R. (2003). Young people's higher education choices: The role of family and friends. *British Journal of Sociology of Education, 24*(3), 283–297.

Cheung, C. K. (2001). The use of popular culture as a stimulus to motivate secondary students' English learning in Hong Kong. *ELT Journal, 55*(1), 55–61.

Comanaru, R., and Noels, K. A. (2009). Self-determination, motivation, and the learning of Chinese as a heritage language. *Canadian Modern Language Review, 66*(1), 131–158.

Dörnyei, Z. (1994). Motivation and motivating in the foreign language classroom. *The Modern Language Journal, 78*(3), 273–284.

Dörnyei, Z., and Ottó, I. (1998). Motivation in action: A process model of L2 motivation. *Working Papers in Applied Linguistics (Thames Valley University, London), 4*, 43–69.

Dörnyei, Z., and Schmitt, R. (2001). *Motivation and second language acquisition.* Honolulu, HI: University of Hawai'i, Second Language Teacher & Curriculum Center.

Gardner, R. C. (1985). *Social psychology and second language learning: The role of attitudes and motivation.* London, UK: Edward Arnold.

Gardner, R. C. (2001). Language learning motivation: The student, the teacher, and the researcher. *Texas Papers in Foreign Language Education, 6*(1), 1–18.

Gardner, R. C., and Lambert, W. E. (1972). *Attitudes and motivation in second-language learning.* Rowley, MA: Newbury House.

Gurney-Read, J. (2013, December 20). English-Mandarin bilingual free school to open next year. *The Telegraph.* Retrieved from www.telegraph.co.uk.

Jivraj, S., and Simpson, L. (2015). *Ethnic identity and inequalities in Britain: The dynamics of diversity.* Bristol, UK: Policy Press.

Kondo-Brown, K. (2005). Differences in language skills: Heritage language learner subgroups and foreign language learners. *The Modern Language Journal, 89*(4), 563–581.

Kondo-Brown, K. (2010). Curriculum development for advancing heritage language competence: Recent research, current practices, and a future agenda. *Annual Review of Applied Linguistics, 30*, 24–41.

Lage, M. J., Platt, G. J., and Treglia, M. (2000). Inverting the classroom: A gateway to creating an inclusive learning environment. *The Journal of Economic Education, 31*(1), 30–43.

Lee, J. S. (2005). Through the learners' eyes: Reconceptualizing the heritage and non-heritage learner of the less commonly taught languages. *Foreign Language Annals, 38*(4), 554–563.

Li, D., and Duff, P. (2008). Issues in Chinese heritage language education and research at the postsecondary level. In A. W. He and Y. Xiao (Eds.), *Chinese as a heritage language: Fostering rooted world citizenry* (pp. 13–36). Honolulu, HI: University of Hawai'i, National Foreign Language Resource Center.

Lu, X., and Li, G. (2008). Motivation and achievement in Chinese language learning: A comparative analysis. In A. W. He and Y. Xiao (Eds.), *Chinese as a heritage language: Fostering rooted world citizenry* (pp. 89–108). Honolulu, HI: University of Hawai'i, National Foreign Language Resource Center.

Mu, G. M. (2016). *Learning Chinese as a heritage language: An Australian perspective.* Bristol, UK: Multilingual Matters.

Office for National Statistics. (2009). *Population Trends No. 135, Spring 2009.* Retrieved from www.ons.gov.uk/ons/rel/population-trends-rd/population-trends/no--135--spring-2009/index.html.

Reay, D., Davies, J., David, M., and Ball, S. J. (2001). Choices of degree or degrees of choice? Class, 'race' and the higher education choice process. *Sociology, 35*(4), 855–874.

Reay, D., David, M. E., and Ball, S. J. (2005). *Degrees of choice: Class, race, gender and higher education.* Stoke-on-Trent, UK: Trentham Books.

School of Oriental and African Studies (SOAS). (n.d.). Programme specification 2012/13. Retrieved from www.soas.ac.uk/cia/degrees/bachinese/file80699.pdf.

Sillitoe, K., and White, P. H. (1992). Ethnic group and the British census: The search for a question. *Journal of the Royal Statistical Society. Series A (Statistics in Society), 155*(1), 141–163.

Trifonas, P. P., and Aravossitas, T. (Eds.). (2014). *Rethinking heritage language education.* Cambridge, UK: Cambridge University Press.

Ushioda, E., and Dörnyei, Z. (2012). Motivation. In S. M. Gass, and Mackey, A. (Eds.), *The Routledge handbook of second language acquisition* (pp. 396–409). London, UK: Routledge.

Zhang, Q. (2013). The attitudes of students in the northwest of England towards Mandarin Chinese and their intercultural sensitivity. *Journal of Second and Multiple Language Acquisition–JSMULA, 1*(3), 21–37.

10

TRAINING FOR TRANSNATIONALISM

Chinese Children in Hungary[1]

Pál Nyíri

The Context: Migrant Entrepreneurs from China in Low-Income Countries

This chapter discusses the children of a recent wave of Chinese migrants: entrepreneurs who leave Mainland China for low-income countries to exploit demand for cheap consumer and industrial goods there. The scale of this migration is quite large: it probably encompasses more than 1,000,000, although available numbers are notoriously unreliable (see Nyíri, 2010, pp. 41–44). This migration began in the former Soviet Union and South America in the late 1980s, but has since expanded to Eastern and Southern Europe, the Middle East, the Pacific region, Indochina, and most prominently Africa. Research suggests that entrepreneurial migrants to these different regions share a number of common features, including forms of economic organization, a high degree of transnationalism—that is, structural embeddedness in both the society of residence and that of China—and extremely high international mobility (Nyíri, 2011).

Given the diversity of societies in which these entrepreneurs live, modes of local incorporation obviously differ. Overall, however, it can be said that the societies of residence are much more incidental to them than to other groups of Chinese migrants. The transnational social field, anchored in China, is much more centrally the one from which they derive meaning. This is not to say that there are no local emotional attachments in the lives of some individuals. But the countries of residence do not tend to be part of their ideas of a desirable future life, and local recognition matters little to them.

I have discussed reasons for this elsewhere: the undesirability of countries of residence on the global imagined scale of modernity and development; higher income than the local population, which enables Chinese merchants to hire local help expected to learn rudimentary Chinese rather than learn the local language;

scarcity of jobs they see as desirable for their children; and a high degree of socioeconomic and political exclusion. While migrant entrepreneurs gain kudos from transnational Chinese media and the Chinese state, they rarely gain local recognition and often face hostility (Nyíri, 2005). The position of these migrants is in some ways reminiscent of the "middlemen minorities" of the colonial era: the Chinese, Indians, and Lebanese who were essential for the rural economies of the colonies but were denied political and social recognition by both the rulers and the populace (Nyíri, 2011).

The first-generation migrant cohort discussed in this chapter shares a number of sociodemographic features that are central to migrants' identities and relationship to China. They came of age, or at least lived most of their active lives, during China's reform period. Immigration data and surveys suggest that they tend to be more highly educated than the national average and than earlier cohorts (see, for example, Yang and Wang, 1998), although of course less so than the students and highly skilled professional migrants who constitute another major current flow of migration from China. The overwhelming majority remain Chinese citizens, and their identification with the People's Republic of China (PRC) is largely unambiguous. Their shared status as private "bosses" (*laoban*) of small to medium-sized enterprises serves to some extent to level internal differences in education and pre-migration social status. It also accentuates a distinction between them and the managers of large Chinese state enterprises, who command much greater resources and thus enjoy elite status within the new Chinese populations in a number of African and Southeast Asian countries. But this situation is changing as some large private companies have begun to emerge, particularly in South America.[2]

Furthermore, the relative homogeneity of local status and lifestyles does not obliterate differences in family lives that are associated with education, rural versus urban, and southern versus northern origin. Thus, a higher-educated urban couple from northern China or Shanghai tend to have both fewer family members migrating with them and, conversely, fewer family resources in China than rural migrants from northern Fujian or the Wenzhou area, who plug-in into extensive local transnational networks. They are also likely to be more intent on higher educational aspirations for their children, and less likely to expect them to help out in the family enterprise while at school. These factors have an impact on the upbringing of children in these transnational families, on their relationships with their families, and on their expectations for the future.

In their introduction to this issue, Gregor Benton and Terence Gomez (2014) caution against exaggerating the validity of transnationalism as an analytical framework and warn of the political consequences of doing so. Others, too, have argued that transnationalism tends to generalize an experience that is limited to elites. These caveats are to be taken seriously, but the migrants discussed in this chapter offer an example of a strong non-elite transnationalism. It remains to be seen to what extent this transnationalism will be continued by their locally born or raised children. Since the oldest of these are now in their early to mid-twenties and are just entering the labor market, now is the time to ask this question.

Chinese Children in Hungary[3]

Between 2002 and 2004, we studied the situation of non-Hungarian-speaking migrant children in Hungary's schools. Hungary's state schools have no special provisions for non-Hungarian speakers, and some deny them admission. Although these schools do not thematize the integration of foreign children, some of the migrant students, often benefiting from teachers' individual help, become high achievers and are invoked as positive examples for Hungarian children. But the schools appear to achieve these relatively positive results at the cost of "screening out" those students who may be expected to require special measures to remedy their disadvantage in the knowledge of Hungarian, differences in educational background, or difficulties in "fitting" into the student community.

We found that these children were directed to schools that, formally or informally, specialized in those children with "special needs." Often, these schools had very high pupil turnover. At the beginning of our research, one such school we studied had 14 migrant children on the books; four months later, it had only eight, all of them Chinese. This school, although not officially designated a "special education" school, admitted many students who had not "fitted into" other schools, including a large number of Hungarian children from underprivileged ethnic (namely Gypsy) or class backgrounds, as well as migrant children. The school advertises special "slow-paced" classes, and hardly any of its graduates go on to secondary school. The Chinese pupils had come to the school in the first form, but all were significantly older than their classmates, ranging from a 15-year-old third-former to a 17-year-old eighth-former. Yet even among these eight students, we were able to track down only four; the rest had vanished. The teachers assumed that the parents had taken them to an English-language school. A teacher told us that "Chinese children don't have to obey the same rules as the others. They don't have to come to class. If they don't come for a long time, someone might look for them, but that's increasingly rare." The four Chinese students who were still there spoke hardly any Hungarian after six years of education. They had no Hungarian friends, and sat in a cluster in the classroom.

We expected that these divergent school experiences of success or failure would strongly shape the life-choices and trajectories of migrant children later on. Yet in the case of Chinese families—unlike those from other ethnic groups—we found that parents who could afford yearly fees of US$4,000 to US$12,000 preferred to transfer their children to English-language schools no matter what their initial experience and level of achievement in Hungarian schools. This was particularly striking at the secondary level: we found few migrant children in state-run secondary schools even in those areas with a strong migrant presence at the primary

180 Pál Nyíri

level. This was in stark contrast to the massive presence of the same age group in "international schools."

At the time of our research, such schools operated only in Budapest, the capital, and had a total enrolment of about 2,000. Some of the English-medium schools catered specifically to the children of Chinese, Russian-speaking, Israeli, and Arab migrant entrepreneurs, for example by maintaining websites in their languages or advertising in their newspapers. These schools had adapted to the situation of migrant children with diverse educational backgrounds, often without adequate knowledge of either Hungarian or English, and who, in several cases, had spent only a year or two at school. The schools offered remedial English and native-language classes, placed students within their peer groups, and were often flexible about allowing students to graduate faster by "jumping" classes, reducing the number of final examination subjects, and so on. Being "international" schools, they did not integrate migrant children into the Hungarian educational system, but aimed at strengthening their self-respect and at teaching communication skills that would help them progress within a global, commodified educational system of the Anglo-American type. The cultural capital they offered in the form of knowledge, language skills, patterns of behavior, and discourse was meant to be globally rather than locally convertible. The handbook of one of the schools stated its main aim as "prepar[ing] its students for a mature and purposeful participation in a multicultural, international and technological society." Graduates usually went on to English-language higher education in Hungary or to universities in the USA or UK.

The attractiveness of "international education" makes particular sense for groups that are marginalized by local society or have only a weak identification with it but are connected to global information flows through their cultural or economic capital. This is the case of the 10,150,000 Chinese migrants in Hungary, who constitute the largest non-white migrant group in a population of 10,000,000. The overwhelming majority were born in China, migrated to Hungary after 1989 and retained PRC citizenship. Almost all are small entrepreneurs who operate shops or import or wholesale companies. They attract an attention and hostility quite out of proportion to their numbers (Nyíri, 2005). Most Chinese migrants came to Hungary in the 1990s, and their children joined them only after having received some years of schooling in China, and arrived at the Hungarian school with no knowledge of Hungarian. Since the 2000s, as immigration slowed, the share of local-born children has increased. But many parents still send their children back to China for several years at preschool or early school age in order to learn Chinese.

Educational Strategies of Chinese Families[4]

An 18-year-old student whom we called Rick had completed four years of primary school in a village in South China before leaving for Budapest, aged 11, to join his parents. He first joined relatives at a state school, where he studied up to the seventh form, and then left to study Hungarian at a private school, where he spent one year. After that, he went back to the state school, but stayed only for a few months and left without graduating. He told us:

> I think it wasn't the school's fault. It was me who didn't like studying, or rather, it's not that I didn't like to, but if a kid's family background is such that his parents don't push him to study, then he won't study by himself. Hungarian schools don't suit us foreigners; international schools do. Hungarian schools don't have language classes [for non-native speakers], only international schools do. If a foreigner doesn't know Hungarian and finds himself in a Hungarian school in sixth or seventh form, of course he'll be unable to keep up.

During our interview, Rick was enrolled at one of Budapest's English-language schools. According to his teacher, he was the best male student in his class, and he was voted the "cleverest boy" in a survey. He considered himself at home in Hungary, but mentioned that his family was planning to move away. Would he attend university? That depended on the family's demands on his time. If they required his help, he would probably not be able to. For them, education was a means to an end rather than an end in itself. They were not particularly interested in their children's school performance, except for math and language, skills they considered useful. Rick's older sister, Fang, then a student at an English-language college, was in charge of decisions about her own and her brother's education. Like Rick, she had left primary school to join a language school and had also returned, in the eighth form, managing to graduate, but only by scraping through. Although she was still unable to follow all classes, she graduated, but her marks were rather poor. She tried to get into a *gimnázium* (a grammar school, which prepares students for university entrance), but her applications to two such schools were turned down. She ended up doing economics at a vocational school, but she was unhappy there and soon left. Like other friends, she opted instead to study English:

> I used to do a lot of interpreting [from Hungarian to Chinese], it paid well, [so] I wanted to work. And my [Chinese] friends were either already in college or at university or working. I thought I had nothing to do in a secondary school, it would be a waste of time. So I did what others did. . . . Eighty per cent of the Chinese kids I knew were studying in English, and also, there were problems among the Chinese in Hungary, so I didn't know whether we'd stay. Our homeland is China. But English is good everywhere. Hungary has lots of unemployment, and even if the situation improves they won't give the jobs to the Chinese.

182 Pál Nyíri

So Fang studied English for six months and was then accepted on to her college's foundation course, which she thought (wrongly) was the Hungarian branch of a well-known UK university. She was happy there, and had Hungarian as well as Chinese friends. Her plan was to switch to the school's British center, but that plan seemed to lapse. Instead, she was keen to take a degree in marketing, and also to do a master's, since she felt that one degree was no longer enough for a decent job.

It was Fang's decision that Rick ended up at the school that he did. There were two grounds for choosing this particular school: it taught in English and it was "cheap." Led by Fang, both Rick and another brother signed up for a foundation year.

According to the students we interviewed, their parents mostly wanted their children to attend a Hungarian school to acquire knowledge of the Hungarian language. For Chinese parents in Hungary, a schooling in English is a means to both social and geographic mobility in the sense of going to a university in the UK or the USA. So whether or not their Hungarian schooling is good is rarely uppermost in their minds. They expect their children to do well but make little effort to find out what goes on at school. Rick told us: "Here, no one uses their degree to look for a job. They see how little money Hungarians have. A Chinese [vendor] at the market, with a good turnover, makes more money than a graduate."

The lack of interest and faith that Chinese students and their parents seemed to have in the quality of education in Hungarian schools contrasted starkly with their interest in and knowledge of distinctions and rankings among Chinese, British, and American universities.

This reflects the fact that, because children of migrant families that follow transnational life strategies are in a position to circumvent or manipulate seemingly hegemonic institutions of public education, the discourse of goals that those institutions employ does not appear relevant to them. In "international education," the dominant national narrative of knowledge is replaced with a pragmatic and opportunistic narrative of learning that is constructed from pieces of information about education systems, degrees, and career opportunities gleaned from the transnational networks of parents and children locally, in China, and in third countries. The following excerpt from a conversation with three 16-year-old female classmates exemplifies this narrative:

Student 1:	We have to spend another three years here; by the time we get to university we'll be too old! Still so many years! We can't wait!
Student 2:	Maybe we'll finish school somewhere else!
Student 3:	Life is short!
Student 2:	We want to be successful earlier than the usual.
Researcher:	What does "successful" mean?

| Student 1: | Go to a very good university, good salary, high position. If we don't have a good job how are we going to have money? |

In 1991, Frank Pieke observed that Chinese children in the Netherlands tended either to do better in school than majority Dutch children or to drop out. He explained this by suggesting that the parents of these children—restaurant owners with low education levels who had come to the Netherlands from rural South China between the 1960s and the 1980s—aimed to maximize family, rather than individual, accumulation. Schooling was an investment in the family's future upward mobility, but this investment was seen as worthwhile only if the child had a good chance of succeeding at school. If a child's school performance was not outstanding, then the family restaurant's loss of his or her labor outweighed the expected benefit. Pieke found that some of the children were themselves uncertain of the benefits of studying, as opposed to entering early employment. Others, however, had internalized the dominant Dutch view of learning as an end in itself or as a strategy of individual advancement, sometimes leading to conflicts with parents.

Significantly, Chinese migrants' strategies of success in the Netherlands of the 1980s, as far as their children were concerned, were framed entirely by the Dutch education system. Some saw their children's integration into that system as necessary for their success; others regarded it as largely superfluous. (At the time, mother-tongue education received significant state support in the Netherlands, so parents could send their children to Chinese weekend schools without much cost, but these schools were not integrated into the state education system.)

Today, however, national education systems are no longer the only choice. "International education" is now a widely known, if usually unaffordable, option not only for migrants but also for families in China. In parallel, transnationalism— put simply, a way of life in which the migrant remains socially, economically, and sometimes politically embedded in two or more societies (Basch et al., 1994)— has become more widespread. Stories of global success and images of entrepreneurs who have struck rich abroad beckon incessantly in China's official and popular media (Nyíri, 2005). In these stories, "Western" education appears not as a source of specialized knowledge or even a way of entering a specific society, but as means to a generalized "developed-country citizenship" (Fong, 2011), seen as important for succeeding in the global economy. This was particularly so in Hungary, where there were few desirable corporate jobs. Even parents who could not afford to send their children to "international schools" hoped to be able to do so eventually. Our research suggested that children largely identified with the transnational fantasies that their parents dreamt up for them, and that, because of that identification, even children who had spent a lot of time at a Hungarian school and formed bonds of friendship there slipped fairly effortlessly out of these networks when moving to a more international environment. Naturally, there are exceptions, namely of two kinds: children who indicate that they will fail to

184 Pál Nyíri

live up to the fantasy of a transnational future—for example, because they study poorly or do not find their place within the school—and retreat to a largely online Sinophone world of chat and games while perhaps making themselves useful around the family business; and those who integrate too successfully into their Hungarian school communities, refuse to be part of the transnational fantasy, and follow more independent educational and career trajectories, for example, in the arts.

The Hungarian-Chinese Bilingual School: A State-Sponsored Experiment in Transnational Education

At the time of our research, the Hungarian government, keen to develop good relations with China, proposed, on the occasion of a Chinese state visit, to open a school in Budapest that would allow Chinese children to continue to study the Chinese curriculum while also learning Hungarian. The head of the international department in Hungary's Ministry of Education, who initiated the project, said that such a school would assure Chinese parents that if they moved back to China their children could continue their education there, and the government hoped that this prospect would attract more Chinese investors. In line with this idea of "training for transnationalism," the school opened in the autumn of 2004 and operates, uniquely in Europe and perhaps anywhere, as a state-supported school that combines local and Chinese curricula and—according to its website— "enjoys the distinguished attention of the Embassy of the People's Republic of China." In total, 65% of the lessons are in Hungarian and 35% in Chinese; the principal is Hungarian and the vice-principal Chinese; and, quite remarkably, the school celebrates the official holidays of both countries. Anti-communism is central to the legitimizing ideology of the current Hungarian government, but it shares the desire of the Chinese government to centralize and control school curricula, which results in the absurd situation that pupils commemorate the victory of the Chinese Communist Party on October 1, and the victory of the people over "communist tyranny" in Hungary on October 23. (It would be fascinating to research the view of history that these children develop.) The Chinese government does not provide financial support for the school—only textbooks and three teachers—and the director of the Confucius Institute in Budapest, a Hungarian sinologist, is its adviser.

Remarkably, the school website says that only 60% of Chinese pupils speak Hungarian "relatively well." Although this indicates that the school caters to the needs of Chinese children who speak little Hungarian, the school's popularity with Chinese pupils is in fact limited and decreasing: it had only 96 non-Hungarian pupils in 2013, as against 176 Hungarians. In contrast, for Chinese parents, the promise of connecting to further studies in China or Hungary, despite its explicit transnational orientation, is probably a poor alternative to the promise of the "intercontinental life" that an international school offers.

Emerging Trajectories of the Second Generation

At the time of the study, the first locally raised Chinese children were reaching college age. Since then, that cohort has entered the labor force. Although we have conducted no systematic follow-up research, it is clear that some young Chinese have remained in Hungary despite their parents' wishes, the unfavorable economic situation, and burgeoning local xenophobia. Some are continuing their parents' businesses or working in the ethnic economy (e.g., in Chinese travel agencies); these individuals have usually remained within the transnational Chinese social field and socialize largely among co-ethnics both offline and online (on Mainland China-based social networking sites such as QQ and Tianya). But most have graduated from English-language university courses in Hungary and found jobs with foreign-invested companies that need a multilingual staff, particularly call centers, of which there are quite a few in Hungary, and have made inroads into an international Budapest party scene that, in at least some situations, tolerates foreigners. Their online socializing centers on international networking sites such as Facebook. The primary language of communication for the former group is Chinese; for the latter, Hungarian; and for those who have moved along the expected trajectory of "international education," Chinese and English. These young people describe themselves as cosmopolitans who feel at home in Hungary but who keep a wary eye on economic and political developments and are open-minded about where life might take them. Thus, the life paths of part of the second generation seem to be developing along lines more similar to those of their peers in Western Europe, where second-generation Chinese are subjected to much stronger localizing influences, and especially Southern Europe, where most Chinese youth are children of labor migrants who arrived in the 1990s (see Ceccagno, 2004; Parker and Song, 2006; Pedone, 2011). Still, it is important to stress that mingling with non-Chinese is not necessarily typical of second-generation Chinese in Hungary.

Let me illustrate the range of personal trajectories with two cases. I met 26-year-old Yan on the Facebook site of a Hungarian news magazine; subsequently, she sent me several Hungarian-language Facebook invitations to parties in Budapest. Yan graduated from the Budapest College of Economics in 2009. All her classmates were Hungarian. Soon after graduating, she was hired by an international pharmaceuticals company to work at its international technical support center in suburban Budapest. The center had a multilingual staff and the language of communication was English. Yan had two Chinese colleagues, both of whom attended international schools and one of whom has also studied in the USA. A year later, she quit and moved to the regional logistics center of a major US-based multinational. Here, her colleagues are mostly Hungarian, but her knowledge of Chinese is considered an asset because she deals with Chinese clients.

Yan's mother was a physical education teacher in China. She moved to Hungary in 1991 and quickly established herself as a shopkeeper in Kecskemét, a county

186 Pál Nyíri

town with a population of about 100,000, where the number of Chinese has remained very small. Yan joined her in 1994, having finished second grade in China. Yan's father stayed in China, remarried, and subsequently moved to the USA with his wife, who went there to study. Yan's mother found another Chinese partner in Hungary and had a second daughter with him. Yan went to Hungarian school throughout. Her mother, she says, "tried to take her out of the Chinese community" and preferred her to spend time with Hungarians. This was because she felt it was important for Yan to learn the language and was worried that she would get into the "bad company" of "rich kids." Since the Chinese weekend school was in Budapest, sending her there would in any case have been impractical. Yan has not been back to China often because of the cost, but she spent a year in the USA with her father, an experience that, interestingly, had no lasting impact.

As a result, Yan grew up with only Hungarian friends, and when it came to choosing a university, she followed the choice made by a Hungarian classmate. At university she met other young Chinese. She "tried to make friends" with them but found that she had "no common topic" with most, had "different values," and "wasn't interested in [Chinese] KTV." Nonetheless, she now has one close Chinese friend. She is "still" a Chinese citizen but says that she feels at home everywhere. Although she says her expectations for the future are "95% satisfied . . . whether I want to stay in Hungary is a question." She "likes to change places every now and then," but also she finds Hungarians "pessimistic and prejudiced," although she has no experience of discrimination at her workplace. Despite these plans—or precisely because of them—Yan is considering applying for Hungarian citizenship in order to be able to work freely in Western Europe, but she feels no particular urgency to do so.

Yan's cautious attitude concurs with the low rate of citizenship applications among young Chinese in Hungary. Her Hungarian-born half-sister, in contrast, became a Hungarian citizen at the age of ten by special dispensation: since she was a top-level chess player for her age group, the Hungarian chess federation wanted her to be able to compete for the country, and her parents did not oppose the suggestion. According to Yan, her mother is both more permissive and emotionally closer to her sister than she was with Yan: Yan was brought up according to the strict "Chinese scheme," "through me, my mother learned how to handle a child who is growing up in Europe."

The Zheng twins, now 18, are following a trajectory closer to the one that emerged from our earlier research. They have long-term Hungarian residence permits but, after having lived in Nyíregyháza, a town in northeastern Hungary, for a few years when they were younger, they were sent back to Henan to be looked after by their grandparents. When they reached upper secondary school, they went to study as boarders in Beijing, where their uncle lives. After graduating, they, or their parents, decided that they should go to university in the Netherlands, a country that in their view offered tertiary education in English at a lower cost than the USA or the UK, and was close to Hungary, where their parents still live. The Zhengs speak no Hungarian and only go back to visit their parents and renew their residence permits.

Detailed studies of the children of new entrepreneurial migrants from China remain to be done. In the next decade, they will begin reaching working age around the world, including in many countries that older waves of Chinese emigration did not reach or where the descendants of those migrants have developed local identities. On the basis of the Hungarian study, one might hypothesize that they will face a range of choices that might include relatively strong identification with, and ties to, the country of birth or residence. In most of these countries, however, ethnic Chinese in ten to 20 years' time are likely to face a situation different from that with which we are familiar in other settings: lack of institutionalized management of ethnic diversity (as in Southeast Asia or North America) or a state strategy of integration (as in Western Europe); continued economic reliance on ties with China, whether in trade or as employees of multinational corporations; and, in some countries, high levels of xenophobia. Unlike any previous generation of Chinese born outside China, most of these young people will have grown up in a world of online and satellite media that binds them strongly with peers in China and consolidates their identification with the Chinese political nation. Fulfilling their parents' transnational dreams and becoming globetrotting corporate men/women with a cultural fluency in the Anglo-Saxon and Chinese worlds, and with ephemeral and perhaps somewhat incidental places of residence, will, then, be a more realistic and attractive option for them than for previous generations.

Notes

1 Originally published as Pál Nyíri (2014), Training for transnationalism: Chinese children in Hungary, *Ethnic and Racial Studies*, *37*(7), 1253–1263. Taylor & Francis Ltd, www.tandfonline.com. Reprinted by permission of the publisher.
2 For ethnographic examples, see Nyíri (2007) on Eastern Europe; Ceccagno (2007) and Nieto (2007) on Southern Europe; Dobler (2009), Bourdarias (2010), and Kernen (2010) on Africa; and Lausent-Herrera (2010) and Tjon Sie Fat (2010) on South America.
3 This section draws on Nyíri (2006). The study, reported more fully in Nyíri and Feischmidt (2006), included a questionnaire administered to 71 schools with a total of over 2,000 foreign students, one school year of fieldwork in 30 schools and three refugee reception stations, focus group discussions with 40 migrant children, and 60 interviews with children, 30 with parents, and 40 with teachers.
4 This section is based on Nyíri (2006).

References

Basch, L., Schiller, N. G., and Blanc, C. S. (1994). *Nations unbound*. Langhorne, PA: Gordon and Breach.
Benton, G., and Gomez, E. T. (2014). Belonging to the nation: Generational change, identity and the Chinese diaspora. *Ethnic and Racial Studies*, *37*(7), 1157–1171.

188 Pál Nyíri

Bourdarias, F. (2010). Chinese migrants and society in Mali: Local constructions of globalization. *African and Asian Studies*, *9*(3), 269–285.

Ceccagno, A. (2004). *Giovani migranti cinesi. La seconda generazione a Prato*. Milan, Italy: Franco Angeli.

Ceccagno, A. (2007). The Chinese in Italy at a crossroads: The economic crisis. In M. Thunø (Ed.), *Beyond Chinatown: New Chinese migration and the global expansion of China* (pp. 115–136). Copenhagen, Denmark: NIAS Press.

Dobler, G. (2009). Chinese shops and the formation of a Chinese expatriate community in Namibia. *The China Quarterly*, *199*, 707–727.

Fong, V. (2011). *Paradise redefined: Transnational Chinese students and the quest for flexible citizenship in the developed world*. Stanford, CA: Stanford University Press.

Kernen, A. (2010). Small and medium-sized Chinese businesses in Mali and Senegal. *African and Asian Studies*, *9*(3), 252–268.

Lausent-Herrera, I. (2009). Tusans (*tusheng*) and the changing Chinese community in Peru. In W. L. Lai and C. Tan (Eds.), *The Chinese in Latin America and the Caribbean* (pp. 143–184). Leiden, Netherlands: Brill.

Nieto, G. (2007). *La inmigración China en España. Una comunidad ligada a su nación*. Madrid, Spain: Catarata/UAM.

Nyíri, P. (2005). Global modernizers or local subalterns? Parallel perceptions of Chinese transnationals in Hungary. *Journal of Ethnic and Migration Studies*, *31*(4), 659–674.

Nyíri, P. (2006). The nation-state, public education, and the logic of migration: Chinese students in Hungary. *The Australian Journal of Anthropology*, *17*(1), 32–46.

Nyíri, P. (2007). *Chinese in Eastern Europe and Russia*. London, UK: Routledge.

Nyíri, P. (2010). *Mobility and cultural authority in contemporary China*. Seattle, WA: University of Washington Press.

Nyíri, P. (2011). Chinese entrepreneurs in poor countries: A transnational "middleman minority" and its futures. *Inter-Asia Cultural Studies*, *12*(1), 145–153.

Nyíri, P., and Feischmidt, M. (Eds.). (2006). *Nem kívánt gyerekek? Külföldi gyerekek magyar iskolákban [Unwanted children? Foreign children in Hungarian schools]*. Budapest, Hungary: Centre for International Migration and Refugee Studies, Institute for Political Sciences, Hungarian Academy of Sciences.

Parker, D., and Song, M. (2006). New ethnicities online: Reflexive racialisation and the internet. *The Sociological Review*, *54*(3), 575–594.

Pedone, V. (2011). "As a rice plant in a wheat field": Identity negotiation among children of Chinese immigrants. *Journal of Modern Italian Studies*, *16*(4), 492–503.

Pieke, F. N. (1991). Chinese educational achievement and "folk theories of success." *Anthropology and Education Quarterly*, *22*, 162–180.

Tjon Sie Fat, P. B. (2010). Old migrants, new immigration and anti-Chinese discourse in Suriname. In W. L. Lai and C. Tan (Eds.), *The Chinese in Latin America and the Caribbean* (pp. 185–210). Leiden, Netherlands: Brill.

Yang, Y., and Wang, Z. (1998). 欧洲华侨华人妇女研究报告 *[Research report on Chinese women in Europe]*. Submitted to the European Federation of Chinese Organisations, Budapest, Hungary.

PART III

Teaching, Schooling, and Pedagogical Possibilities for Chinese–Heritage Learners

11

A MULTI-CASE STUDY OF THE LANGUAGE EXPERIENCES OF CHINESE CHILDREN IN AUSTRALIAN EARLY CHILDHOOD CENTERS

Jiangbo Hu

Children's language skills are recognized as a key element in their literacy development (Vellutino et al., 2007). High-quality language experiences in preschool are known to foster children's development in literacy in kindergarten and the primary school years (Dickinson and Porche, 2011). Yet little is known about the language experiences that young children have in Australian early childhood centers, especially those of young English language learners (ELLs) who learn English as an additional language. This chapter focuses on the language experiences of Chinese children, a rapidly increasing group of ELLs in Australian educational settings (NSW Department of Education and Communities, 2011). It investigates the specific features of the language experiences that Australian early childhood educators provide to Chinese children through daily interactions. Employing multi-case research method, the study investigated six Chinese children (two of them are twin sisters) and five educators. Interactions between the educators and the children involving both verbal and non-verbal language were recorded and analyzed using the framework of interpersonal functions of systemic linguistic theories. Based on the analysis of the language, the conclusions and implications were drawn for educators to support Chinese children's language development in early childhood centers.

Introduction

Chinese children are recognized as good academic achievers in many Australian schools and this trend is also documented for other English speaking countries (Feniger and Lefstein, 2014). The research into Australian Chinese students has explored the factors contributing to Chinese children's success in schools. Dandy and Nettelbeck (2002) compared Australian Chinese children with Anglo-Celtic children and investigated the relationship between IQ, homework, aspirations, and academic achievement. They found that parents' support and occupational aspiration play a critical role in motivating Chinese children to pursue academic achievement. Feniger and Lefstein (2014) explored Australian Chinese children's performance by examining International Student Assessment (PISA) data, comparing the PISA scores of Chinese children studying in Shanghai and in Australia. They demonstrated that Chinese children in Australia performed as well as, or even better than Chinese children in Shanghai, and the Australian Chinese children achieved much higher scores than their Australian peers in general. These studies emphasize that cultural heritage rather than educational system is a vital factor determining Chinese children's academic performance.

While the outstanding achievement of school-aged Chinese children has attracted some research attention in Australia, the experiences of preschool-aged Chinese children in Australian early childhood settings seem to be overlooked in the research agenda. Within the very limited literature, Richards' (2010) ethnographic research sheds an insight in this area. Richards (2010) analyzed the drawings of a Chinese boy—Lee. He reported on Lee's ideas of his identity and friendships and notes the disjunction between Lee's home and preschool experiences. Lee is an English language leaner (ELL) who speaks Chinese at home but uses English to interact with people in his preschool. At preschool Lee is a quiet, serious, and solitary child who is far from the midst of a social network. He has little interaction with his educators and peers, which is in contrast with his active, socially centered roles at home as a son and a brother.

Many Chinese children attending early childhood centers are ELLs like Lee. Australian Chinese parents tend to use their home language to interact with their children at home and these children have little opportunity to learn English language before attending early childhood centers (Hu et al., 2014). The experience of Chinese children in early childhood centers could be very different from their experience in primary or high schools, yet little research has been undertaken in this area. This study is designed to address this gap by investigating Chinese children's language experiences in Australian early childhood centers, specifically focusing on the interaction between Australian educators and Chinese children. Such a perspective is chosen based on the following considerations.

First, early language development supports the success and speed of literacy acquisition, which significantly determines a child's future academic success (Catts et al., 2006; Dickinson et al., 2003; Storch and Whitehurst, 2002). Vellutino, Tunmer, Jaccard, and Chen (2007) found that preschool children's semantic knowledge, such as understanding of word concepts, is related to context-free word identification that strongly influences reading comprehension of children at Year 2 and Year 3. This finding is partly supported by the evidence from another study involving children from kindergarten to Year 8 (Catts et al., 2006). The study identified that mild deficits in semantic knowledge and syntactic processing (e.g., grammatical understanding) could lead to poor reading comprehension. Poor comprehenders have difficulty in gaining full understanding of text even when these texts are read aloud.

Second, language development of preschool-aged children is heavily influenced by the language experiences that their educators provided in early childhood centers. There is a correlation between the type of language experiences that preschool educators provide and children's language skills and their literacy abilities. Dickinson and Porche (2011) undertook a longitudinal study of 57 children from preschool to Year 4. They found that the type of educators' talk, for example, the frequency of the use of sophisticated words, predicts the language comprehension and word recognition of these children when they are in kindergarten and even in Year 4. Hamre (2014) reviewed the recent research relating to preschool educators' interactions with children. He points out the importance of educators' interactions with children in early childhood programs as well as the risks existing among early childhood settings in United States. A major risk emerging from the research he reviewed is that some children cannot experience high-quality interactions, such as interactions involving higher-order thinking (e.g., logical thinking). Hamre (2014) urged that the quality of educator–child interaction should be an essential part of early childhood programs due to its importance in the education of children.

Third, there is little research relating to language experiences of Chinese children in early childhood centers. The majority of research into educator–child interaction focuses on the interactions between educators and English-speaking children. As stated above, many preschool-aged Chinese children are ELLs who are at a very initial stage of developing their English language skills. Their language experiences and interactions with educators may be very different from those of English-speaking children. Investigating language use in daily interactions between educators and Chinese children addresses the research gap. This study is designed to address two questions:

1. What type of language do educators use in the interactions with Chinese children?
2. How do Chinese children use verbal and non-verbal language in their interactions with their educators?

Theoretical Orientation: Systemic Functional Linguistic Theory—Interpersonal Functions

Systemic functional linguistic (SFL) theory is applied in this study for the analysis of educator–child interactions. SFL acknowledges that the process of language development is embedded in the social contexts of interactions. The social context of an interaction shapes the text of language and, in turn, the produced language forms a new context (Halliday and Matthiessen, 2004). The process of

194 Jiangbo Hu

language development requires a child to learn the appropriate use of language functions in a range of social contexts rather than simply learning words and grammatical structures.

The social roles and relationships between the participants are a significant aspect in the context of interaction. The social power between the participants and the role that participants play are vital factors influencing the organization of the text of language. Conversely, the text of language reveals the nature of the contextual features through the linguistic options selected from those that are available. Using modality as an example, a speaker's choices from the system of modal expressions (the use of "might," "could," "must") helps to construct the interpersonal relationship of the interlocutors.

According to Halliday and Matthiessen (2004), the basic speech role of a speaker is either *giving* or *demanding*. Cutting across the basic roles is another dimension, the commodity being exchanged in the interaction, which is either *goods-&-services* or *information*. There are four primary interpersonal functions when the two variables come together: *offer*, *command*, *statement*, and *question*.

> Offer—giving goods-&-services: *Would you like this teapot?*
> Command—demanding goods-&-services: *Give me the teapot!*
> Statement—giving information: *He's giving her the teapot.*
> Question—demanding information: *What is he giving her?*

In accordance with the primary functions, there is a matched set of responses:

> Accept or reject an offer: *Yes, please do; No thanks.*
> Undertake or refuse a demand: *Here you are; No, I won't.*
> Acknowledge or contradict a piece of information: *Is he? No, he isn't.*
> Answer or disclaim a question: *He is giving her a teapot; I don't know.*
> (Halliday and Matthiessen, 2004, pp. 107–108)

Halliday and Matthiessen (2004) point out that when goods-&-services are being exchanged, the choices open to the listener are limited. Only two of sets of choices are available: accept or reject the offer, undertake or refuse the demand. In many situations, listeners can respond to an *offer* or a *command* without verbal language because what is exchanged is a good-&-service for which the requirement for a response is taking action. In contrast, when information is exchanged, language itself is the commodity that is being exchanged. Language is necessary for an adequate response to a *statement* or a *question*, no matter whether the information is affirmed, denied, doubted, contradicted, or insisted on. From this perspective, giving information in *statements* and requesting information through *questions* provide more opportunities for supporting children's language development than do *offers* and *commands*. This is because these two types of speech roles provide more opportunities for language use and serve to extend conversations between participants.

SFL theory provides an effective approach for the analysis of language and it has been used recently in early childhood settings. Davis and Torr (2016) applied the interpersonal functions of SFL theory to investigate educators' use of questioning as a pedagogical strategy in the interaction with infants in Australian long day care nurseries. They categorized questions as pedagogical (demanding information) or regulatory (in forms of command and offer). Their analysis revealed that some questions, like "open questions," which are beneficial to preschool-aged children, may not be appropriate for infants whose developmental needs are different from older children. In this study, the language used by Australian educators in their interaction with Chinese children is analyzed and categorized with the four interpersonal functions (*offer*, *command*, *statement*, and *question*). Based on the analysis of the language functions, language experiences provided by the educators to the Chinese children in daily practice is presented and discussed. The details of the application of the interpersonal functions of SFL theory in this study will be further explained in the next section.

Methodology

Multi-case study is the overarching method in this study. The decision to employ this method was made with the following considerations. First, the case study method is advantageous in investigating phenomena in social contexts (Baxter and Jack, 2008). This method aligns with the theoretical framework utilized in this study that considers language in the social contexts of interactions, allowing for a rich explanation and interpretation of the findings drawn from the language analysis. Second, a multi-case study is a good research method for exploring a group phenomenon (Yin, 2009). Language experiences of Chinese children in Australian early childhood centers are a group phenomenon and so a multi-case study approach serves the objectives of this study. Third, a multi-case study allows for a comparison among the cases. The validity of the study is strengthened and the findings become more robust when the similarities and differences among a variety of cases can be considered (Yin, 2009).

The Participants

The participants are six preschool-aged Chinese children (two of them are twin sisters) and five educators from five early childhood centers in the Northwestern Sydney area where the Chinese community had been expanding. Ethical approval was obtained from the Human Research Ethics Committee of Macquarie University for the recruitment of participants. The selection criteria of Chinese children were: 1) speaking home language (Mandarin) at home most of the time; and 2) attending an Australian early childhood center from three years of age. These criteria were set because children who are exposed to the second language after three years old are defined as successive second-language learners (Baker,

196 Jiangbo Hu

2011). The process for these children's second-language acquisition is very different from those of simultaneous learners who have the opportunity to access and use the second language before three years of age. Many Australian Chinese children are successive English language learners who have little opportunity to use English at home and learn English in Australian early childhood centers (Hu et al., 2014). The educators who participated in this study are all from an English-speaking background and they only use English in their interaction with children. These educators are diploma or bachelor-qualified who are the room leaders and main caregivers of these six Chinese children and have substantial opportunities to interact with the children. The five early childhood centers are all good quality childcare services according to their accreditation records. They ranked high in the quality area of "Relationships with Children" in their Assessment Report, which indicates that the educators actively engage in the interaction with the children in their room. The reason for the choice of this type of center is to place the investigation of Chinese children's language experience in a context that represents the trend of Australian early childhood education. A summary of the participant information is listed in Table 11.1.

TABLE 11.1 Educators' and children's information

Children's name	Age	Gender	Months of attending early childhood centers	Educator's name	Qualification relating to early childhood education	Years working in early childhood
Lucas	4 years and 5 months	Male	12	Lindy	Diploma	32
Elli	3 years and 9 months	Female	9	Anna	Bachelor's degree	8
Emma and Imogene	3 years and 7 months	Female	3	Mary	Diploma	4
Jacky	4 years and 8 months	Male	6	Rae	Bachelor's degree	7
Riana	4 years and 9 months	Female	12	Virginia	Bachelor's degree	4

Data Collection and Analysis

The data for this study were collected through observations. The author visited the five early childhood centers and captured the interactions between the educators and the focus Chinese children using a small unobtrusive video camera. The observation lasted for one day in each center for 7–10 hours approximately.

It commenced when the focus child arrived at the center and finished when he/she was picked up by his/her parents. The main contexts of the interactions included free play, structured activities (e.g., group time), mealtime, and transition time. The video clips were reviewed and transcribed. Some non-verbal interactions such as hand gestures that make meanings in the contexts were noted.

For the convenience of analysis, the recorded interactions were broken into dialogues. Dialogue in this study refers to an interaction between the educators and the children on one topic. It could be initiated either by the educators or the children, involving both verbal and non-verbal language. For example, Lucas (four years and five months old) found an empty cat food carton box from a bag. He saw the picture of a cat on the box and said "cat!" He then showed the box to his educator Lindy.

Dialogue 1

Lucas: Miss Lindy! [Pointing to the picture of cat]
Lindy: Oh, a cat. Do you have a cat at home?
Lucas: Yeah.
Lindy: You do?
Lucas: [Shrug his shoulders]
Lindy: No?

Dialogue 2

Lucas: [Looking into the cat food box from the open part]
Lindy: Oh, I hope it is empty before you use it. [Tipping out the litters from the box] Just little bit. How are you going to use it?
Lucas: [Smile and take the box away]
Lindy: You got a plan, Lucas?
Lucas: Yeah! [Tipping out litters like Lindy did before]

This is an ongoing interaction during indoor free play. A few dialogues were identified in this session of the interaction according to the small topics occurring in the process. In Dialogue 1, Lucas felt a bit uncomfortable (shown in his facial expression and body language) by admitting that he has a cat at home, which might not be the truth. He then tried to cover this by moving his focus to the inside of the box, changing the topic of the interaction, which was identified as Dialogue 2. Lindy, as an experienced educator fully understood Lucas' intention and soon moved into the new topic cooperatively.

After the dialogues were identified according to the topics as stated above, the clauses and turn-taking in the dialogues were then examined. A clause refers to a group of words containing a subject and a verb. It can be a sentence or a sub-sentence, for example, the sentence "Little Miss Muffet sat on a tuffet, eating her curds and whey" includes two clauses: "Little Miss Muffet sat on a tuffet/

198 Jiangbo Hu

eating her curds and whey" (Halliday and Matthiessen, 2004, p. 8). For the purpose of this study, a sentence with one word such as "Yes" or "No" is recognized as a clause. These words actually have a subject and a verb in implicit, for example, "Yes, you do" or "No, I don't." Turn-taking in dialogues is important because it shows the extent of engagement of participants in the interaction. A dialogue with more turn-taking shows participants being more active and engaged in the interaction. Turn-taking is calculated from the first response of the listener in the dialogue. The first response is the number one turn-taking, and then each time of change of the speaker or responder is a turn-taking, for example, Dialogue 1 shown above contains five turn-takings. Lucas' first utterance "Miss Lindy!" is not counted as a turn-taking, it's more the initiating event. The clauses spoken by educators were classified according to the interpersonal functions of SFL theory (*offer*, *demand*, *statement*, and *question*). The responses of the children were categorized accordingly as well. The analysis of Dialogue 1 is displayed here as an example showing the process of data analysis:

TABLE 11.2 Analysis of Dialogue 1

Turn-taking of the dialogue	5
Clauses in the educator's language	4 (Oh, a cat/Do you have a cat at home?/You do?/No?)
Types of the educator's language	1 statement (Oh, a cat)
	3 questions (Do you have a cat at home?/You do?/No?)
Responses from the child	1 answer to the question, using simple word "Yeah"
	1 disclaim to the questions (shrugs his shoulders)

One thing that needs to be clarified is that the numbers of children's responses are not fully matched with the number of clauses in educators' language. In many situations, a statement, an offer, a command, or a question contains more than one clause. For example, an educator says "Can you please pick out the blocks and put them in the red box? Thank you." This command contains three clauses. "Thank you" in this context is a part of the command semantically. In this study it is considered as a polite way to give the command, not exactly conveying the information of appreciation. The child could only have one response to this command. Likewise, a lot of dialogues have more clauses in the educators' language than in the responses from the children, and this is shown in the findings reported in the next section.

Chinese in Australian Early Childhood Centers **199**

Findings

The findings of this study are presented separately for each of the five cases. In each case, the number of dialogues in different contexts, turn-taking in the dialogues, the speech functions of the educators' language, and the responses of the children—both verbal and non-verbal—are reported. Non-verbal responses in this study include facial expression, eye contact, and any sort of body languages (e.g., head nodding and hand gestures).

Case 1: Lucas and His Educator Lindy

The interactions between Lindy and Lucas occurred frequently during free play, and there were more dialogues with four or more turn-takings in this context. Lindy seemed to create some one-to-one opportunities to interact with Lucas during play. Most of Lindy's language was in the types of *statement* and *question* that helped extend Lucas' interest and engagement in play. For example, when she saw Lucas made an airplane with carton boxes and sticky tape, she commented, "You know what I like most, Lucas? I like the way you made the sticky tape touches the sides [of the boxes]." This praise is a *statement*, giving the information that Lindy noticed what Lucas had done very well in his play, which brought

TABLE 11.3 Dialogues between Lindy and Lucas

Dialogue context	1 turn-taking	2 and 3 turn-takings	4 or more turn-takings	Total
Free play	1	1	20	22
Mealtime	2	2	0	4
Structured activities	3	0	3	6
Transition time	1	2	1	4
Total	7	5	24	36

TABLE 11.4 Types of Lindy's language and responses from Lucas

Types of Lindy's language (clause)		Responses from Lucas (verbal and non-verbal)	
Offer	15	Accept	10
		Reject	0
Command	12	Undertake	8
		Refuse	0
Statement	120	Acknowledge	58
		Contradict	5
Question	48	Answer	32
		Disclaim	8
Total	195	Total	121

200 Jiangbo Hu

Lucas a feeling of achievement and encouraged him to be more engaged in the play. Most *commands* and *offers* that Lindy used occurred in the contexts of transition and mealtime. The dialogues using *demand* and *offer* were short with one to three turn-takings. Lucas responded to all the *offers* and *commands* in a cooperative way. He made less responses to *statements* as he could not understand Lindy's language in many situations. He seemed to use "yeah" to answer most *questions*, and only disclaimed a small amount of *questions* when he was really not sure.

Case 2: Elli and Her Educator Anna

The interaction with Elli and her educator was rare. Only two dialogues were identified in free play time. Most of the interactions occurred in the contexts of transition and mealtime where *command* was Anna's main function of language. The dialogues were short with only one or two turns. Elli seemed to be timid in the interactions with Anna. She accepted and undertook all *offers* and *commands* from Anna. For example, when Anna asked "Do you want to go out to play [*offer*]?" when she was playing in dress up corner inside by herself. She quickly put down the scarf in her hand and went out. Elli answered most *questions* using simple word "yes" or nodded her head, similar to Lucas.

TABLE 11.5 Dialogues between Anna and Elli

Dialogue context	1 turn-taking	2 and 3 turn-takings	4 or more turn-takings	Total
Free play	0	0	2	2
Mealtime	2	1	0	3
Structured activities	0	1	0	1
Transition time	3	3	1	7
Total	5	5	3	13

TABLE 11.6 Types of Anna's language and responses from Elli

Types of Anna's language (clause)		Responses from Elli (verbal and non-verbal)	
Offer	2	Accept	2
		Reject	0
Command	25	Undertake	15
		Refuse	0
Statement	8	Acknowledge	3
		Contradict	0
Question	12	Answer	10
		Disclaim	0
Total	47	Total	30

Case 3: Emma and Imogene and Their Educator Mary

Mary initiated some interactions with Emma and Imogene during free play and structured activities. She put effort into guiding and encouraging the twins to join in group activities, giving instructions and explanations to them clearly. On the observation day, Mary conducted a musical activity: statue game. Emma was the final winner of the group statue game by following Mary's instruction effectively. She understood the rules of the game and enjoyed it very much. Mary had many *offers* in her language when interacting with Emma and Imogene, and the twins rejected almost half of the *offers*. This pattern of interaction is different from other children in this study who tended to accept *offers* from their educators. Sometimes it seemed that the twins said "no" to Mary in order to enjoy using the power of rejection. They always regretted their choices soon. For instance, during free play, Mary asked Emma "Do you want to sit down and do the finger painting?" "No," said Emma and ran away. A couple of minutes later, Emma came back to the table and sat down, waiting for her turn to do the painting. However, the twins undertook all the *commands* from Mary.

TABLE 11.7 Dialogues between Mary and Emma and Imogene

Dialogue context	1 turn-taking	2 and 3 turn-takings	4 or more turn-takings	Total
Free play	1	2	5	8
Mealtime	1	2	0	3
Structured activities	0	4	4	8
Transition time	1	2	0	3
Total	3	10	9	22

TABLE 11.8 Types of Mary's language and responses from Emma and Imogene

Types of Mary's language (clause)		Responses from Emma and Imogene (verbal and non-verbal)	
Offer	36	Accept	13
		Reject	12
Command	12	Undertake	6
		Refuse	0
Statement	35	Acknowledge	10
		Contradict	0
Question	15	Answer	8
		Disclaim	2
Total	98	Total	51

Case 4: Jacky and His Educator Rae

Rae had few opportunities for individual interaction with Jacky on the observation day. She seemed to be busy with preparing some materials for the next week's program. The main language function that Rae used was *command*, and the dialogues were short with one or two turns. *Commands* usually occurred in the context of transition time where Rae asked Jacky to follow instructions, such as "Jacky, can you please sit next to Miss Bronwyn to have lunch?" Two dialogues containing *command* were also recorded in group reading when Rae used language to regulate Jacky's behaviors (e.g., touching another child). Jacky, although unsettled frequently, undertook most *commands* from Rae.

TABLE 11.9 Dialogues between Rae and Jacky

Dialogue context	1 turn-taking	2 and 3 turn-takings	4 or more turn-takings	Total
Free play	2	0	3	5
Mealtime	0	0	0	0
Structured activities	0	3	0	3
Transition time	3	1	0	4
Total	5	4	3	12

TABLE 11.10 Types of Rae's language and responses from Jacky

Types of Rae's language (clause)		Responses from Jacky (verbal and non-verbal)	
Offer	14	Accept	5
		Reject	1
Command	24	Undertake	12
		Refuse	1
Statement	7	Acknowledge	3
		Contradict	0
Question	4	Answer	2
		Disclaim	0
Total	49	Total	24

Case 5: Riana and Her Educator Virginia

The majority of interactions between Riana and Virginia occurred in the context of free play and transition time. Virginia encouraged Riana to interact with her and other children during free play. For example, when Riana sat at the table for art and craft activity and was making flags, Virginia noticed that Riana needed a piece of paper from beside another child. She encouraged Riana to talk to this child, "Do you want to ask Felix to give you the paper?" Riana nodded her head

Chinese in Australian Early Childhood Centers **203**

but didn't say anything. Virginia then asked Felix "Can you please pass the paper to Riana?" Felix followed the instruction. Virginia said to Riana again "Say thank you to Felix." Riana then said "thank you" as Virginia guided in a small voice. Like the other children in the study, Riana accepted and undertook most *offers* and *commands* from her educator. She acknowledged Virginia's *statements* even though she sometimes had difficulty in understanding the information.

TABLE 11.11 Dialogues between Virginia and Riana

Dialogue context	1 turn-taking	2 and 3 turn-takings	4 or more turn-takings	Total
Free play	0	2	7	9
Mealtime	0	0	0	0
Structured activities	0	2	0	2
Transition time	3	3	1	7
Total	3	7	8	18

TABLE 11.12 Types of Virginia's language and responses from Riana

Types of Virginia's language (clause)		Responses from Riana (verbal and non-verbal)	
Offer	9	Accept	3
		Reject	1
Command	17	Undertake	13
		Refuse	0
Statement	22	Acknowledge	8
		Contradict	0
Question	14	Answer	5
		Disclaim	1
Total	62	Total	31

Summary

While the individual cases differ, there are some common attributes across the cases. First, most "long dialogue" with four or more turn-takings arose in the context of free play. It seems to be easier for educators to extend the dialogues during free play. The children were active in using verbal language to respond during play, although their verbal language was simple English words or phrases. Second, the "short dialogue" with one or two turn-takings were more likely to happen in the context of transition time and mealtimes, where educators generate more language in the form of *command*, which they use to ask the children to follow instructions. Third, *command* and *offer* take a big part of the educators' language. Anna, Rae, and Mary used more *command* and *offer* than *statement* and *question* in their interaction with the focus children. Fourth, four out of six of

204 Jiangbo Hu

the focus Chinese children seemed to be timid and obedient in most interactions with their educators. They tended to accept and undertake most *offers* and *commands* from the educators. Fifth, the individual interaction between the educators and the Chinese children is limited. Except for Lindy, the educators produce less than 100 clauses in their interaction with the Chinese children. Anna and Rae had the least interactions with only 47 and 49 clauses identified irrespectively. In some situations, such as mealtimes, educators (Rae and Virginia) didn't have any interaction with the focus children because they didn't sit at the table.

Discussion and Conclusion

Implications of the Findings

The purpose of this study was to gain some insight into the language experiences that Chinese children had in Australian early childhood centers. Research in this field is scarce despite the fact that Chinese children are one of the most rapidly increasing groups of ELLs in Australian educational settings (NSW Department of Education and Communities, 2011), and despite the importance of language experiences during preschool years for these children's future literacy development. This study contributes to the field by investigating Australian educators' language use during interactions with Chinese children and those children's responses to their educators. Some implications generated from this study may provide educators with enhanced awareness about how to use more appropriate language in daily interactions with Chinese children in order to enrich their language experiences.

The findings resonate with research by Richards (2010) who describes a young Chinese boy's experience of marginalization in his preschool. The Chinese children in this study also seemed to be in a similar position in their interactions with the Australian educators. The data from this study shows that the opportunity for the interaction between the Chinese children and their educators is quite limited. Four out of five educators had about 20 or fewer dialogues with the focus children, and most of these dialogues were short conversations with three or fewer turn-takings. Considering that the centers involved in the study had been assessed during accreditation as being good quality in terms of relationships with children, and the interactions between educators and children were generally active, the focus Chinese children were disadvantaged in gaining opportunities for the individual interactions with their educators. Research shows that individual interactions with adults provide an important avenue for children to improve their language skills. In the context of one-to-one interaction, adults are able to adjust their language to meet children's individual needs, for example they can scaffold children's language skills in a subtle way (Hall et al., 2003). In the education of ELLs, individual interactions not only are the key method for educators to model and foster ELLs' English language use, but are also an important avenue for the development of ELLs' sense of belonging to the new language environment (Cummins, 2007). The findings from this study indicate that there is a need for the educators to increase the individual interactions with the Chinese children. Due to their limited English skills, Chinese children may not actively initiate interaction with educators as other children do and could be easily ignored. In many situations, they need the educators' initiative to start a conversation.

The finding that a large portion of educators' language is made up of *offers* and *commands* raises a concern as to the quality of the limited interaction between the educators and the Chinese children. According to Halliday and Matthiessen (2004), interactions in the form of *command* and *offer* do not necessarily invite a response in language because the commodity being exchanged in the interaction may be an action, not a linguistic commodity. When children are exposed to language mainly in the form of *commands* and *offers*, their opportunities for developing language are limited. In early childhood centers, the use of *commands* and *offers* are necessary for giving children instructions or regulating children's behaviors. However, when *commands* and *offers* become the dominant language types in the limited individual educator–child interactions, it restricts the exposure to rich and meaningful English language that is essential for the development of the Chinese children's English skills. ELLs need to hear all types of language to foster their language skills. *Statements* and *questions* are important language types because they contain more opportunities for vocabulary and grammatical structures than *commands* and *offers* provide (Halliday and Matthiessen, 2004). Chinese children would benefit from a higher quality of interaction with their educators if the educators adjust their language to include a greater proportion of *statements* and *questions*.

The data also shows that some educators' *commands* were supplemented in ways that changed the overall language function of the interaction. Some *commands* were with a *statement* or a *question*. For example, when Lindy found Lucas playing with another boy at the lunch table, she said "Hands down please, Lucas. We don't put our hands up now because we need our hands to eat lunch." Lucas followed Lindy's instruction and stopped playing. This is a one-turn-taking dialogue in which the first clause is a *command*. Lindy then adds a *statement* to explain her *command*. The *statement* of a reason shifts the commodity of the interaction from service to information and increases the language to which the child is exposed. Compared with the other educators, Lindy used the most *statements* in her language across all the different contexts. Her *commands* and *offers* are always accompanied with a *statement*. The type of language Lindy used seemed not to be restricted by the context of interaction. This finding indicates that while the use of *offers* and *commands* is necessary in early childhood centers, they can be used in ways that extend children's language opportunities.

The responses from the children in this study also deserve some comment. Except for Emma and Imogene, who rejected some *offers* from Mary, the Chinese children accepted and undertook most *offers* and *commands* from their educators. This finding is in line with the previous research stating that Chinese students tend to be quiet and obedient to their educators (Sit, 2013). Sit suggests that this is because, in Chinese culture, educators have full authority and students are encouraged to respect educators by following their instructions. If this is the case, it highlights the importance of educators supplementing their *commands* and *offers* with *statements*. This strategy may help Chinese children to gain more understanding about educators' instructions, enabling them to learn that following the instructions is for "good reasons," not only because it is the "teachers' words." This type of language is of the high-quality interaction as Hamre (2014) suggests that involves high-order thinking, such as understanding the cause-and-effect relation.

Finally, the data demonstrate that different contexts may trigger different types of language. Most dialogues with four or more turn-takings occurred in the context of free play when educators extended the children's play with *statements* and *questions*. For example, when Lucas played with a floor puzzle with his friend, Lindy guided "Which one comes next, Lucas? . . . Look at the plan, is it right?" The play itself provides a topic for the extension of the dialogue so that *statements* and *questions* are needed. However, in the context of transition or mealtimes, there were more short dialogues made up of *commands*. In such contexts, commands were used by educators to facilitate children's compliance with routine tasks. For example, when children moved from indoor to outdoor play, Anna reminded Elli "Can you please put your hat on?" Elli undertook this *command* and ran out. "Hat on" is a sun protection rule for all Australian early childhood centers for outdoor play. Anna used a simple *command* here to make Elli follow the rule. She didn't explain to Elli why a hat is needed for outdoor play. She seemed to be busy with "getting things done." This finding demonstrates how the context of interaction influences the language experiences provided to children. The finding highlights the importance of including a continuous and long-lasting free play time in daily routines because this context provides more opportunities for educators to use the language of *statements* and *questions* in the support of children's play.

This study offers insights into the language experiences that Chinese children have in Australian early childhood centers. Language experiences in preschool years have significant influence on children's future literacy and academic development (Dickinson and Porche, 2011). The findings show a substantial variation in the educator–child interaction among the cases and demonstrate some ways in which educators can play a critical role in shaping children's language experiences. In addition, the study provides evidence and practical suggestions for educators to effectively use language for the improvement of their interaction with Chinese children to support these children's language development during preschool years.

Limitations and Directions for Future Research

This study is subject to two major limitations. An important consideration is the generalization of some findings from only a few study cases. The criteria for selecting the cases meant that the participants shared some similar characteristics. According to Yin (2009), it is difficult to generalize findings from cases sharing similar characteristics, particularly when there is little reference in previous research. The other consideration is that the data was collected in the form of snapshots rather than longitudinal design. Undertaking more observations over different days may provide extra data that could lead to more nuanced findings. Future research involving more participants, supported with richer observational and interview data would assist in better understanding in educators' thoughts and practices regarding their daily interactions with Chinese children.

The findings indicate that Chinese children may be in a disadvantaged position in interactions with their educators during the preschool years. This disadvantage could impact their early literacy development and their academic performance in future years. However, numerous reports show that many Chinese children achieve successful schooling outcomes in primary schools and high schools. This triggers a thought regarding how Chinese children positively turn their schooling experiences around throughout the schooling years. Further research exploring Chinese children's schooling experiences in language and literacy development, using longitudinal design is needed.

Finally, the method for this study has the potential to inspire a new approach for research of Chinese children in an educational setting. This study is based on the analysis of the language spontaneously occurring in educator–child interactions, using SFL theory. Language is a powerful communication tool rooted in speakers' social and cultural roles (Hasan, 1992). Investigating language occurring during spontaneous contexts is very useful in revealing speakers' social roles and ideologies in a subtle and unconscious way. Language could be a rich resource for future research exploring Chinese children's language, literacy, and social experiences in various contexts.

References

Baker. C. (2011). *Foundations of bilingual education and bilingualism* (5th edn). Toronto, Canada: Multilingual Matters.

Baxter, P., and Jack, S. (2008). Qualitative case study methodology: Study design and implementation for novice researchers. *The Qualitative Report, 13*, 544–559.

Catts, H. W., Adlof, S. M., and Meismer, S. E. (2006). Language deficits in poor comprehenders: A case for the simple view of reading. *Journal of Speech, Language, and Hearing Research, 49*, 278–293.

Cummins, J. (2007). Language interactions in the classroom: From coercive to collaborative relations of power. In C. Baker (Ed.), *Bilingual education: An introductory reader* (pp. 108–136). Clevedon, UK: Multilingual Matters.

Dandy, J., and Nettelbeck, T. (2002). The relationship between IQ, homework, aspirations and academic achievement for Chinese, Vietnamese and Anglo–Celtic Australian school children. *Educational Psychology, 22*, 267–275.

Davis, B., and Torr, J. (2016). Educators' use of questioning as a pedagogical strategy in long day care nurseries. *Early Years: An International Research Journal, 36*(1), 97–111.

Dickinson. D. K., and Porche. M. V. (2011). Relation between language experiences in preschool classrooms and children's kindergarten and fourth-grade language and reading abilities. *Child Development, 82*(3), 870–886.

Dickinson, D. K., McCabe, A., Anastasopoulos, L., Persner-Feinberg, E., and Poe, M. D. (2003). The comprehensive language approach to early literacy: The interrelationships among vocabulary, phonological sensitivity, and print knowledge among preschool-aged children. *Journal of Educational Psychology, 95*, 465–481.

Feniger, Y. and Lefstein, A. (2014). How not to reason with PISA data: An ironic investigation. *Journal of Education Policy, 29*(6), 845–855.

Hall, G., Burns, T. C., and Pawluski, J. (2003). Input and word learning: Caregivers' sensitivity to lexical category distinctions. *Journal of Child Language, 30*(3), 711–729.

Halliday, M. A. K., and Matthiessen, C. M. (2004). *An introduction to functional grammar* (3rd edn). London, UK: Edward Arnold.

Hamre, B. K. (2014). Teachers' daily interactions with children, and essential ingredient in effective early childhood program. *Child Development Perspectives, 8*(4), 223–230.

Hasan, R. (1992). *Rationality in everyday talk: From process to system*. Berlin, Germany: Mouton de Gruyer.

Hu, J., Torr, J., and Whiteman, P. (2014). Australian Chinese parents' language attitudes and practices relating to their children's bilingual development prior to school. *Journal of Early Childhood Research, 12*(2), 139–153.

NSW Department of Education and Communities. (2011). *Students with language background other than English in NSW public schools: 2011*. Retrieved from www.det.nsw.edu.au/media/downloads/about-us/statistics-and-research/key-statistics-information/lbote_students.pdf.

Richards, R. D. (2010). Narratives within narratives: One young Chinese-Australian boy's exploration of ideas of difference, identity, and friendship through his drawing. *Current Narratives, 7*(2), 84–103.

Sit, H. H. W. (2013). Characteristics of Chinese students' learning styles. *International Proceedings of Economics Development & Research, 62*(8), 36–39.

Storch, S. A., and Whitehurst, G. J. (2002). Oral language and code-related precursors to reading: Evidence from a longitudinal structural model. *Developmental Psychology, 38*, 934–947.

Vellutino, F. R., Tunmer, W. E., Jaccard, J. J., and Chen, R. (2007). Components of reading ability: Multivariate evidence for a convergent skills model of reading development. *Scientific Studies of Reading, 11*, 3–32.

Yin, R. K. (2009). *Case study research: Design and methods* (4th edn). Newbury Park, CA: Sage.

12

CHINESE LANGUAGE INSTRUCTION IN SINGAPORE

Voices of Children and Views of Teachers

Baoqi Sun and Xiao Lan Curdt-Christiansen

As a city-state with 5.31 million inhabitants, Singapore is known as a multiracial and multilingual nation, composed of three main ethnic groups—76.8% Chinese, 13.9% Malays, and 7.9% Indians (Singapore Department of Statistics, 2012). The official languages recognized by the government are English, Chinese (Mandarin), Malay, and Tamil. English, although not of Asian origin, is promoted as the "working language" and used as a lingua franca for government administration, education, commerce, science, technology, and communication between different ethnic communities (Dixon, 2005; Wee, 2003). The other official languages are considered as the "mother tongues" of the major ethnic groups. Despite the Chinese being the largest ethnic group, Chinese as a heritage language (mother tongue) is declining, and a noticeable language shift to English has taken place in recent years (Curdt-Christiansen, 2014a, 2014b; Zhao and Zhang, 2014). Researchers/educators express their concerns over children's deteriorating Chinese proficiency and the greater challenges faced by teachers in engaging and motivating students (Curdt-Christiansen, 2016; Dixon, 2005; Wee, 2003; Zhao and Liu, 2008). Some members of the public also worry about children's ability to learn two languages at the same time (Goh, 2004). In order to rectify the language shift situation and improve students' mother tongue learning experience, the government has initiated various language curriculum reforms. However, little research has examined how these Chinese language instructional practices, when carried out in the classroom, are perceived by children and teachers. This chapter reports on two independent yet interrelated studies aimed to understand the "insiders'" (i.e., the children's and teachers') perspectives on Chinese learning and Chinese instruction in Singaporean primary school classrooms. The first study is an ethnographic study involving the Chinese learning journey of three

Singaporean Chinese children (aged 7–11). The second study is an intervention study on morphologically enhanced instruction, involving six primary school Chinese teachers. By identifying both similarities and differences between the teachers' and children's views, we hope that our work can make timely contributions to the current Chinese language teaching and learning in schools.

Chinese Language Education in Singapore

The emphasis of Singapore's bilingual education is grounded in the belief that English is important for the economic development of the country and the management of its ethnic diversity; and mother tongues (MTs) can help children to learn about their culture, to identify with their ethnic roots, and to preserve cultural traits and Asian values. Research has shown that the bilingual policy is essential for the country's economic development and cultural continuity (Curdt-Christiansen and Silver, 2012; Dixon, 2005). However, even though the policy-makers give due status of imparting Asian cultural values to MT languages, the bilingual policy has inevitably tilted the balance in favor of English: in schools, Chinese is taught as a single subject (5–7 hours per week), but English is the medium of instruction for English language and all non-language subjects (17–19 hours per week), which means that around 70% of all instruction is in English. At society level, English is established as the language of economic advantage and the lingua franca across communities. This has led to the use of English not only in homes but also in workplaces, markets, and streets (Curdt-Christiansen, 2016; Vaish, 2007). Consequently, Chinese has a reduced social function despite the government's repeated ideological emphasis on Chinese as repository of tradition and culture. Predictably, people's attitudes toward English and Chinese have been influenced, resulting in changes in language behavior. Recent data show that the number of Chinese children whose dominant language is English when entering primary school has increased from 35% in 1996 to 50% in 2006 (Singaporean Ministry of Education [MOE], 2006), which suggests an accelerated language shift towards English. Moreover, there is a noticeable decline of Chinese proficiency, as most Chinese Singaporeans use Mandarin for everyday conversations only, and opt for English when discussing more complicated topics (Lee, 2012). In response to these trends, various language curriculum reforms have been implemented in schools.

The most recent reform places greater emphasis on listening, speaking, and reading skills than on writing Chinese characters. The principle "Recognize First, Write Later" is clearly specified in the curriculum guidelines, and the number of characters to be learned has been reduced across all levels. For the majority of students, the goal of Chinese learning is to achieve a high level of oral proficiency to help keep Chinese language and culture alive; whereas for those who are interested in and have aptitude for Chinese language and culture, the goal is to achieve a balanced bilingual and bicultural competence. To promote continual learning and professional development for teachers, the Ministry of Education (MOE) has introduced the Teachers Network Learning Circle concept, in which teachers engage in open, reflective dialogue and deal with their concerns regarding teaching and learning. The motivation for this educational renewal is a wish to improve the current classroom practice and to create pedagogical practices where Chinese learning is interesting for the students and corresponds to their various levels of Chinese proficiency.

To date, however, little is known about how children and teachers view Chinese learning and Chinese instruction in this context. In this chapter, we will examine the perspectives of three children and six teachers on the learning and teaching of Chinese language.

Findings

Study 1

This study is an ethnographic inquiry of the Chinese learning journey of three Singaporean Chinese children. The participants were Chengcheng (boy, aged 11), Xiaohong (girl, aged 9), and Eric (boy, aged 7); their names are the pseudonyms they chose to use for the study. All three children go to the same government school and live in the same neighborhood. To gain understanding of the participants' perspectives on Chinese language learning and Chinese instructions, biweekly home visits were made by the first author over seven months, each visit lasting 30–40 minutes. During each visit, field observations of the children's daily literacy activities, recordings of their homework routines, and semi-structured interviews were conducted to obtain participant perspectives. In this study, the first author negotiated her multiple identities as neighbor, family friend, and bilingual researcher. Therefore, she participated in the study as an insider, which allowed her to share her insider view with the participants' perspectives.

The fieldnotes, audio recordings, and interviews were subsequently transcribed by the researcher (named R in the transcription), and data were coded and thematically analyzed to allow patterns to emerge. In the following section, we present the children's views on Chinese learning and the Chinese instruction they received.

On Chinese Language Learning

When sharing their point of view with regard to learning Chinese language, cultural factors appeared to be the primary driving force, as most children take the importance of mastering Chinese as axiomatic. For instance, Xiaohong asserts, "我们是华人，所以要懂华语。如果你是华人但不懂华语就很奇怪。[We are Chinese, so we need to understand Chinese. It is a bit weird if you don't understand Chinese if you are Chinese]." Her comments point to the symbolic

212 Baoqi Sun and Xiao Lan Curdt-Christiansen

value that a language represents, which according to Baker (2006) can be perceived as a carrier of culture and provides means to construct, define, and frame people's identity.

Another underlying factor for Chinese language learning that emerged from the data is the economic aspect, which can be seen from the following excerpts. All excerpts are transcribed in the original language; code change is indicated in italic font. Translation is placed right below the original text.

Excerpt 1

After lunch, Xiaohong was choosing a Chinese book to read.

R: 你选华文书啊？喜欢吗？
Xiaohong: [smile] 不是很喜欢
R: 那为什么还要选？你不是有很多英文书吗？
Xiaohong: 我爸爸说要我多读华文书。他说中国发展很快，我长大了也许会去那边工作，所以要华语要很好才行。

R: You chose a Chinese book? Do you like it?
Xiaohong: [smile] Not really.
R: Then why did you choose it? Don't you have many English books?
Xiaohong: My dad said that China develops very fast, and I may need to work there when I grow up, so my Chinese needs to be very good.

Excerpt 2

Eric did not have homework from school. His mother asked him to do some English worksheets and Chinese worksheets.

Eric: 做好啦, yeah, 我要去读故事书。
Mother: 那个华文练习册做好了吗？
Eric: 啊，那个也要做啊？不是做了吗？
Mother: *That was English. You need to practice your Chinese also. So you will be good at both. See, China is developing so fast.*
Eric: Done, *yeah*, I am going to read story books.

Mother Have you done your Chinese worksheets?
Eric What? Do I need to do that? Haven't I done it?
Mother *That was English. You need to practice your Chinese also. So you will be good at both. See, China is developing so fast.*

These responses confirm English as a form of economic capital that can create wealth and job opportunities, although the importance of Chinese is also acknowledged. The parents of the participating children realize the growth of

China and the important role Chinese language plays in this process and understand that knowing two languages will put the children in a more advantageous position in terms of more and better job opportunities and higher income. Therefore, the children, like Xiaohong and Eric, were asked to read more Chinese story books and complete extra worksheets to boost their Chinese proficiency. It should be noted that even though the parents understand the importance of Chinese learning, they may unconsciously use English, just as Eric's mother did. We will further elaborate on this in later sections.

Despite their clear consensus about the importance of learning Chinese, learning to read Chinese is by no means an easy task, as articulated by Chengcheng.

Excerpt 3

Chengcheng was vexed by a Chinese composition.

Chengcheng:	唉，又要写作文了。
R:	很难写吗？
Chengcheng:	很难啊。华文要比英文难。
R:	为什么呢？
Chengcheng:	是因为那个，华文的话，我那些写那个东西，我得，我得用中文来表示，英文的我得用英文来表示，英文写起来很容易的 A P P L E, apple 哈哈
R:	可是我觉得你华文很好啊。
Chengcheng:	对，但是，写华文的那个时候，我就要想华文的那个词语，还要想，华文词语时，我还要想它们，那个怎么写，英文我只需要把它们拼出来就行了。
R:	哦，就是说你华文好多字都不会啊。

Chengcheng:	[Sigh] Need to write Chinese composition again.
R:	Is it difficult?
Chengcheng:	Yes, it is very difficult. Chinese [composition] is more difficult than English [composition].
R:	Why?
Chengcheng:	Because, for Mandarin, when I write those things, I have to, I have to express them in Mandarin, for English, I have to use English to express. I find writing in English is easier, *A P P L E, apple* [laugh].
R:	But I think your Chinese is very good.
Chengcheng:	Yes, but when writing in Chinese, I have to think of the words in Chinese, and think of the Chinese words, I also need to think how to write them; for English, I just need to spell them out.
R:	Oh, that means there are many Chinese characters you don't know how to write.

The challenge of learning Chinese, as pointed out by Chengcheng, seems to have language-specific reasons. Unlike the letter-to-phoneme correspondence found in alphabetic languages such as English, Chinese is often considered to be a "morphographic" language in which the graphemes represent syllables that are morphemes rather than phonemes. Chinese learning thus entails the acquisition of grapheme–morpheme correspondences. Moreover, there are a large number of homophones in Chinese, and each morpheme is less distinctively represented in spoken form, because a spoken syllable in Chinese may represent several different morphemes. Hence analyzing characters in spoken Chinese into morphemes is not a straightforward task. For instance, without exposure to written Chinese, it is virtually impossible for learners to distinguish the *hong*'s in *hong hua* (红花, red flower), *hongs shui* (洪水, flood), *hong wei* (宏伟, magnificent), and *cai hong* (彩虹, rainbow). To learn to read in Chinese, mastering basic word-reading skills and the commonly used 2,500 characters is very necessary. Children, teachers, and parents alike often regard this as a formidable task (Li and Rao, 2000; McBride et al., 2008), and the participating children in the present study are no exception.

On Chinese Instruction

Regarding children's perceptions of Chinese instructions, when asked about the teaching activities conducted during class, the children provided the following responses.

Excerpt 4

Xiaohong, Chengcheng, and Eric were playing cards at Chengcheng's house.

R:	说一说平时你们上华文课是怎样的？
Xiaohong:	老师会给我们读课文，讲故事，教我们写字。
Chengcheng:	*Teacher will pepper with stories*，有时也会让我们读课文，回答问题。
Eric:	我的老师有时还会给我们看录像，听故事。
R:	上华文课时老师会让你们自己讨论吗或者小组功课那些？
Chengcheng:	有的时候老师会让我们回答问题，或者和旁边的朋友讨论。
Xiaohong:	我们没有，老师要我们好好听课。 英文课就有很多小组功课，英文老师也会让我们说很多。
Eric:	*Yeah, show and tell* ... 我喜欢英文课，因为 *more fun*，也比较容易说，华文课 *not fun*.

R:	Tell me about what your Chinese class is like.
Xiaohong:	Teacher will read the passage for us, tell stories, and teach us how to write characters.

Chengcheng:	Teacher will pepper with stories, and sometimes will ask us read the passage and answer questions.
Eric:	My teacher will let us watch videos and listen to stories sometimes.
R:	During Chinese class, will teacher ask you to discuss or do group work?
Chengcheng:	Sometimes teacher will ask us to answer questions, or discuss with friends next to us.
Xiaohong:	We don't. Teacher asks us to pay attention to class. There are many group works in English class, English teacher will also let us to talk a lot.
Eric:	Yeah, show and tell . . . I like English class, because [it is] more fun, and it is easier to speak [English], Chinese class [is] no fun.

Unlike the stereotype of the monotonous Chinese class perceived by the public (Goh, 2004), responses from children show that there were diversified pedagogical activities offered in the classrooms. Most of these activities (e.g., storytelling, text reading, etc.), however, were teacher-centered rather than student-centered. As Xiaohong and Eric noted, they had more student-centered teaching activities during their English classes and they found them more appealing. The children's responses reveal an important feature of their literacy development that usually went unnoticed by the teachers or policymakers: being bilingual children who receive formal schooling in both English and Chinese concurrently, they are exposed to two pedagogical approaches. In Singapore, current English language teaching at the primary level is based on an instructional program that incorporates both communicative and structural components (MOE, 2010). It aims to provide enjoyable experiences for children with authentic literature and emphasizes learner-centeredness and seeks to develop in children strong communication skills in non-threatening contexts. Besides, it provides a highly structured curriculum with instructional materials and scripted lesson plans, including discussion points and specific prompts for teachers to use. Hence there is a qualitative difference in language teaching that stems from the pedagogical approaches adopted to teach the two languages. Tasks or activities in English classes are usually student-centered and children's central position in the learning process is emphasized, thus they are more likely to take up an active role during class time because group work is encouraged and projects are interesting. By contrast, pedagogical activities are not explicitly specified in the Chinese curriculum, even though it places great emphasis on making "Chinese learning fun and interesting" (MOE, 2007). Chinese teaching and learning involves, as noted by the children earlier, mainly memorization of characters, reading exemplary texts, and practicing isolated tasks. Such a teaching approach may inevitably impede Chinese learning and dampen children's learning interest.

216 Baoqi Sun and Xiao Lan Curdt-Christiansen

As discussed earlier, mastering the Chinese characters poses great challenges to Chinese learners. In the recent curriculum reform, the number of characters for writing as well as the opportunities for writing characters have been greatly reduced, for the purpose of giving "greater emphasis to character recognition and less emphasis to script writing in the lower primary years to facilitate early reading" (MOE, 2006, p. 3). However, such reforms do not seem to ease the learning challenge. Rather, children often encounter difficulty with Chinese characters writing, as shown in the excerpt below.

Excerpt 5

Xiaohong was doing her Chinese homework, which was filling blanks according to the passages taught in class. The researcher noticed that she wrote the character "我" in a very peculiar sequence: she first wrote "我" without the lower strokes Tí (提 "Rise") and Piě, 撇 (撇 Falling leftwards), then she realized something was missing. After examining the character for a while, she added the two strokes.

R:	等一下，你写字好像画画儿啊，这个'我'，怎么最后才写这个提和这个撇啊？上面那个点不是最后才写吗？
Xiaohong:	哎呀，一样的啦。老师不会算错的。
R:	你上课也是这样写吗？
Xiaohong:	嗯，我们上课很少写的。
R:	很少写啊？那老师是怎么教你们生字的呀？
Xiaohong:	老师会读课文，然后把那些要读的字要写的字让我们画线，然后再写在白板上，告诉我们它们的意思。然后 *once in a while*，会给我们讲个故事。
R:	什么样的故事？
Xiaohong:	就是字的故事。
R:	是把那个字拆开，一部分一部分的讲吗？
Xiaohong:	对。
R:	很经常这样讲吗？
Xiaohong:	嗯，*not really always*.
R:	那老师教一个字先写什么后写什么吗？
Xiaohong:	有的时候有，有的时候没有。只要写对就可以啦。

R: Wait a moment, the way you wrote the character is like drawing. The '我', why [did you] write the Tí and Piě last? Isn't the Diǎn the last stroke?

Xiaohong: Aiya, [they are] the same. Teacher won't mark [it] wrong.

R: Do you write like this in class?

Xiaohong: Erm, we seldom write [characters] in class.

R: [You] seldom write? Then how does your teacher teach you the new characters?

Xiaohong:	My teacher reads the passage, then asks us to underline those characters for writing and characters for recognition, after that [the teacher] writes [the characters] on the white board, tells us their meaning. Then once in a while, [the teacher] will tell us a story.
R:	What kind of story?
Xiaohong:	Just stories about the characters.
R:	Is it like breaking one character [into several sections], and teach section by section?
Xiaohong:	Yes.
R:	[Does the teacher] teach like this very often?
Xiaohong:	Erm, *not really always.*
R:	Then does the teacher teach you which section [of the character] to be written first and which section to written next?
Xiaohong:	Sometimes [the teacher] does, sometimes [the teacher] does not. So long as [we] write all the strokes of [the characters].

From the above excerpt, the third-grader, Xiaohong, was observed to be unfamiliar with writing even the most common Chinese characters. Her comments show that writing Chinese characters was seldom practiced in class and taught mainly in a "look-and-say" approach, while instructions focused on the unique Chinese morphological structures were only incidental. Moreover, the sequence of the strokes was not emphasized. While these pedagogical practices are consistent with the "Recognize First, Write Later" principle specified in the curriculum, they do not seem to help children retain the Chinese characters, as shown in Xiaohong's experience. Recent research has shown that frequent practice of the sequence of the strokes that form Chinese characters is necessary to understand and retain Chinese words (McBride et al., 2013; Shu et al., 2006). Hence reducing teaching on Chinese character writing may not ease children's learning burden nor promote their motivation. Instead, it may lead to a weaker foundation of decoding skills, which is a critical building block for the mastery of the commonly used Chinese characters. Such curriculum reforms, as Curdt-Christiansen (2014b) points out, have diluted the content of Chinese teaching rather than facilitated Chinese learning.

Study 2

To gain understanding of how teachers view Chinese teaching and learning, we retrieved part of the collected data from an intervention study which aims to promote a group of Primary 3 children's Chinese morphological awareness and help them apply morphological analysis in learning Chinese characters. The rationale behind the intervention came from the important role that morphological awareness plays in learning to read Chinese, due to the unique morphological features of the Chinese language (Anderson et al., 2003; Sun and Curdt-Christiansen, 2016). The study was an extension of a research project "Biliteracy Development: Metalinguistic Knowledge and Bilingual Academic Performance" (Curdt-Christiansen and Hu, 2010), funded by the Education Research Funding Programme, National Institute of Education, Nanyang Technological University, Singapore. A group of Chinese teachers in one of the participating schools expressed interest in further collaboration as part of their Learning Circle project to enhance Chinese teaching. Their major concern was how to help students in lower primary grades master Chinese characters. After careful discussion, the authors and teachers decided to conduct an intervention study on morphological awareness, due to its critical role in early Chinese literacy acquisition.

The Learning Circle group consisted of six Chinese language teachers (Teachers A, B, C, D, E, and F), who were all in their thirties and had taught in primary schools for more than seven years. The intervention session for the Learning Circle was held every other week and lasted for a year. Before the commencement of the study, the researchers conducted two workshops on how to apply morphological instruction methods in classroom teaching. Throughout the year, the researchers participated in the teachers' biweekly discussions, during which the pedagogical practices adopted to strengthen systematic teaching of Chinese morphology as well as the difficulties encountered by the teachers were documented and discussed. By the end of the intervention study, reflection notes from the teachers were gathered. In general, teachers viewed the intervention study as a positive experience and perceived that their theoretical understanding of the morphological-enhanced instruction had increased. For the purpose of the current chapter, the recordings of workshops, semi-structured interviews and reflection notes were transcribed and coded. The teachers reviewed and responded to the transcripts of their interviews. The authors served as peer debriefers for the process. In the following analysis, we will report the teachers' views on Chinese learning and teaching.

On Chinese Learning

Consistent with the children's view, the teachers unanimously acknowledged the importance of learning Chinese. As Teacher D said, "虽然在新加坡英文很重要，哪里都用得到，但现在中国发展这么快，华语以后会有很多机会用得到，所以学华语应该是越来越重要了。 [Even though English is very important in Singapore, and you can use it everywhere, China is developing so fast and there will be more opportunities to use Chinese, therefore learning Chinese should be more and more important]." Moreover, they pointed out that language can also connect to the past, as Teacher C elaborated: "想象一下，如果我们的孩子不讲华语的话，他们怎样和父母或祖

父母沟通呢？ [Imagine if our children don't speak Chinese, how can they communicate with their parents or grandparents?]" This comment acknowledges that language can serve as identity marker and provide a connection to the older generation, which is in line with the bilingual policy position that mother tongues are repositories of cultural values and tradition.

In terms of the challenges in Chinese learning, the teachers identified poor decoding skills and deteriorating Chinese language environment as two major difficulties. Regarding children's poor decoding skills, Teacher E said that "一个很严重的问题就是他们[学生]好多字不会写 [one serious problem is that there are many characters that they [students] do not know how to write]"; and Teacher D agreed that "小三小四的时候还要去复习小一小二学过的字 [when teaching Primary 3 and Primary 4, it is necessary to revise the characters learned in Primary 1 and 2]." When considered together with Chengcheng's lament about writing Chinese characters, it is evident that learning Chinese characters is a serious problem.

The teachers revealed also another challenge in Chinese learning, as indicated in the following excerpts.

Excerpt 6

During one discussion, the teachers were sharing their views about the challenges of teaching Chinese.

R:	你觉得华语教学有什么困难吗？
Teacher B:	不大好教啊，很多学生可以讲华语，但是常常会掺进来英文，就要一直纠正他们。然后好象父母呢，也都是蛮希望他们的孩子学华语的，但是呢，又会跟我说他们的华语不好，在家里很少讲。
Teacher F:	对，现在很多学生家里都是讲英文的，爸妈讲英文，和朋友也是讲英文。你要他多讲华语啊，他就不讲了。
R:	What do you think are the challenges that Chinese teaching are facing in Singapore?
Teacher B:	It is not easy to teach. Many children can speak Chinese, but they also mix it with English, so [I] have to remind them not to do that. Then, their parents are also hoping their children can learn Chinese, but at the same time, [they] also tell me that their (the parents') Chinese is not so good and they do not speak much Chinese at home.
Teacher F:	Yes, many children nowadays are from English-speaking families. They use English when talking to their parents and friends. If you want him/her to speak more Chinese, he/she won't speak at all.

The above comments confirm that bilingual children in Singapore have declining proficiency in Chinese language. Both teachers attributed the primary difficulty

220 Baoqi Sun and Xiao Lan Curdt-Christiansen

they had encountered to less frequent Chinese use within home domains. The comments seem to suggest that parents should be responsible for speaking more Chinese at home, which in turn would make children speak more Chinese. Implicitly, the teachers seem to suggest that there are inconsistencies between what the parents say and what they do, and it is what they actually practice at home that indexes their ideological positions and attitudes towards Chinese language. The teachers' articulation is consistent with other studies on language ideologies in Singapore. For instance, Curdt-Christiansen (2016), in her study of family language policy, found that parents often express pro-bilingual ideology but practice "English only" at home. The finding suggests that it is difficult to change the parents' longstanding, covert and ideologically negative perception of the mother tongue language. Very often, the use of English has become so habitual in the families that the bilingual expectations of parents and teachers are illusory.

The inadequate parental collaboration in providing Chinese exposure at home reveals an intrinsic limitation of the Singapore bilingual policy, which establishes English as more dominant than mother tongues. Inevitably, this will affect the frequency and extension of Chinese language use in home domains. Just as noted in Excerpt 2, Eric's mother made an effort in English when persuading Eric to read Chinese.

On Chinese Teaching

Given the focus of the intervention study, in what follows we discuss the morphological instructions conducted by the teachers. Excerpt 7 presents how new Chinese characters are taught in most classrooms.

Excerpt 7

R:	生字是怎么教的呢？
Teacher C:	读写字要重点教，写在白板上或者用幻灯片。识读字相对花的时间少点，主要是教怎样读和字的意思。
R:	会讲解字的结构吗？比如说偏旁部首什么的？
Teacher C:	那些都有教，但不是很经常。好像 '山' '田' 这些字，一开始学华文的时候都是从它们的结构像什么学的，但那是幼儿园教的。小学后一般很少教那么细了。部首的话，像口字旁，提手旁，学生都很熟悉了，就不太会讲了。
R:	How do you teach the new characters?
Teacher C:	[Our] focus is on the written characters (productive characters). [I will] write them on the white board or present them in slides. Less time is spent on the receptive characters. Primarily, it is to teach the pronunciation and the meaning of the characters.

R:	Do you teach the structures of the characters? Such as radicals?
Teacher C:	Those are taught, but not very often. For example, characters like 山 [mountain], 田 [field], we always start with the structures of characters when we begin learning Chinese, but that is taught in kindergarten. For primary school, usually [we] do not teach such details. As to radicals, students are very familiar with radicals such as 口 扌, so we don't spend much time [on that].

Consistent with children's responses, the above dialogue shows that some Chinese teachers in Singapore, but by no means all, do occasionally adopt an analytical approach to teaching some Chinese characters. The instruction, however, mainly focused on learning to pronounce and write the characters correctly rather than on analyzing their morphological structures. One excerpt during the discussion before the commencement of the intervention study provided answer for the absence of morphological instructions.

Excerpt 8

During the discussion on morphological-enhanced instruction, Teacher A expressed her reservations.

Teacher A:	其实这些方法我们上课的时候都会用的。
R:	但是就我们的观察，并不是很经常。
Teacher A:	是的，但是大纲里也没要求这样教啊。而且，我担心时间不太够，因为本来教生字的时间就不是很多。
Teacher A:	Actually we did use these [morphological instructions] methods in class.
R:	But based on our observation, it is not done very often.
Teacher A:	I agree. But the curriculum does not specify these teaching methods. Moreover, I am worried about that there is not sufficient time, because the time allocated to new characters is not that much in the first place.

The curriculum, as Teacher A denoted, neither provides clear guidance nor allocates adequate time for teaching Chinese characters. Learning Chinese, however, requires both clear morphological guidance and adequate practicing time. As noted earlier, learning to read Chinese relies greatly on understanding and manipulating morphological features of Chinese characters (Kuo and Anderson, 2006; Nagy and Anderson, 1998), which differs drastically from learning alphabetic languages as it does not have the graphic–phonic association. Therefore, the early stages of Chinese literacy acquisition require children to practice and memorize various morphemes that are basic elements of characters (Ho and Bryant, 1997).

222 Baoqi Sun and Xiao Lan Curdt-Christiansen

Failing to consider this language-specific feature will inevitably pose great challenges for both children (as noted in earlier sections) and teachers. Hence provision of explicit and systematic morphological instruction into the current Chinese teaching in Singapore may help to promote and sustain children's attention to the morphological structure of Chinese characters, which may help to lay a sound foundation for the acquisition of Chinese characters (Wu et al., 2009).

Regarding other teaching activities, the curriculum places a clear emphasis on changing the current "unproductive" classroom practice and on pedagogical practices where Chinese learning should be fun and interesting. The following excerpt provides an example of the common pedagogical activities.

Excerpt 9

During one biweekly discussion.

Teacher A:	基本上就是按照大纲的要求和课本的内容，讲解课文，还有生字，识读字，识写字，活动本练习这些。因为现在的学生对华文没什么兴趣，大纲里也是这样强调，所以要想办法生动才能吸引他们。
Teacher D:	对，我们会利用ICT来给他们放一些短片，听一些课文朗读和小故事，这样会让学生有兴趣。
R:	这些方法是大纲里的？
Teacher A:	那倒不是，大纲里没这么具体。它里面虽然说教学时要考虑到孩子来自不同的语言环境，但是，没有给出些具体的例子说怎么教。我们平时用的方法大部分是经过我们讨论，或者根据自己教课的经验，这样来的，要想怎样吸引学生，比如说有时讲解生字生词的时候会编出有意思的故事来，吸引他们的注意力。 对，现在的上课就像说相声（笑）说学逗唱都要有一点 (笑)。
Teacher A:	Basically it is to follow the requirement of the curriculum and the textbook, teach passages and new characters, characters for writing, characters for recognition, and activity book. Since students nowadays do not have much interest in Chinese, as emphasized in the curriculum, [we] need to make the lesson vivid so to entice them.
Teacher D:	Yes, we make use of the *ICT* to show some video clips, listen to the passage reading and short stories, to arouse the students' interest.
R:	These methods are from the curriculum?
Teacher A:	Not really, it is not specified in the curriculum. Even though it [the curriculum] mentions that teaching approaches need to take children's various language backgrounds into consideration, it does not provide

	specific methods to teach. Most of the teaching activities have been discussed among us or based on our teaching experiences. [We] need to think about how to motivate the students, such as making up some interesting stories when teaching new characters, to attract their attention.
Teacher E:	Yes, nowadays [we] teach like cross-talkers [laugh], need to make use of speech and drama techniques [laugh].

From the excerpts, we can see that the teachers generally reckon with the curriculum in that children lack interest in Chinese learning, and are concerned about how to entice children in order to enhance teaching efficacy. Hence, they are making an effort in utilizing various resources in their teaching, such as "pepper [the class] with stories" as mentioned earlier by Chengcheng and "teach like cross-talkers" as remarked by Teacher E.

The teachers also voiced the discrepancy between the desired Chinese learning outcome and the pedagogical support provided by the curriculum. As Teacher A pointed out directly, even though the curriculum emphasizes that changes in teaching approach are necessary to cater to children's need, it does little to help facilitate her everyday teaching. The interpretation and implementation of the curriculum thus is largely up to the teachers' past teaching experience (as shown above). Such discrepancy, if not dealt with, may present further obstacles for effective Chinese teaching.

Conclusion

Based on the data of two studies, this chapter examined children's voices and teachers' views on Chinese language learning and Chinese instruction in Singapore. Admittedly, the foregoing results are by no means a comprehensive representation of Chinese learning in Singapore, but they do provide some understanding of how children and teachers perceive the Chinese pedagogical practices and the underlying factors that shape these perceptions.

The results indicate that both the children and the teachers regard the significance of mastering Chinese as self-evident, which indicates that the national bilingual policy is successful in shaping people's views on the importance of Chinese learning. With regard to the underlying factors for learning Chinese language, the data indicate that cultural and economic factors are the most important driving forces.

Both children and teachers agreed that mastering common Chinese characters was one of the challenges of Chinese learning. This is very likely due to the lack of Chinese morphological instruction. In light of the findings of the present study, it seems that the task could be made less daunting if teachers cultivate children's insights into the morphological structures of the Chinese characters they are learning.

Another challenge for Chinese learning, voiced by the teachers, is that the language environment in home domains may not be optimal for Chinese learning. Home language use patterns, however, are profoundly influenced by national language policy (Curdt-Christiansen, 2009; Curdt-Christiansen and Silver, 2012). As a result of its inherent limitations discussed earlier, even though the current bilingual policy gives equal official status to English and Chinese, English has occupied a privileged position. In addition to its role as a "neutral" language among the different ethnic communities, English is also used as working language in government administration, law, commerce, science, and technology. The major goal of Chinese learning, on the other hand, is to develop awareness and nurture children's appreciation of Chinese culture. While possessing a high level of proficiency in English can ensure access to higher education and a good career with a high income, the same cannot be said about a high level of proficiency in Chinese. Therefore, the separation of functions of English and Chinese can arguably generate very different attitudes towards these two languages, which has led to a tendency that English is taking over Chinese. In order to change parental attitudes towards Chinese and increase Chinese language use at home, policies need to focus on other values that Chinese has in addition to cultural affiliation. For instance, Sun (2015) has demonstrated home language use significantly predicted reading comprehension and composition writing for Primary 3 Singaporean English-Chinese bilingual children. Policies may consider emphasizing these results in order for parents and children to appreciate the educational value of Chinese.

Moreover, our results also underscore the importance for the curriculum to provide adequate pedagogical support for teachers. It has been shown that teachers are not equipped with sufficient instructional activities that cater to children with different proficiency levels and different home language backgrounds. Hence, there is a need to integrate these topics into current pre-service and in-service training programs for Chinese teachers in Singapore.

References

Anderson, R. C., Li, W., Ku, Y.-M., Shu, H., and Wu, N. (2003). Use of partial information in learning to read Chinese characters. *Journal of Educational Psychology*, *95*, 52–57.

Baker, C. (2006). *Foundations of bilingual education and bilingualism*. Clevedon: Multilingual Matters.

Curdt-Christiansen, X. L. (2009). Invisible and visible language planning: Ideological factors in the family language policy of Chinese immigrant families in Quebec. *Language Policy*, *8*(4), 351–375.

Curdt-Christiansen, X. L (2014a). Family language policy: Is learning Chinese at odds with leaning English in Singapore? In X. L. Curdt-Christiansen and A. Hancock (Eds.), *Learning Chinese in diasporic communities: Many pathways to being Chinese* (pp. 35–58). Amsterdam, the Netherlands: John Benjamins.

Curdt-Christiansen, X. L. (2014b). Planning for development or decline? Education policy for Chinese language in Singapore. *Critical Inquiry in Language Studies, 11*(1), 1–26.

Curdt-Christiansen, X. L. (2016). Conflicting language ideologies and contradictory language practices in Singaporean bilingual families. *International Journal of Multilingual and Multicultural Development.*

Curdt-Christiansen, X. L., and Hu, G. W. (2010). *Biliteracy development: Metalinguistic knowledge and bilingual academic performance.* Report No. OER 35/09 XLC. Singapore: National Institute of Education/Nanyang Technological University.

Curdt-Christiansen, X. L., and Silver, R. E. (2012). Educational reforms, cultural clashes and classroom practices. *Cambridge Journal of Education, 42*(2), 141–161.

Department of Statistics. (2012). *Census of the population: Education, language and religion.* Retrieved from www.singstat.gov.sg.

Dixon, L.Q. (2005). Bilingual education policy in Singapore: An analysis of its sociohistorical roots and current academic outcomes. *International Journal of Bilingual Education and Bilingualism, 8*(1), 25–47.

Goh, N. W. (2004). *Huayuwen zai xinjiapo de xianzuang yu qianjing [Chinese language in Singapore: Reality and prospect].* Singapore: Cuangyiquan Chubanshe.

Ho, C. S. H., and Bryant, P. E. (1997). Phonological skills are important in learning to read Chinese. *Developmental Psychology, 33*(6), 946–951.

Kuo, L.-J., and Anderson, R. C. (2006). Morphological awareness and learning to read: A cross-language perspective. *Educational Psychologist, 41*(3), 161–180.

Lee, K. Y. (2012). *My lifelong challenge: Singapore's bilingual journey.* Singapore: Straits Times Press.

Li, H., and Rao, N. (2000). Parental influences on Chinese literacy development: A comparison of preschoolers in Beijing, Hong Kong, and Singapore. *International Journal of Behavioral Development, 24*(1), 82–90.

McBride, C., Tardif, T., Cho, J. R., Shu, H. U. A., Fletcher, P., Stokes, S. F., . . . and Leung, K. (2008). What's in a word? Morphological awareness and vocabulary knowledge in three languages. *Applied Psycholinguistics, 29*(3), 437.

McBride, C., Shu, H., Chan, W., Wong, T., Wong, A. M. Y., Zhang, Y., . . . and Chan, P. (2013). Poor readers of Chinese and English: Overlap, stability, and longitudinal correlates. *Scientific Studies of Reading, 17*(1), 57–70.

Ministry of Education. (2006). Chinese Language Primary Syllabus. Retrieved from www.moe.gov.sg/education/syllabuses/languages-and-literature.

Ministry of Education. (2007). Chinese Language Primary Syllabus. Retrieved from www.moe.gov.sg/education/syllabuses/languages-and-literature.

Ministry of Education. (2010). English Language Syllabus for Primary and Secondary Schools. Retrieved from www.moe.gov.sg/education/syllabuses/languages-and-literature.

Nagy, W. E. and Anderson. R. C. (1998). Metalinguistic awareness and literacy acquisition in different languages. In D. Wagner, R. Venezy, and B. Street (eds.), *Literacy: An International Handbook* (pp. 155–160). Boulder, CO: Westview Press.

Shu, H., McBride-Chang, C., Wu, S., and Liu, H. (2006). Understanding Chinese developmental dyslexia: Morphological awareness as a core cognitive construct. *Journal of Educational Psychology, 98*, 122–133.

Sun, B. (2015). *Metalinguistic awareness and its relationship with academic language performance: A comparative study of bilingual and monolingual children.* Unpublished PhD dissertation, National Institute of Education/Nanyang Technological University, Singapore.

Sun, B., and Curdt-Christiansen, X. L. (2016). Morphological awareness and reading development in bilingual English-Chinese children in Singapore. In R. Silver and W. Bokhorst-Heng (Eds.), *Quadrilingual education in Singapore: Pedagogical innovation in language education* (pp. 84–101). Berlin, Germany: Springer.

Vaish, V. (2007). Globalisation of language and culture in Singapore. *International Journal of Multilingualism, 4*(3), 217–233.

Wee, L. (2003). Linguistic instrumentalism in Singapore. *Journal of Multilingual and Multicultural Development, 24*(3), 211–224.

Wu, X., Anderson, R. C., Li, W., Wu, X., Li, H., Zhang, J., . . . and Chen, X. (2009). Morphological awareness and Chinese children's literacy development: An intervention study. *Scientific Studies of Reading, 13*(1), 26–52.

Zhao, S., and Liu, Y. (2008). Xinjiapo huazu shequn jiating yongyu de shehui yuyanxue fenxi [A sociolinguistic study on home-language use in Singapore Chinese community]. *Shehui Kexue Zhanxian [The Social Science Frontier], 158*, 131–137.

Zhao, S. H., and Zhang, D. (2014). Conflicting goals of language-in-education planning in Singapore: Chinese character (汉字 *Hanzi*) education as a case. In X. L. Curdt-Christiansen and A. Hancock (Eds.), *Learning Chinese in diasporic communities: Many pathways to being Chinese* (pp. 35–58). John Benjamins.

13

OVERSEAS CHINESE–HERITAGE STUDENTS LEARNING TO BE CHINESE LANGUAGE TEACHERS IN TAIWAN

A Journey of Comparisons and Affirmations

Ya-Hsun Tsai and Jason D. Hendryx

Overseas Chinese students have been actively recruited to come to Taiwan for study since 1962 (Lin et al., 2011, p. 793). Such recruitment is quite logical in light of the large number of overseas Chinese around the world. Some researchers estimate their number to be as high as 60 million (e.g., Rae and Witzel, 2008), while others put the number at around 40 million. In particular, Southeast Asia has witnessed their continued growth in recent decades. For example, Skinner (1959) put the number of overseas Chinese in Southeast Asia at around ten million, but by the time of Kuhn's (2008) work this number had increased to somewhere near 26 million.

Perhaps then it should be of no surprise that in one of the more well-established universities in Taiwan you will find a bell tower with Chinese words carved along its side that read, "Overseas Chinese are the mother of revolution." Commenting on this motto, Huang (2011, p. 224) suggests that, "The slogan had the necessary magnetism and resonance to assist in re-territorializing and linking the far-flung Chinese diasporic communities back to China. That explains its continuous currency and efficacy up to the present."

In overseas Chinese communities, sustaining established cultural traditions and maintaining educational ideals are considered imperatives. Barrett (2012, p. 125) offers that, "Perhaps the most interesting aspect of overseas Chinese organizations in general is the concerted effort they directed towards maintaining the social and cultural integrity of their settlements abroad." Meanwhile, Yen (2008, p. 282) unpacks the sustainability of overseas Chinese communities by suggesting,

"For the purpose of survival and development, the ethnic Chinese communities . . . have to modernize themselves so as to strengthen their competitive capacity . . . modernization of the economy, social structure, thinking, education, and culture." In addition, Wei (2016, p. 6) identifies three areas of considerable importance to overseas Chinese communities, "The collective coping strategies for the immigrants often involve building the so-called 'three pillars of the diaspora', namely, a community . . . association, a school, and a communication network." From these various studies it becomes clear that overseas Chinese communities are seen as placing great value on their communities, cultures, languages, and education, as well as it even being suggested that the continued survival of these communities will be contingent on continuing effort to modernize in these areas.

Narrowing these areas of importance to a focus on language, two overarching theoretical frames will be employed here to situate the Chinese languages of overseas Chinese students in Taiwan within regional and global frames. The first draws on the terms "mobility" and "immobility" from a review of the literature concerning cultural geographies provided by Blunt (2007). Those terms will allow us to consider the mobility Mandarin Chinese, as a teachable commodity, provides for overseas Chinese within Asia, and at the same time also reflect on any immobility that might be embedded in that commodification of language as well.

The second involves taking de Swaan's (2001) global language system and reworking it to include only Chinese languages in order to provide a construct that might assist us in better comprehending the relationships between instructed Chinese languages around the world. De Swaan's original model is comprised of four hierarchal levels of languages: peripheral, central, supercentral, and hypercentral, with English being the only hypercentral language. Interestingly de Swaan suggests that, "language learning occurs mostly upward, in a 'centripetal' mode: people usually prefer to learn a language that is at a higher level in the hierarchy" (p. 5).

By taking de Swaan's global language system and modifying it to include just instructed Chinese languages, with Beijing Mandarin as the sole hypercentral language, we have a global model for examining prestige values associated with various forms of Chinese language being taught. In such a model, peripheral Chinese languages would be found in places like Thailand, Burma, and Indonesia, central Chinese languages would be in Malaysia and Hong Kong, and supercentral Chinese languages would be linked to Taiwan, Singapore, and various cities in China proper like Harbin.

Background for the Study

In 2009 the Department of Applied Chinese Language and Literature in Taiwan piloted a program that invited approximately 30 overseas Chinese students to their department in 2010 as a separate student cohort. This initiative was aimed at meeting the growing demand for qualified Chinese language teachers in Southeast Asia and around the globe. Indeed, as Chan (2016) remarks, "a shortage of well-trained teachers" is one reason why Mandarin Chinese still has somewhat limited use in Hong Kong (p. 197).

As with any pilot program there were some issues that revealed themselves with this first cohort. Some of these issues were the need for additional support in English and Chinese as well as clarifications concerning university policies. In terms of academic performance, this initial cohort generally preformed much differently than their Taiwanese counterparts. For English, this meant that some of them had command of a much smaller vocabulary and less willingness to communicate, while others came with a very high level of fluency. Meanwhile, the cadence of the Chinese language these students spoke varied according to the region they grew up in, as did their ability to present and teach Chinese tones and characters.

Currently there are three overseas Chinese cohorts working their way through the same university program and there are still questions about how these overseas Chinese students—and the Taiwanese faculty teaching them—understand the learning and teaching realities these students are facing in Taiwan. It is hoped that the current study will provide further insights into what these students are dealing with in their chosen course of study. By so doing, this research will contribute to discussions Ma and Li (2016) began with their investigations into the contexts of Chinese-heritage students studying in North America by extending those conversations to include overseas Chinese-heritage students studying in Taiwan.

For overseas Chinese students, the questions in this study will focus on two areas. The first is a self-evaluation of their own Chinese language abilities. The second is how they situate Taiwan, and the education they are receiving there, as helping them realize their life goals and further support their Chinese identities. For Taiwanese faculty, the questions focus on what they think of the overseas Chinese students they have worked with, and continue to work with, in terms of strengths and weaknesses, as well as the potential obstacles these students will need to face and overcome after they graduate in order to be successful Chinese language educators.

Method

Data Sources

Overseas Chinese-heritage students currently studying to be Mandarin Chinese language teachers at a university in Taiwan were given the opportunity to complete a survey that presented the questions of this study. The survey instrument was offered in both paper and online formats and was accessible to overseas Chinese students studying in this university for a period of two months. The survey instrument was offered in Mandarin Chinese (see Appendix A for English version), consisted of 25 items, and took approximately 10–15 minutes to complete. The accuracy of the Chinese language used in the survey was checked by several native speakers of Chinese who are currently working in higher education in Taiwan.

The first two items of the survey asked participants to rate their Chinese language abilities and then identify from these the abilities that they would need the most additional support in to become an effective Chinese language teacher. The next ten questions had participants rate their perceptions toward how Taiwan was aiding them in reaching their life goals and supporting their Chinese identities. The next seven items were short-answer and further explored the role Taiwan was playing in these overseas Chinese students' lives as well as the continuing formation of their Chinese identities. The following five questions asked for some basic background and demographic information. The final question of the survey asked if they had any additional information they wished to share. The ordering and types of questions on the survey instrument followed those suggested in the relevant literature (Zoltán and Taguchi, 2010).

To further ground and complement the survey data, three overseas Chinese students were interviewed about topics similar to those found in the survey instrument. These interviews were audio-recorded and then transcribed. The interview was semi-structured in nature, consisted of nine questions in Mandarin Chinese, and took approximately 10–30 minutes to complete (see Appendix B for English version). The overseas Chinese student interviews focused on three primary areas: 1) Their perceptions of the teaching effectiveness of their Taiwanese faculty; 2) their views of their own Chinese language abilities; and 3) how they have gone about situating themselves in the realities they are facing in Taiwan and how those adjustments might have impacted their Chinese identity.

The final dataset of this study involved the collection of faculty interviews (see Appendix C for English version). These interviews with three faculty members were also semi-structured in nature, consisted of ten questions in Mandarin Chinese, and took 10–30 minutes to complete. Interview questions with faculty explored three primary areas: 1) what they identified as the strengths and weaknesses of the overseas Chinese students they have worked with; 2) how these students could be better supported in Taiwan; and 3) how they view the identities of the overseas Chinese students they have worked with in Taiwan.

The Participants

Twenty-nine overseas Chinese students currently enrolled in an applied Chinese language program in a university in Taiwan (40% return rate) completed the survey for this study. From these surveys, three students were contacted and asked to complete the related interview. Meanwhile, three faculty members (25% of the total number of faculty in this program) were invited to complete the faculty interview for this study.

From the data provided on the surveys (eight of which were only partially completed), the majority of respondents were female (n = 17/59%) with only four respondents reporting being male. In terms of age, 18–20 years old had the most responses with 18 (62%), followed by 21–23 years old with four (14%) and only one respondent reporting being 24 years old or older. For place of origin, the greatest number of respondents reported coming from Hong Kong (11/38%), followed by Malaysia (9/31%), Indonesia (2/7%), Macau (2/7%), and Japan (2/7%).

For the amount of time participants had spent in Taiwan, 15 (52%) reported being in Taiwan a year or less, while 12 (41%) reported being in Taiwan from between one and a half to four years. They identified Cantonese (12), Malaysian (7), Mandarin Chinese (3), Indonesian (2), Japanese (2), Portuguese (1), and English (1) as the primary language of their country of citizenship.

Data Analysis

All survey data for this study were collected and compiled with frequency counts and percentages generated for fixed range items. Eight surveys were only partially completed and the data provided in those surveys were included in the current study. Short answers provided on the survey were coded and major themes identified. For interviews, both with students and faculty, some light coding on participant answers was employed to collapse and align the data collected between students and between faculty.

Results

Survey

Language Abilities

The highest rated aspects of their own Chinese language abilities with either a "good" or "excellent" marking were listening (26), speaking (23), and reading (in traditional script) (23). Meanwhile, the areas overseas Chinese students identified most as needing either "some" or "a lot" of support in order to be an effective Chinese language teacher were speaking and culture (26 each), grammar (24), and writing (traditional and simplified) (23).

Views on Taiwan

The role of Taiwan in helping survey respondents realize their professional and personal goals was mostly positive with 21 and 22 responses of agree or strongly agree for these two items (72% and 76% respectively). Only one respondent disagreed with the statement that "Taiwan has helped you realize your professional goals." Seventeen (59%) agreed or strongly agreed with the statement that "Taiwan has helped you more fully understand your Chinese-heritage identity," while 11 selected "neutral" for this item. Meanwhile, 25 (86%) agreed or strongly agreed that "Taiwan has helped you more fully understand your Chinese language abilities," with only three respondents remaining neutral on this item.

As for participants' views on government and university policies that benefited them during their time there, 15 (52%) responded with agree or strongly agree, with only one response of disagree being reported for this item. Being proud about their Chinese-heritage speaker identity and more in touch with who they are and want to be generated 20 and 21 responses of agree and strongly agree for these items (69% and 72% respectively), with all remaining recorded responses being neutral. Four respondents (14%) were not looking forward to returning to their home countries and four felt that people in Taiwan did not appreciate their heritage identity. Only one respondent marked that her or his experiences in Taiwan were not "mostly positive."

Moving to the short-answer responses of the survey, for what Taiwan has specifically offered them that their home country could not, the most numerous response offered centered around Taiwan providing, "A good Chinese language learning environment" (5), followed by education and resources (4), training in Chinese (3), a degree (2), specific course choices (2), and cheap goods and transportation (1). Particularly representative comments for this item were "wherever I go they speak my mother tongue," "strong Chinese culture vibes everywhere," and "makes me realize that studying languages other than my mother tongue is important."

As for how Taiwan could have been more supportive, ten comments (40% of all comments provided) were directed at providing them with more opportunities for internships, scholarships, and financial support. More support for English language learning, more support for Chinese language learning, and Taiwan has already done enough (for them) were each mentioned twice.

Participants wanted to tell the people of Taiwan that they have appreciated their kindness (5), passionate natures (5), and helpfulness (4). Representative comments were, "I really like Taiwan," "I love Taiwan, thank you!", "Thanks for giving me this opportunity," "Most Taiwanese are very generous hosts, thanks for your tolerance for foreigners!", "Taiwan is better than my country." Some comments spoke to more complicated understandings, "most Taiwan people are friendly but because our cultural backgrounds are different, we have some different values" and "Taiwan people are all very passionate, but a portion of them like to make mountains out of molehills, magnifying their own interests." One respondent hoped Taiwan people could "be a little more passionate."

As for respondents' roles in promoting Chinese language they saw themselves as helpers (2) and transmitters (1) with small roles (1) to play. One respondent suggested that, "We are all pieces on a chessboard." An interesting comment from this item was, "through training overseas Chinese it has indirectly broadcast the excellence of Chinese education in Taiwan and furthermore pushed the development of Chinese in the world."

In a question about what respondents have learned about themselves and their Chinese-heritage identities while in Taiwan, answers varied. Some respondents mentioned they better understood the importance of Chinese culture (5) and language (3). Meanwhile, some were not sure about any impact (3).

More detailed comments concerning heritage identity development ranged from "We are all Chinese, from different places with cultural backgrounds which are not entirely the same" to

> after coming to Taiwan in addition to understanding my identity as an outsider, I also better understand my Chinese-heritage identity, when I confirm my identity with a Taiwan student, I must spend a great deal of time to explain to them the current conditions of my country and my own story, which results in making me feel uncomfortable about my Chinese identity, through more effort I hope to gain people's acceptance.

In regards to their future careers, the majority wrote that they were going to be a Chinese language teacher (19) or Chinese translator (5) with two considering being a Chinese language materials developer or editor (2). Other possible career paths offered included administrator (2), Japanese language teacher, writer, and boss. Three respondents were unsure about their future careers.

Asked if they would come to Taiwan all over again knowing what they know now, all but two said they would. Reasons for still coming to Taiwan again if given the chance included, it was an excellent environment to develop in (4), it was realizing a dream to come here (3), there is "a lot to experience here that one cannot experience in one's hometown," love for Chinese, so many channels to learn Chinese, Taiwanese relatives and "attending university is better than not attending university." The two respondents who would not come to Taiwan if given the chance again arrived at that decision for very different reasons. The first mentioned, "No, because of the differences in my expectations about the society and people here. There are other places I would rather go." The second said, "No, because I miss home."

In the final question of the survey, in which respondents had the opportunity to provide additional comments about their time in Taiwan, all comments provided (11) were positive and covered a broad range of topics. Remarks offered included, "Taiwan is a great place!", "people are very considerate," "made lots of friends here," and "the university is a very open place."

Student Interviews

Three overseas Chinese-heritage students who were surveyed also completed an audio-recorded interview. From these interviews, the strengths the interviewees

234 Ya-Hsun Tsai and Jason D. Hendryx

saw in their Taiwan faculty were foreign language knowledge, cultural knowledge, and language teaching knowledge. Faculty members were also seen as rich in overseas experiences and in their abilities to write and conduct research. Faculty offered clear explanations, answered student questions, and used PowerPoint slides to teach that were "easy to understand and had pictures." In addition, the faculty members were viewed as being very involved with, and providing opportunities for, out-of-class activities. Weaknesses of faculty mentioned by overseas Chinese students were that faculty only taught to their strengths, and had narrow understandings of teaching, interaction, and questioning strategies.

Overseas Chinese interviewed felt their strengths with the Chinese language were listening (2), reading and writing in both kinds of Chinese script (1), and being logical, careful, and patient with the language. Meanwhile, they offered their weaknesses with Chinese as pronunciation (2), cultural knowledge (2), being able to teach Chinese (2), the four tones, grammar, and their own non-standard speaking discourse patterns because of the influences of home language uses. In terms of how they have tried to develop themselves while in Taiwan, all students interviewed mentioned taking a broad range of classes, inside and outside their home department, as well as participating in school clubs and activities.

As for limitations Taiwan may impose on these students, one mentioned that becoming accustomed to a primarily Chinese speaking environment could be a hindrance later on. Another student mentioned that where the student comes from they don't have an environment for reading and writing Chinese, so how to bring that knowledge back and teach it would be problematic. Finally, a student mentioned that family relations in Taiwan were much closer than those in the student's home country and that intimacy between family members was difficult to comprehend.

Responses about the development of their Chinese identity while in Taiwan revealed extremely different perceptions. One student said, "I have always known my Chinese identity so there has been no change in this understanding from my time in Taiwan." Another student remarked,

> I didn't really understand my Chinese identity when I first came to Taiwan. However, I gradually worked past some feelings of inferiority about my identity and started to feel proud. I gradually found I have the ability to change and breakthrough!

The third student felt "[m]ore accepted here in Taiwan." In sharing any additional comments about Taiwan, one student offered,

> I have changed a lot during my time in Taiwan. Not only because of the different environment, but also because of my ever-broadening contact with different levels of society, my thinking has become more mature. Even so, there is still much to improve.

Faculty Interviews

Three university faculty were interviewed about their perceptions of the overseas Chinese-heritage students they have worked with in Taiwan. In terms of the strengths seen in overseas Chinese students, faculty saw them as having "multiple abilities" and success with a number of languages, international perspectives and understandings, and maintaining more traditional Chinese study habits than Taiwanese students. In addition, they felt these students' connections with, and understanding of, the local languages and cultures from their home regions were great advantages. Their ability to make and sustain social contacts in their home areas was also seen as an advantage. Having the ability to compare and align Chinese expectations and realities from different areas, connections with Chinese culture, and the ability to absorb Chinese knowledge quickly conclude what faculty offered as the strengths they see in overseas Chinese-heritage students.

For weaknesses, all faculty spoke to the Chinese language abilities of these students needing further development. Issues with proper pronunciation were mentioned (2), some have problems with English, and Chinese cultural understandings differ. Ineffective study habits and unwillingness to form bonds and operate outside their own cultural background groups were also mentioned.

As for obstacles, these students must face and successfully overcome, one faculty reiterated, "Chinese language abilities, utilizing effective study habits, and moving outside their same cultural background groups." Other faculty comments were framed differently: "They don't really have any issues they cannot overcome. They only have advantages," and "They can make improvements. The biggest obstacles are pronunciation and characters use."

Faculty feel that Taiwan can better support overseas Chinese students by continuing to clarify and improve government and university policies related to overseas Chinese, providing career guidance, and more types and kinds of support after they graduate and return home. One specific kind of support suggested by faculty was to provide teaching resources, as the students' home countries may have limited access to such resources.

Faculty would like to "provide them practical language teaching and cultural experiences" if there was the opportunity to do so. Sometimes overseas Chinese students may not know the precise language used and the proper cultural norms of, say, going to a fancy department store. Another faculty member offered, "I would create more opportunities for Taiwan students to have quality interactions with heritage students and overseas students. I would continue to instill confidence in overseas students so they can integrate themselves successfully into Taiwan organizations and environments." A faculty member's hope was to be able to "provide them with the resources they need to be successful after returning home."

When asked to describe overseas Chinese-heritage students with a word, the words faculty chose were, "multidimensional," "independent," and "pure." In regards to if the faculty believed their overseas Chinese students were proud of their own Chinese identity, one faculty member said, "I don't know. They don't show this in my interactions with them." Another faculty member mentioned, "not really about their Chinese identity or comparing their Chinese identities with others. But they are very united in being Chinese." The final faculty member felt that,

> This is an individual issue. Some are proud and this may be the result of where the overseas Chinese students come from. But some areas students are from they may not feel that proud about being Chinese. There may also be economic reasons. Many are not very proud of their identity.

When asked to comment whether Taiwan appreciates these overseas Chinese-heritage students and what they contribute to Taiwan one faculty member said, "I don't know. Some do, but many may not appreciate what they contribute to Taiwan. Taiwanese are not prejudiced in any way, but many would not think to appreciate what overseas Chinese offer to Taiwan." Meanwhile, the other two faculty members framed the impact these overseas Chinese students have in much more familiar contexts, "Overseas students provide an international perspective which the Taiwan students they work with can appreciate." In addition, a faculty member remarked, "In the classroom, I like the interactions between Taiwan students and overseas Chinese students as there are differences and you can understand how overseas Chinese go about learning Chinese and the difficulties they face in this process."

As to whether these overseas Chinese-heritage students come to better understand their Chinese identities in Taiwan, two believed this was the case. "Yes, through the education process they better understand and can access their Chinese identity," and "A little. They understand their Chinese identity." Meanwhile, one faculty member commented, "Not necessarily. You need to understand the individual student. Some students already have a very concrete overseas [heritage] Chinese identity . . . it will depend on why they are coming to Taiwan and where they are coming from."

In the opportunity faculty had to offer any additional comments about their work with overseas Chinese-heritage students, one said, "You need a little more care in supporting them. Giving them encouragement is very helpful." Another remarked,

> Actually, for most overseas Chinese students coming to Taiwan is a process. The overall influence on these students by coming here is very great . . . Most of the overseas Chinese student experiences in Taiwan are positive. Taiwan society gives them a good impression. The education they receive here makes them more competitive for their future local contexts.

A faculty member's comment was very appreciative of overseas Chinese students in Taiwan, as shown in the following remark:

I really look forward to overseas Chinese students coming to Taiwan because of their international capabilities. I can feel their gentleness, and see their willingness to work hard, and their multiple and varied abilities. I am very grateful for having the opportunity to work with them and respect their multiple abilities and contributions.

Discussion

Overseas Chinese-heritage students in this study believe they have strong Chinese listening and readings abilities. These are passive language skills which only require them to interpret, not actively create or produce language. While they also believe their ability to speak Chinese is a strength, they list it along with Chinese culture, grammar, and written Chinese as areas they will need further support in to be successful Chinese language teachers. For support with writing Chinese, as one student mentioned earlier, this may just be a result of the fact that their home environments do not widely employ written Chinese. All other aspects of Chinese language overseas that students in this study list as potential weaknesses could actually be unrealized strengths. This is especially true if what these Chinese-heritage students are learning in Taiwan is seen as in addition to their local language realities and not normed to what is expected in Taiwan.

To further unpack this framing, Liu (2015, p. 186) suggests that, "Increasing connectivity means that cultures circulate in different ways . . . We define our own identities and those of others within the realm of an interdependent and interconnected network of a global society." An interconnected network is certainly something these overseas Chinese-heritage students in Taiwan are experiencing firsthand. These experiences are providing them with opportunities to compare Chinese languages and cultures, reflect on the similarities and differences they encounter, and develop their own conceptualizations for how to situate these multiple linguistic and cultural realities in relation to those they already possess.

Overseas Chinese-heritage students are also surely no strangers to operating appropriately in intricate linguistic environments. Wei provides a description of such environments as,

> a complex pattern of polyglossia has emerged . . ., with the local language as the socioeconomically High variety, the regional variety of Chinese as the community High variety, Putonghua as the politically High variety within certain contexts, and the other Chinese regional languages that do not belong to the immediate community . . . Low varieties.
>
> (Wei, 2016, p. 8)

Coming from such varied and nuanced linguistic environments would seemingly provide those who have successfully functioned in such spaces a unique skill base to work from and potentially expand upon.

238 Ya-Hsun Tsai and Jason D. Hendryx

As for where these overseas Chinese-heritage students are returning to after they leave Taiwan, Wang (2008, pp. 129–132) proposes that, "the types of overseas Chinese communities which have the potential to survive into the future [are] . . . the faithful, the peripheral, and the marginal." If Taiwan is categorized as a faithful community, then the overseas Chinese going to Taiwan for study are from what Wang would categorize as peripheral and marginal overseas Chinese groups. For the peripheral, "Much depends on their numbers and their connection with Chinese education" (p. 130). Peripheral communities are suggested to be those found in Malaysia and Singapore. Meanwhile, for marginal overseas communities, "Their educated members have combined older Chinese cultural artefacts with indigenous and modern Western cultures and moulded their own sub-cultures" (p. 131).

Data from this study would suggest that overseas Chinese students from peripheral communities have more established Chinese identities, while students from marginal communities experience much more growth and development in their knowledge about what it means to be Chinese during their time in Taiwan.

In returning to understanding how self-identified problem areas with the Chinese language by overseas Chinese-heritage students could actually be unrealized strengths, it would seem that these weaknesses are only identified through the lens of comparison when these students are in Taiwan and exposed to the kind of Chinese language and culture that is prevalent there. That being the case, the new Chinese language and cultural elements they meet with in Taiwan can continue to grow and improve in them after initial contact and instruction. So that when they return home it will be with additional understandings of Chinese languages and cultures that should only be advantageous for the returnees.

It is important to consider that the continued willingness of overseas Chinese to seek out and align themselves with what being Chinese means in China, and by extension in Taiwan, will be dependent on a number of factors. Wang suggests,

> What will be decisive is the quality of the modern culture that China projects to the outside world. If that is neither imperial nor heavily Confucianized but contains attractive universal attributes that invite admiration from a global audience, diaspora cultures could reinvent themselves regularly and never lose their claims to Chineseness.
>
> (Wang, 2008, p. 132)

In some regards this seems to be happening in Malaysia, for example, where Wang (2016, p. 215) notes that some Malaysian Chinese feel that, "Chinese language has already become one of the international languages, which they are proud of."

Returning to the two theoretical frames aimed at situating the Chinese languages of overseas Chinese students in Taiwan introduced earlier; for the first, data collected here suggest that while these students do experience some mobility while engaged in making Mandarin Chinese a commodity, this mobility is temporary, and eventually requires that they return to their home countries where their new Chinese language knowledge can be effectively utilized. Faculty views shared here seem to echo earlier observations. Song (2005), for example remarks overseas Chinese language teachers who study Mandarin Chinese in Taiwan, "can gain the acceptance of learners with similar backgrounds . . . and also use their own learning experiences as a guide" (p. 103).

There is no mention in Song (2005), or in data collected for this study, about overseas Chinese going outside of Asia to teach Mandarin Chinese. Perhaps there are conceptions about overseas Chinese that place them clearly outside of what it means to truly be Chinese. For example, not too long ago Su, Xu, and Li (2006, p. 218), said that overseas Chinese students, "aside from having the same yellow skin and black eyes, actually, they are just like foreign students."

The second theoretical frame, the proposed four hierarchies of instructed Chinese language tied to prestige (as well as economic) values, seems to be somewhat confirmed here. This is evidenced by overseas Chinese students continuing to travel to places like Taiwan and China to learn more mainstream Mandarin Chinese. Wang (2016, p. 215) also, "noted a rise in Mandarin use by young people with a resulting decline in ancestral Chinese dialects" in Malaysia, which would suggest that young people there are in the process of attempting to move their Chinese language up within that hierarchy.

Implications

Some suggestions for further supporting overseas Chinese-heritage students studying to be Chinese teachers in Taiwan would be to understand the potential differences in the Chinese identities they possess. Chinese students coming from Wang's (2008) peripheral and marginal overseas communities require different levels of Chinese identity support. Being aware of the range of overseas Chinese identities students might have and developing various types of techniques for different kinds of Chinese student identities would potentially be of benefit not only for these students' academic success, but also for their future attachments to the language and culture.

In addition, to acknowledge the rich international and multilingual knowledge and experiences these overseas Chinese students possess, they could be provided with opportunities to speak about how Chinese languages and cultures function in their home realities at formal events, taking on expert status in front of their peers. Such speaking opportunities could also be encouraged in less formal gatherings at local schools and community centers.

Enhanced clarity in government and university policies concerning overseas Chinese students as well as additional scholarships, internships, and funding opportunities for them would be well received and has been suggested previously

(Song, 2005). Career guidance and continuing support for them and their teaching of Chinese after graduation would also be extremely prudent (Huang, 1995).

While there is always room for continuing improvement in any program or department, it seems that the data here confirms earlier work conducted on overseas Chinese students studying in Taiwan universities,

> the extent of the problems faced by international and overseas Chinese students studying in Taiwan were relatively minor . . . given the fact that the actual problems experienced by students in our sample were minor . . . it is clear that the sampled universities in Taiwan are doing something right.
>
> (Jenkins and Galloway, 2009, p. 167)

For the particular case of overseas Chinese students in this department studying to be Chinese language teachers, whether by chance, plan, or a combination of both, these students are for the most part being well prepared for having successful learning experiences in Taiwan.

In this regard, Lin, Hsu, and Lai (2011) comment about overseas Chinese in their study, which also seem to be describing students in this study, where those "who were satisfied with their university experience in Taiwan . . . were responsive to overcoming difficulties, establishing interpersonal interaction and social support networks, integrating cultural experiences, and developing their self-identity" (p. 804). In addition, it also seems that this particular department is providing their overseas Chinese students support with many of the areas Huang (1995) calls for, such as: class homework, economic difficulties, adapting to (a different) society, language, personal relations and social support systems, health and entertainment, and continuing to promote the functions of overseas Chinese support offices.

In closing, the overseas Chinese-heritage students studying to be Chinese teachers in Taiwan described by their teachers as multidimensional (and multi-competent), independent, and pure, can certainly be considered as the mothers of a future Chinese language revolution. The questions that remain are how far will such a language revolution reach, what forms will it take, and what Chinese languages will it use? Programs and students like the ones described here will be instrumental in creating the answers to those questions and many others.

References

Barrett, T. C. (2012). *The Chinese diaspora in South-East Asia: The overseas Chinese in Indo-China.* London, UK: I. B. Tauris.

Blunt, A. (2007). Cultural geographies of migration: mobility, transnationality and diaspora. *Progress in Human Geography, 31*(5), 684–694.

Chan, S.-D. (2016). Putonghua and Cantonese in the Chinese territories. In G. Leitner, A. Hashim, and H.-G. Wolf, (Eds.), *Communicating with Asia: The future of English as a global language* (pp. 188–204). Cambridge, UK: Cambridge University Press.

de Swaan, A. (2001). *Words of the world*. Cambridge, UK: Polity.

Huang, J. (2011). Umbilical ties: The framing of the overseas Chinese as the mother of the revolution. *Frontiers of History in China, 6*(2), 183–228.

Huang, L. H. (1995). Qiaosheng shiying wenti zhi tantao [The adjustment problems of Chinese students from overseas]. *Huli Yanjiu, 3*(3), 211–224.

Jenkins, J. R., and Galloway, F. (2009). The adjustment problems faced by international and overseas Chinese students studying in Taiwan universities: A comparison of student and faculty/staff perceptions. *Asia Pacific Education Review, 10*, 159–168.

Kuhn, P. A. (2008). *Chinese among others: Emigration in modern times*. Lanham, MD: Rowman & Littlefield.

Lin, Y.-N., Hsu, A. Y.-P., and Lai, P.-H. (2011). Life experiences of overseas Chinese university students in Taiwan. *College Student Journal, 45*(4), 793–805.

Liu, S. (2015). *Identity, hybridity, and cultural home: Chinese migrants and diaspora in multicultural societies*. London, UK: Rowman & Littlefield.

Ma, W., and Li, G. (Eds.). (2016). *Chinese-heritage students in North American schools: Understanding hearts and minds beyond test scores*. New York, NY: Routledge.

Rae, I., and Witzel, M. (2008). *The overseas Chinese of South East Asia: History, culture, business*. Basingstoke, UK: Palgrave MacMillan.

Skinner, W. (1959). Overseas Chinese in Southeast Asia. *The Annals of the American Academy of Political and Social Science, 321*, 136–147.

Song, R. Y. (2005). Cong [xuexizhe] dao [jiaoxuezhe]-Daxue qiaosheng huayuwen shizi peiyu yanjiu [From [learners] to [teachers]: Research in university-level overseas Chinese Mandarin teacher training]. *21 Shiji Huayu Jigou Yingyun Celüe yu Jiaoxue*, 101–108.

Su, Y. L., Xu, Y. H., and Li, X. (2006). Haiwai qiaosheng huiguo shengdu daxue zhi zhiyuan qingxiang, zaixue qingkuang yuqi xueye biaoxian [The orientation and school achievements of overseas Chinese students studying in Taiwan]. *Jiaoyu Ziliao yu Yanjiu, 68*, 197–220.

Wang, G, (2008). Flag, flame, and embers: Diaspora cultures. In K. Louie (Ed.), *The Cambridge companion to modern Chinese culture* (pp. 115–134). Cambridge, UK: Cambridge University Press.

Wang, X. M. (2016). The Chinese language in the Asian diaspora: A Malaysian experience. In G., Leitner, A. Hashim, and H.-G. Wolf, (Eds.), *Communicating with Asia: The future of English as a global language* (pp. 205–215). Cambridge, UK: Cambridge University Press.

Wei, L. (2016). Transnational connections and multilingual realities: The Chinese diasporic experience in a global context. In L Wei (Ed.), *Multilingualism in the Chinese diaspora worldwide: Transnational connections and local social realities* (pp. 1–12). New York, NY: Routledge.

Yen, C.-H. (2008). *The Chinese in Southeast Asia and beyond: Socioeconomic and political dimensions*. Hackensack, NJ: World Scientific.

Zoltán, D., and Taguchi, T (2010). *Questionnaires in second language research: Construction, administration and processing* (2nd edn). New York: Routledge.

242 Ya-Hsun Tsai and Jason D. Hendryx

Appendix A

Overseas Chinese-Heritage Student Survey

Data collected in this survey will be used as the content of an academic article to be published in a journal or as a book chapter. Data you provide will not be linked back to you and will not keep you from receiving any benefits you are entitled to in the future. Thank you for your participation.

1. How would you rate your Chinese language abilities in the following areas:

Area	Poor	So-so	Fair	Good	Excellent
Speaking:					
Listening:					
Reading (Simplified):					
Reading (Traditional):					
Writing (Simplified):					
Writing (Traditional):					
Grammar:					
Translation (into first language):					
Culture (from China or Taiwan):					
Other: ( ):					

2. In what areas do you think you need improvement in to be an effective Chinese language teacher?

Area	Needs Improvement		
	None	Some	A Lot
Speaking:			
Listening:			
Reading (Simplified):			
Reading (Traditional):			
Writing (Simplified):			
Writing (Traditional):			
Grammar:			
Translation (into first language):			
Culture (from China or Taiwan):			
Other: ( ):			

Question	Strongly Disagree	Disagree	Neutral	Agree	Strongly Agree
3. Taiwan has helped you realize your professional goals	1	2	3	4	5
4. Taiwan has helped you realize your personal goals	1	2	3	4	5
5. Taiwan has helped you more fully understand your Chinese heritage identity	1	2	3	4	5
6. Taiwan has helped you more fully understand your Chinese language abilities	1	2	3	4	5
7. Taiwan government and university policies have benefited you in your time here	1	2	3	4	5
8. You are proud to be a Chinese-heritage speaker	1	2	3	4	5
9. You feel more in touch with who you are and want to be in Taiwan	1	2	3	4	5
10. You look forward to returning home after you graduate	1	2	3	4	5
11. You feel people in Taiwan don't appreciate your heritage identity	1	2	3	4	5
12. Your experiences in Taiwan have been mostly positive	1	2	3	4	5

13. What specifically has Taiwan offered you that your home country could not?
14. In what areas could Taiwan have been more supportive in helping you reach your goals?
15. What would you like to say to Taiwan about your feelings toward the country and its people?
16. What do you see your role as in promoting Chinese language in the world?
17. What have you learned about yourself and your Chinese heritage identity in Taiwan that you were not aware of before you came here?
18. What do you think you will do as your future career?
19. If you could go back in time and decide again to come to Taiwan or not, would you? Why? Why not?
20. What is your age? 18–20 / 21–23 / 24 or older
21. What is your gender? Male/Female
22. What country are you from?
23. How long have you been in Taiwan?

24. What is the primary language of your country of citizenship?
25. What else would you like to share about your time in Taiwan? Thank you for your time and assistance!

Appendix B

Overseas Chinese-Heritage Student Interview

Data collected in this survey will be used as the content of an academic article to be published in a journal or as a book chapter. Data you provide will not be linked back to you and will not keep you from receiving any benefits you are entitled to in the future. You can choose not to answer any question and stop your participation at any time. This interview will be audio recorded and last approximately 30 minutes. Thank you for your participation.

1. What are the strengths of the university faculty you have worked with? List at least three strengths if possible and explain why you feel this way.
2. What are the weaknesses of the university faculty you have worked with? List at least three weaknesses if possible and explain why you feel this way.
3. What are three strengths you have as a speaker of Chinese?
4. What are three weaknesses you have as a speaker of Chinese?
5. How have you improved yourself during your time in Taiwan?
6. What are the main differences between Taiwan and your home country and what opportunities have those differences provided for you?
7. What are the main differences between Taiwan and your home country and what limitations have those differences imposed on you?
8. Has your own understandings of your Chinese identity evolved during your time in Taiwan? Why do you think this way?
9. What else would you like to share about your time in Taiwan? Thank you for your time!

Appendix C

Faculty Interview

Data collected in this survey will be used as the content of an academic article to be published in a journal or as a book chapter. Data you provide will not be linked back to you and will not keep you from receiving any benefits you are entitled to in the future. You can choose not to answer any question and stop your participation at any time. This interview will be audio recorded and last approximately 30 minutes. Thank you for your participation.

1. What do you believe to be the strengths of the Chinese-heritage students in your program? List at least three strengths if possible and explain why you feel this way.
2. What do you believe to be the weaknesses of the Chinese-heritage students in your program? List at least three weaknesses if possible and explain why you feel this way.
3. What obstacles will these heritage students need to overcome in the future? Do you think they will be able to?
4. What could Taiwan do more to help these students be successful in their future careers?
5. If you could do one more thing to help your heritage students what would it be?
6. If you were going to describe your heritage students in a word, what word would it be?
7. Do you think your heritage students are proud of their heritage identity? Why? Why not?
8. Do you think Taiwan appreciates these heritage students and what they contribute to Taiwan when they are here? Why? Why not?
9. Do you think your heritage students come to better understand their Chinese identity when they are in Taiwan? Why? Why not?
10. Is there anything else you would like to share about your experiences with Chinese-heritage students? Thank you for your time!

PART IV

Summary and Closing Thoughts

14

CHINESE–HERITAGE LEARNERS DE/RE-TERRITORIALIZING TRANSNATIONAL SOCIAL FIELD

Identities, Conflicts, and Possibilities

Guofang Li and Wen Ma

From its beginning in January 2016 to its completion in January 2017 when the newly elected 45th American president took office, the production process of this volume has witnessed increased nationalism and xenophobia around the world, evidenced by a series of historical events such as the Black Lives Matter movement and the ups and downs throughout the U.S. presidential election, Brexit in Britain, the fight against ISIS in the Middle East, and the refugee crisis in Europe and other parts of the world. Simultaneously, this book-making process has also witnessed increased transnational flow of Chinese people, goods, and businesses around the world in light of China's growing economic power, rising competitiveness in its domestic labor market, worsening air and food pollution, and the recent second-child policy that enabled and encouraged many of its middle- and upper-class citizens to move out of the country and settle elsewhere in the world in search of a better education and a better life. The increased Chinese exodus at a time of awakened nationalism and intensifying xenophobia makes this book even more relevant and timely, as education will no doubt be a central concern as millions of them establish new lives globally.

In this edited volume, we have asked researchers around the world to describe Chinese-heritage students' experiences in language and education in and outside of schools, the educational challenges and difficulties they encounter in their particular local environment, how they make sense of their multiple ethnic and sociocultural identities, as well as how they develop coping strategies to navigate the complex linguistic, cultural, and social landscapes. For each chapter, we have also asked researchers to reflect on educational practices that work for these learners in specific contexts and globally.

Collectively, the chapters reveal Chinese-heritage students' glocalized educational experiences filled with triumphs, challenges, and possibilities. On the one hand, their experiences are inseparably shaped by the place-based educational policies, politics, and practices as well as the sociolinguistic realities in their host environment. On the other, they actively align their educational experiences with transnational identities that are placeless and limitless, afforded by unceasing territorialization of their relations to the homeland.

According to Robertson (1992), territorialization involves a dual process of de-territorialization characterized by cultural distancing from the locality and/or national identity (i.e., loss of natural the natural relation between culture and the social ad geographic territories) and re-territorialization characterized by relocalizations of old and new symbolic productions. For the second or third generation, such de/re-territorialization is realized through following their parents' or grandparents' transnational fantasies or their root-finding educational journeys; for the Chinese students leaving China, this dual process of territorialization is through engaging in a renewed sense of homeland and their prior educational experiences enabled by their transnational mobility. Central to all of their experiences is multilingualism, which provides both possibilities and limitations to the educational trajectories of Chinese-heritage learners in their glocalized experiences.

The Glocalization of Educational Experiences: Challenges and Dilemmas

Although globalization is inevitably a process of the global meeting the local, resulting in "the simultaneity—the co-presence—of both universalizing and particularizing tendencies" (Robertson, 1992, p. 16), the process and its effects on social identities (i.e., how people identify about themselves in relation to others) have been subject to different interpretations (Ariely, 2016; Louie, 2000). While some scholars (e.g., Beck, 2008; Sassen, 2003) believe that globalization, with the increasing blurring of borders and cultures, has created transnational, cosmopolitan identities that transcend national identities, others argue that people may cling to their national identities as a safety net in the process of transnational mobility; globalization therefore reinforces the sense of national belonging (see Ariely, 2016). Research on the Chinese diaspora has documented both tendencies. For example, L. J. C. Ma (2003), in his groundbreaking work on space, place, and identity of Chinese transnational mobility, described contemporary Chinese transnational experiences as both place-based (e.g., influenced by place of origin) and place-nourished (as affected by local contexts of reception), resulting in dynamic and fluid identities that must be interpreted both within the local environments and across global contexts.

Across the chapters in this book, we see both place-based and place-nourished effects on Chinese-heritage students' educational experiences and identity development. For the Chinese learners pursuing higher education in Hong Kong (Chapter 6, this volume), Japan (Chapter 2), and New Zealand (Chapter 5), their transnational experiences were shaped both by their prior schooling experiences, in China and their current institutional culture, social experiences, and political climate in the host context. Similarly, for the second or third generation born in the host context such as Hong Kong (Chapter 1), Indonesia (Chapter 3), Spain (Chapter 7), South Africa (Chapter 4), Singapore (Chapter 12), and Hungary (Chapter 10), their schooling experiences are simultaneously shaped by their parents' and grandparents' nostalgic memories (or fantasies) of their motherland China and an increased flow of culture and information through media (despite their lack of identification with China as motherland) and the local racial relations and tensions (e.g., in South Africa and Spain), racial and sociopolitical climate (e.g., Indonesia), language policies (e.g., Singapore), and local economy (e.g., Hungary) in their adopted motherland.

Formation of these dual-referenced transnational identities is apparently not a process void of struggles and challenges. While the China-born transnational migrants struggled with learning and socializing in local languages (such as Cantonese in HK, Japanese in Japan, and Hungarian in Hungary) and English as an international language, local-born second or third generation struggled with gaining and maintaining literacy skills in their heritage languages and in some cases, cultures. For the Chinese-heritage students born in the UK who were seeking a degree in Chinese (Chapter 9), those born in Asian countries who attended a root-searching program in Taiwan (Chapter 13), they also experienced what Louie (2000) called "a cultural gap" as a result of such educational experiences and contacts with native-speaking, China-born peers. That is, even though they shared the same physical features, they were a culturally different group from their China-born peers. This is why a student from Chapter 13 felt like an "outsider" in Taiwan and felt "uncomfortable" about his/her Chinese identity. They were also not accepted as *real Chinese*. As a Chinese professor in Taiwan in Chapter 13 commented, "aside from having the same yellow skin and black eyes, actually, they are just like foreign students." Similar cultural gaps were also experienced by Mainland Chinese students studying in Hong Kong, who found themselves not only linguistically but also culturally different from their Cantonese-speaking HK-born peers (Chapter 6).

The complication is that they were considered different from those "foreign students" (referred to as students of non-Chinese backgrounds, especially those from Western countries), too. The status and experiences of being a "middle-man minority" (Ma, 2003) who are considered neither as locals in the host environment nor as Chinese nationals born in China was shared by both groups of learners. Jie's words in Chapter 2 well illustrate this status, "That makes me be in another position to be looked at . . . Like a totally different, like a third position. I'm neither this nor that."

Being "neither this nor that" and belonging neither here nor there can be challenging to these heritage learners. While the China-born students expressed a love-and-hate feeling toward their education in China (e.g., Chinese students in New Zealand, Chapter 5), local-born second or third generation struggled with a love-and-hate relationship with learning Chinese and being Chinese in local contexts. For example, the two Indonesian-Chinese youths in Lie's chapter struggled with finding affiliation with peers who did not speak Chinese or immediate incentive to maintain their investment in learning Chinese other than potential career benefits in the distant future. Some, like Andrew and Bill who grew up in South Africa, and Yan in Hungary, decided to forego their Chinese identities in order to fit in with the local peers (see Chapters 4 and 10). Some, as the Zeng brothers demonstrated in the Hungarian contexts, retreated to the ethnic social networks both offline and online within the transnational Chinese social field. Despite the challenges, some, such as James and Sarah in the South African contexts, had managed to take up hybrid identities and seek sense of belonging in both worlds.

In sum, the "multi-scalar scapes" (Appadurai, 1996) of both the global and the local influences have resulted in tensions and challenges in their transnational social lives and educational experiences, which, in turn, engendered the Chinese-heritage students' complex, shifting, and divergent identities.

Re/De-Territorializing Transnational Social Fields: Strategies and Stratification

The Chinese-heritage learners, however, are not passive in this dual process. As their stories reveal in this volume, they actively rework the social norms and relations in their transnational social fields that increasingly span borders, spaces, and time (Levitt and Schiller, 2003). In the process of navigating their educational experiences in their specific transnational contexts, the Chinese learners have often reinvented alternative possibilities in juxtaposing relationships among Mandarin Chinese, heritage dialect (such as Cantonese or Hakka), local languages (such as Hungarian), and English. As their stories demonstrate, the students and their families engage in active processes of both de-territorializing (i.e., distancing from) their affiliations to motherland, mother tongue Mandarin Chinese, local languages, and English, and re-territorialization by innovatively reorganizing the existing social relations and establishing new patterns of affiliation and avoidance.

The case of de-territorialization is exemplified by the Chinese international students in New Zealand (Chapter 5) who were eager to throw away their educational baggage from the Chinese education system (which they referred to as "poisonous") to embrace the more liberal education offered in the host country. Similarly, the Chinese students in the Japanese English-medium university engaged in an educational experience where the Chinese language was irrelevant in the formal curriculum and in the job market. As a result, the students increasingly recognized the importance of the local language, Japanese, followed by English in the labor market.

For the local-born second or third generation such as those in South Africa and in Hungary, de-territorialization took the path of de-association from the Chinese language and/or culture. As illustrated above, several participants in the South African study deliberately moved out of the Chinese language and/or cultural communities in order to establish complex racial and linguistic relations with peers in their specific social environments. Similarly, situated in economically depressed Hungary, more and more of the second-generation Chinese were being trained for transnationalism that increasingly diminished the need to know Hungarian or Chinese.

The Chinese-heritage learners also engaged in an active re-territorialization process to realign different social relationships. The elite Hong Kong-Chinese students (Chapter 1), for example, grew up in HK but received English education due to their families' transnational educational goals for them. As a result, they had very limited proficiency in Mandarin or Cantonese. Their elite education with a global mobility, however, mismatched their localized university education based in HK. To fit in the new institutional culture, these students actively repositioned themselves and transformed the current linguistic hierarchies among the Chinese language dialects by "changing toward a more translingual perspective with great flexibility" between Mandarin and Cantonese.

Re-territorialization is also evident in Chapter 13 about Chinese-heritage learners born in Asian countries with varied levels of Chinese proficiency and cultural knowledge who sought improvement in Chinese in Taiwan in hope to gain "acceptance" as Chinese and become Chinese teachers in their home countries. As a result of their educational experiences, many of them overcame "feelings of inferiority" about their Chinese identity and "started to feel proud." Similar feelings of inferiority are also reflected in Australian Chinese students' low self-perception despite their superior performance in both English and math assessments as compared to their English speaking peers (Chapter 8). Re-territorializing the hierarchical social relations often help learners regain a sense of self and pride in one's ethnic identity. Mei Ling, a Chinese student situated in Spain (Chapter 7) who felt inferior and was considered "different" due to systematic discrimination in her K-12 schooling experiences, for example, eventually repositioned herself after a series of negative experiences through gaining a set of survival skills, "the picaresque, when and how to act, when to be careful and when to be just there." Her sense of empowerment in the reconstructed self-identity was evident after this painful process of re-territorialization: "there always is a winning . . . We knew we were different, but we were not worse, we were better."

It must be noted that amid the complex processes and cycles of de/re-territorialization, English language's "hypercentral" status (de Swaan, 2001) remained unaltered across the transnational social fields. Education with this monolingual habitus across the transnational social fields that are inherently multilingual may limit Chinese-heritage students' future possibilities and mobilities.

Limitations and Possibilities of Multilingualism

Intuitively one would agree that multilingualism should be an important part of Chinese-heritage learners' linguistic capital in the transnational social fields that must be maximized. The experiences documented in this volume, however, suggest the preference of English over Chinese (Mandarin or Cantonese or other dialects) and other languages in the glocal education contexts. Gramling (2009) calls this intimate, yet adverse relationship between multilingual practices and monolingual policy and ideology the new "cosmopolitan monolingualism." This monolingual transnational habitus neglects the Chinese learners' non-English competences and capacities and limits their possibilities of achieving their full potential in the transnational social fields.

Cases in point are the international schools in Hong Kong and Hungary and English-medium university in Japan where the elite schooling is built on the monolingual framing of international education characterized by an emphasis on knowledge created in and communicated through English and little attention to the linguistic and cultural context in which such knowledge will be used (Liddicoat and Crichton, 2008). As a result of this monolingual mindset, few actually achieved true multilingualism that fully extended their potential in different languages. The learners in HK failed to learn their mother tongue in their motherland, which in turn affected their college education in HK. Similarly, the students in Japan failed to learn functional Japanese, which affected their employment opportunities in Japan; the students in Hungary failed to learn Hungarian (and Chinese), which made their integration into the local communities difficult and unattainable. For these learners, there is a need to reconsider what international education means and how it can promise or block their future development trajectories.

Although Chinese-heritage language learning is affected by an array of factors (e.g., availability of materials, policies, and environment) (Li and Wen, 2015), this monolingual transnational habitus has definitely been taken up by Chinese-heritage learners and affected their motivation to learn Chinese. For example, Zeth in Indonesia (see Chapter 3) showed a preference to English over Chinese for which he had to study for a future with increasingly growing Chinese economy, but he admitted that, "if I speak Chinese, I can't connect with my friends. They won't understand me. And besides, I can't say things in Chinese like in English." Similarly, Mei Ling in Spain and learners in South Africa and Hungary found little incentive to invest in Chinese learning due to the limited use in the local contexts that emphasized the promising future of learning and knowing English. These learners' lack of awareness of the power of multi-lingualism, therefore, contributed to their low levels of proficiency in Chinese both in oral language and in literacy. The limitations in their Chinese literacy skills will be no doubt affect their future employment in transnational settings (e.g., as Chinese teachers or in companies that require high levels of Chinese reading and writing).

Nevertheless, despite these limitations, the chapters also show promising possibilities to address these conflicts. Different educational programs (such as root-searching cohort programs in Taiwan; and degree programs for Chinese-heritage learners in the UK) and different ways of teaching Chinese such as a morphological approach experimented by Singaporean teachers (Chapter 12) all show promises of affirming the leaners' Chinese ethnic identities and improving their proficiencies in Chinese literacy. More innovative language and cultural programs that address these learners' needs to achieve full multilingualism and multiculturalism will provide more opportunities in their transnational social lives.

Conclusion

In conclusion, this volume presents a picture of heterogeneous ways of being Chinese-heritage learners in the local-global nexuses. As we noted in the Introduction, the heterogeneity and fluidity of Chinese-heritage students' pathways in education necessitates a socially situated perspective of their educational experiences that are anchored in their specific local contexts and simultaneously connected with various transnational space and time. Collectively, the Chinese-heritage learners' experiences demonstrate that while globalization shapes the relations between the places where these learners live and their cultural activities, their educational experiences, and their sociocultural identities; in the meantime, it is also actively transformed by leaners' localized educational and everyday experiences. As their stories reveal, this complex dual process is filled with struggles, dilemmas, and contradictions that can have a profound impact on the learners' being and belonging in the increasingly complex, disconnected transnational spaces across borders and time. The bipartisan nature of this process calls for more research on the relationships between learners' agency and their glocalized educational conditions from an interdisciplinary perspective, including (although not limited to) regional racial relations, transnational communities, multilingualism, cross-cultural China studies, and geography-based identities.

As well, we suggest to move beyond the concept of a unified, essentialized transnational Chinese diaspora (Louie, 2000) to differentiate among the groups, for example, between the China-born and local-born Chinese who have different language and cultural backgrounds as well as different educational needs and challenges. With increasing flows of people, goods, and information across borders, understanding how these different Chinese-heritage leaners engage in life and education and how to help them work against the ideology of cosmopolitan monolingualism will lead to new possibilities in identity formation and transformation in a glocalized world in the twenty-first century.

References

Appadurai, A. (1996). *Modernity at large: Cultural dimensions of globalization.* Minneapolis, MN: University of Minnesota Press.

Ariely, G. (2016). Global identification, xenophobia and globalisation: A cross-national exploration. *International Journal of Psychology*. Retrieved from http://onlinelibrary.wiley.com/wol1/doi/10.1002/ijop.12364/full.

Beck, U. (2008). Mobility and the cosmopolitan perspective. In W. Canzler, V. Kaufmann, and S. Kesselring (Eds.), *Tracing mobilities: Towards a cosmopolitan perspective* (pp. 25–35). Aldershot, UK: Ashgate.

de Swaan, A. (2001). *Words of the world: The global language system*. Amsterdam, the Netherlands: Polity Press.

Gramling, D. (2009). The new cosmopolitan monolingualism: On linguistic citizenship in twenty-first century Germany. *Teaching German, 42*(2), 130–140.

Levitt, P., and Schiller, G. N. (2003). Transnational perspectives on migration: Conceptual-Izing simultaneity. *International Migration Review, 38*(3), 1002–1039.

Li, G., and Wen, K. (2015). East Asian heritage language education in the United States: Practices, potholes, and possibilities. *International Multilingual Research Journal, 9*(4), 274–290.

Liddicoat, A. J., and Crichton, J. (2008). The monolingual framing of international education in Australia. *Sociolinguistic Studies, 2*(3), 367–384.

Louie, A. (2000). Re-territorializing transnationalism: Chinese Americans and the Chinese motherland. *American Ethnologist, 27*(3), 645–669.

Ma, L. J. C. (2003). Space, place and transnationalism in the Chinese diaspora. In L. J. C. Ma and C. Cartier (Eds.), *The Chinese diaspora: Space, place, mobility, and identity* (pp. 1–49). New York, NY: Rowman and Littlefield Publishers, Inc.

Robertson, P. (1992). *Globalization: Social theory and global culture*. Thousand Oaks, CA: Sage.

Sassen, S. (2003). Globalization or denationalization? *Review of International Political Economy, 10*(1), 1–22.

AFTERWORD

Towards *Worlding Practice*

Angel M. Y. Lin

As the editors write in their Introduction to this volume, the notion of "Chinese-heritage learners" is at best a shorthand to denote a great diversity of learners who are in one way or another seen as sharing some "Chineseness" (and that begs the question of what counts as "Chineseness"). The 13 research reports collected in this volume present a great variety of contexts and different challenges, issues and experiences of different kinds of Chinese-heritage learners in different parts of the world. How to make sense of a collection of studies on such a great variety of contexts; what are the emergent and convergent themes coming out of this volume, and what is the way forward in this area of research—these are issues that I hope to address in this Afterword. In the following, I will first outline two emergent themes: 1) individual trajectories of Chinese-heritage learners and the migrant experience, and 2) international education and transnationalism. Then I will discuss a paradox which can be summed up in a remark made by a Chinese-heritage learner in Hungary, "Our homeland is China but English is good everywhere" (Chapter 10, this volume).

Individual Trajectories of Chinese-Heritage Learners and the Migrant Experience

One convergent theme emerging from these chapters is the importance to document and theorize the individual trajectories and life stories of Chinese-heritage learners and their migrant experiences. The research reports speak to the multifarious ways in which these trajectories can take shape and the impossibility of talking about the migrant experience *in the singular*, as it manifests itself in so many different ways in different contexts. Yet, it is still useful to talk about "the migrant experience," which shares some common characteristics; for example,

258 Angel M. Y. Lin

the likelihood of marginalization and discrimination; the perceived need (although not always shared by all Chinese-heritage learners) to integrate into the host society; the (young) immigrants' desire to be the same as their peers, or at least not to be singled out by their peers as "an outsider" or "different"; their desire (or lack of it) to (re-)connect with one's cultural roots through maintaining or (re-)learning the Chinese language, and so on. In a way, these migrant experiences of the Chinese-heritage learners are not too different from other ethnic migrants' experiences. However, what makes the Chinese-heritage learners' migrant experiences stand out (if not unique, as one can argue that many other ethnic migrant groups share a similar value too), as many of the chapters in this volume testify to, is the traditional Chinese value of emphasizing hard work and education (albeit with some exceptions) as a means for survival and socioeconomic mobility in a harsh environment. However, racist and social discrimination does eat into the self-image of the young Chinese-heritage learners; for example, they feel that they are not performing as well as their counterparts in the host country even though they are in fact performing better in key subject areas (see Chapter 8). In some situations, they endure bullying and harsh treatments by their peers and teachers (see Chapter 7). Those who have survived these discriminatory treatments have done so by working hard and achieving good academic results and some form of socioeconomic mobility. But they also need to pay a huge price in terms of their social development—they are either studying or helping out in their parents' shops and they don't have any time of their own. Many chapters in this volume have done a good job documenting individual trajectories and personal stories of migration and settlement, testifying to the resiliency and resourcefulness of many migrant Chinese-heritage learners.

International Education and Transnationalism

Another emerging theme is the rising aspirations of Chinese-heritage learners (or of their parents) to acquire international education as a marker of global citizenship. Many Chinese students leave their familiar sociocultural environments to pursue English medium higher education, and face different challenges of cultural adaptation and clashes of worldviews, whether it is in Hong Kong, Japan, or New Zealand. Some have taken these as opportunities to take a critical, fresh look at their own home country's cultural and social order as well as that of their host country (or "the hidden curriculum," see Chapter 5), and expand their worldviews and cultural horizons. Some have resorted to remaining in their circles of friends from their home country and focus exclusively on their academic studies, as trying to socialize with the local students proves too hard or too unrewarding. English is part and parcel of this dream of internationalization but unsuccessful attempts in socializing with local students often mitigate against their opportunities to interact more in English. Interestingly, international education in the form of English-medium international schools in one's home country has created the

Afterword: Towards *Worlding Practice* **259**

"migrant experience" for otherwise local students. For example, the Chinese-heritage learners in international schools in Hong Kong experience marginalization of their mother tongue in the English-dominant culture of international schools, where speaking any language other than English is frowned upon by teachers and school administrators. While becoming native-like in English, they have lost out on the opportunity to develop high levels of Chinese literacy (see Chapter 1). This strange "bubble"—international schools in Hong Kong—can be seen as providing a kind of self-imposed "migrant experience," paradoxically created in one's own hometown. Similarly, in Hungary, "parallel transnationalism" is sought after when Chinese traders/entrepreneurs in Third World countries send their children to private, fee-paying, English-medium international schools, which cater for Chinese, Russian, and Arab students (see Chapter 10). This brings us to the consideration of the paradox below.

Paradox: "Our Homeland is China but English is Good Everywhere!"

As many authors in this volume have witnessed, Chinese-heritage learners (and their parents) are not necessarily keen on reconnecting with their cultural roots through learning and mastering the Chinese language. The language–identity link can be a fluid, unstable one (see Chapter 4) when it comes to the language hierarchy of cosmopolitan globalism: English is often perceived as a marker of transnationalism and the entry-ticket to the world of "globe-trotting corporate men/women" (see Chapter 10). The promise of a global cosmopolitan life promised by English-medium international schools keeps luring parents to send their children to these schools, even at the expense of developing high levels of Chinese literacies. Migrant Chinese-heritage learners in English-speaking countries also face strong pressure to integrate into the host society and learning English is often their first priority.

The Way Forward: Towards *Worlding Practice*

The chapters in this collection have provided us with some important pointers about what future work needs to be done. They point to the need to engage in research that aims at unpacking some of these paradoxes: for example, English being perceived as the ticket to cosmopolitan transnationalism; the sentiment that it is good to have Chinese too, but English is more important. Future research would need to look at alternative forms of (non-elite) transnationalism that does not hinge on mastery of one single language (often it means mastery of English). Educational research questions such as "What are the appropriate pedagogical strategies (e.g., use of popular culture; see Chapter 9) to motivate Chinese-heritage learners' learning of Chinese?" will be as important as cultural studies research questions such as: How can a non-elite multilingual transnationalism provide alternatives to language hierarchies embedded in global capital-driven transnationalism? What kinds of research and education projects are needed to contribute to the possibility of creating a kind of *worlding practice*—a form of non-elite, non-state-defined, non-capital-governed multiculturalism that embraces "practices that infuse our arbitrary cultural lives with new things from cultural others in ambiguously and open-ended poetic ways to enable us to dwell and be at home with the complexity of the world" (Goh, 2014, p. viii)? In this endeavor, as in many others, educational linguists and language education researchers might find it fruitful to join hands with critical cultural studies scholars and linguistic ethnographers of youth (e.g., Pérez-Milans, 2016). This volume provides a very good beginning of this journey.

References

Goh, D. P. S. (Ed.). (2014). *Worlding multiculturalisms: The politics of inter-Asian dwelling.* London, UK: Routledge.

Pérez-Milans, M. (Ed.). (2016). *Reflexivity in late modernity: Accounts from linguistic ethnographies of youth (AILA Review, Vol. 29).* Amsterdam, the Netherlands: John Benjamins.

NOTES ON CONTRIBUTORS

Xiao Lan Curdt-Christiansen is an Associate Professor at the Institute of Education, University of Reading, UK. Email: x.l.curdt-christiansen@reading.ac.uk

Xuesong (Andy) Gao is an Associate Professor in the School of Education, University of New South Wales, Australia. His current research interests are in the areas of learner autonomy, language learning narratives, language education policy, and language teacher education. Email: andygohteacher@hotmail.com

Feifei Han works as a research fellow at the Centre for Research on Learning and Innovation, University of Sydney, Australia. Her current main research interests are applied and psycho-linguistics, educational psychology, and educational technology. Email: feifei.han@sydney.edu.au

Jason D. Hendryx taught Chinese at the University of Washington and at the United States Air Force Academy. He then went on to prepare future Chinese language teachers at National Taiwan Normal University and is currently the program coordinator for modern languages education at the University of Wyoming. Email: jhendryx@uwyo.edu

Jiangbo Hu is a research assistant in the Institute of Early Childhood Education, Macquarie University, Australia. She completed her PhD study in the Institute of Early Childhood Education of Macquarie University. She has rich working experiences in early childhood field in both China and Australia. Her study focuses on the cross-cultural language experiences of preschool-aged children in home and early childhood centers. Email: jiangbo.hu@students.mq.edu.au

262 Notes on Contributors

Guofang Li is professor and Tier 1 Canada research chair in transnational/global perspectives of language and literacy education of children and youth in the Department of Language and Literacy Education, University of British Columbia, Canada. Email: Guofang.li@ubc.ca

Zhen Li is a PhD student in the Faculty of Education, University of Hong Kong. She received her MPhil degree in second-language education with a distinction from the University of Cambridge, and her MA in anthropology from the Chinese University of Hong Kong. Email: hellozhenzhen@gmail.com

Anita Lie is a professor in the Graduate School and Faculty of Teacher Education, Widya Mandala Catholic University, Surabaya, Indonesia. Her areas of interest include teacher professional development, heritage language learning, and curriculum development. She has published numerous books and articles on those areas. Email: anitalie2003@gmail.com

Angel M. Y. Lin is professor of English language and literacy education at the Faculty of Education, University of Hong Kong. She is well-respected for her interdisciplinary research in multilingual and multicultural education, academic literacies, and language policy and practice in postcolonial contexts. Email: yeonmia@gmail.com

Jun Liu is vice provost for global affairs, dean of international academic programs, and professor of linguistics at Stony Brook University, USA. His research areas include intercultural communication, language education, and teacher development. Email: jun.liu@stonybrook.edu

Wen Ma is an associate professor of education at Le Moyne College, USA. His current research interests include using discussion as an instructional tool, the Eastern and Western learning cultures, English language learners, literacy/content literacy strategies, and teacher education. Email: maw@lemoyne.edu

Iulia Mancila is working at the Theory and History of Education Department, Culture of Diversity and School, Faculty of Education Science, University of Malaga, Campus Teatinos s/n, código 29071 in Spain. Email: imancil@uma.es

Pál Nyíri is professor of global history from an anthropological perspective at the Vrije Universiteit, Amsterdam, the Netherlands. Email: p.d.nyiri@vu.nl

Baoqi Sun is at the National Institute of Education, Nanyang Technological University, Singapore. Email: sunbaoqi@hotmail.com

Notes on Contributors **263**

Jian (Tracy) Tao is a lecturer in the School of Foreign Studies, Shanghai University of Finance and Economics, China. Her current research interests center around language teacher identity and agency. Email: tracy.taojian@gmail.com

Ya-Hsun Tsai is professor of the Department of Applied Chinese Language and Culture at National Taiwan Normal University. She is also the dean of the Division of Preparatory Programs for Overseas Chinese Students. She specializes in Chinese language teacher training, Chinese phonetics, assessment of Chinese language proficiency, and Chinese literature. Email: yahsun@ntnu.edu.tw

Hanae Tsukada is a classroom climate and educational resource developer at the Centre for Teaching, Learning and Technology at the University of British Columbia (UBC), Canada. She received an MA in comparative and international development education from the University of Minnesota, Twin Cities, and a PhD in educational studies from UBC. Email: hanae.tsukada@ubc.ca

Elmé Vivier is in the Department of Business Management, University of Pretoria, and Human Sciences Research Council, South Africa. Email: elmevivier@up.ac.za

Jiayi Wang is subject leader for Chinese and lecturer in Chinese language, cultural studies and interpreting and translation studies at the University of Central Lancashire, UK. She holds a PhD in applied linguistics from the University of Warwick. Her main research interests are language education, pragmatics, intercultural communication, and translation and interpreting studies. Email: jwang11@uclan.ac.uk

Alexander Seeshing Yeung is professor and deputy director of the Institute for Positive Psychology and Education at the Australian Catholic University. His expertise includes motivation, self-concept, cognition and instruction, and large-scale longitudinal research in education and psychology. Email: alexander.yeung@acu.edu.au

Ke Yu is at the Human Sciences Research Council, Pretoria, South Africa. Email: kyu@hsrc.ac.za

Xiudi Zhang is a doctoral student in the critical studies school of the Faculty of Education and Social Work, University of Auckland, New Zealand. Email: x.zhang@auckland.ac.nz

INDEX

Note
Page numbers in **bold** refer to **figures**, *italic* refer to *tables*, followed by 'n' refer to notes

abilities: innate 153; language 67, 71, *73*, 74, 77, 80, 229–232, 235; multiple 235, 237
academic self-concept 8, 141–159; impact of 142–143
Academic Self-Description Questionnaire II 146
academic socialization 105, 109–119; social networks for Mainland undergraduates in Hong Kong 106–108
achievement goals 141–142, 144–147, 150, 152–153, 155; impact of 143
achievements, in mathematics and English 141–159
activities, structured 197, *199–200*, 201, *202–203*
adaptation 7–8, 68, 106–107, 110, 114, 119, 130; strategic 125
affirmations, and comparisons 227–245
Afrikaans 72
Aparicio, R., and Portes, A. 124
apartheid 67, 70, 74–77, 80
Asano, S. 33
assumptions 135; experiences of 129–133
attitudes: discriminatory peer 132–133; distancing 167, 169–170, 173–174
Auerbach, C. F., and Silverstein, L. B. 35
Australian early childhood centers 9; language experiences 191–208

Australian students, Chinese-background 141–159
awareness, morphological 217–218

Baas, M. 41
Baker, C. 212
Barrett, T. C. 227
barriers: ideological 110–117; linguistic 110–117; sociocultural 110–114, 114–117
behaviors, discriminatory peer 132–133
being Chinese 67–83
beliefs, competence 8, 142, 144–145, 152–154
Bentler, P. M. 148
Benton, G., and Gomez, E. 3, 178
bilingual spaces 20–23
bilingualism 41, 69
biliteracy *see* Continua of Biliteracy
Biliteracy Development (Curdt-Christiansen and Hu) 218
biliterate and trilingual education policy 16
Black Economic Empowerment (BEE) court case (2008) 75
Black Lives Matter movement 249
Blunt, A. 228
boundaries, physical 108
Bourdieu, P. 106

Brexit 249
British Council 61, 161
Brown University, Office of International Programs 86
Browne, M., and Cudeck, R. 148
Budapest College of Economics 185

café-style focus groups 91–92
Cairney, T. 54
Campbell, J., and Li, M. 88
Cantonese 164, 166; clean 115
capital: economic 77; psychological 77
Carlson, J. S., and Widaman, K. F. 96
Cartier, C., and Ma, L. 2
Census (PRC, 2011/2012) 16
central language 228
centripetal learning 228
challenges: Mainland undergraduates adapting to Hong Kong 105–121; and motivations 161–176; and opportunities 123–139; of university-level language learners 166–170
Chan, H., and Mak, A. 141
Chan, S.-D. 229
Chao, R. K., and Kim, S. Y. 77
Cheung, G. W., and Rensvold, R. B. 149
children: in Hungary 177–188; language experiences in Australian early childhood centers 191–208; voices of 209–226
China Central Television (CCTV) 52, 57
Chinese for Chinese 173
Chinese Communist Party (CCP) 95–96, 184
Chinese as a foreign language (CFL) 14, 17, 19–23
Chinese problem 47
Chinese scheme 186
Chinese–heritage language (CHL) 7, 49–52, 55–61, 105, 161–167, 169, 172–173, 254; in Hong Kong 13–29
Chineseness 2–3, 50, 70, 74, 77–80, 238, 257
Chiu, M. M., and Klassen, R. M. 145
Christianity 81n4
citizenship, developed-country 183
class gap 36–38
classes, slow-paced 179
classroom practice, unproductive 222
Cohen, R. 79
collective memory 3
command (SFL theory) 194–195, 198, 199, 200–206

communication styles 110–111
communist tyranny 184
communities: faithful 238; marginal 238–239; peripheral 238–239; speech 76, 106
community organization, in Pretoria 75–76
Comparative Fit Index (CFI) 148–149
comparisons, and affirmations 227–245
compensation 130
competence 141–144, 146, 152–155; beliefs 8, 142, 144–145, 152–154
competence–affect distinction 142
competition orientation scale 147
confirmatory factor analysis (CFA) 147–148; and reliability 148
conflicts 249–256
Confucianism 141, 153, 155
Confucius 144–145
Confucius Institute (Budapest) 184
constructivism, social 16, 79
Continua of Biliteracy 13–14, 14–16, **15**; content 15; context 15, 19, 22–23; development 15, 19, 22–23; media 15
Cooc, N., and Oh, S. 125
cosmopolitan globalism 259
cosmopolitan monolingualism 254–255
cosmopolitan transnationalism 259
Coyle, A., and Jaspal, R. 79
Cudeck, R., and Browne, M. 148
cultural background 141–142, 144, 146, 148, 152–153, 232–233, 235
cultural differences 88, 110–111, 135, 152–154
cultural gap 251
cultural groups 49, 142, 147–148; factorial invariance across 149
cultural heritage 47–48, 52, 105–106, 110, 112, 117, 120, 192
cultural identity 7, 24, 47, 49, 51, 57, 60, 68, 80; formation of 52–55, 58–59
cultural issues 144–145
culture 1–10, 128, 141, 144, 146, 148, 152–155; effect of 151; and gender 145; popular 165–166, 172, 174
Curdt-Christiansen, X. 217, 220; and Sun, B. 209–226
curriculum, hidden 7–8, 85–101, 258

Daha, M. 74
Dai, D. Y. 145
Dandy, J., and Nettelbeck, T. 191–192
Davis, B., and Torr, J. 195

266 Index

Dawis, A. 47, 50
De Giorgi, A. 129
de/re-territorializing transnational social
field 249–256
degree in Chinese 164–166
demand 198, 200
developed-country citizenship 183
dialogue: long 203; short 203, 206
diaspora 1–5, 27, 61, 250, 255; three
pillars of 228
Dickinson, D. K., and Porche, M. V.
193
differences: cultural 88, 110–111, 135,
152–154; gender 144–145, 152
disaffiliation, towards schooling 133–135
discrimination 2–3, 33, 67, 69, 74–76,
124, 128, 134–137, 169, 186, 253,
258; attitudes and behaviors of peers
132–133; experiences of 129–133;
mainstream educational policies
129–130; pedagogic practices 130–132
distancing attitudes 167, 169–170,
173–174
domain-specificity 142–144, 150–151
Dörnyei, Z. 162
dual-track programs 168, 173
Duff, P., and Li, D. 50

early childhood centers, Australian 9,
191–208
economic capital 77
Education Research Funding Programme
(NIE) 218
educator–child interaction 191–207
Edwards, J. 77
emotional needs 5, 7, 49, 51, 57–58
engagement, towards schooling 133–135
English 164; achievements in 141–159;
limited usefulness 39–40
English language learners (ELLs) 191–193,
196, 204–205
English as a medium of instruction (EMI)
31, 36, 39, 42–43
English-as-a-foreign-language 165–166
English-medium (EM) education 14, 17,
27, 48, 105–106, 109, 118–119, 180,
252, 254, 258–259; international
students in Japan 31–46
Englishization 31–32, 34, 39, 42, 44; in
Japan 40–41
entrepreneurs, migrant 2, 7–8, 177–179,
180, 183, 187
Essomba, M. A. 130

ethnic identity 52, 69, 74–78, 172, 253,
255
Ethnic and Racial Studies 3
Eurocentrism 132
exclusion, social 4
expectations, higher 167
experiences 88, 100, 106–107, 110, 125,
137, 253, 255; glocalization of
250–252; immigrant 68–69, 74; in
Japan 38–41; learning 9, 26, 88, 105,
209, 239–240; and life strategies 31–46;
lived 1–10; place-nourished 250;
placed-based 250, 253; of prejudices
129–133

Facebook 185
factorial invariance: across cultural groups
149; across gender groups 148–149
faithful communities 238
family: educational strategies of 180–184;
needs 77–78
Feniger, Y., and Lefstein, A. 192
fitting in 68, 179
fluidity 71, 255; role of language in
79–80; of SABC identities 78
focus groups, café-style 91–92
Fong, V. L. 33
fooled generation 112
forced removals 69
foreign language schools 36
foreign students 239, 251
foreigners 21, 129
foul language 114–115
free play 197, 199–203, 206
fresh off the boat (FOB) CHL learners 7
friendships, normal 131
Fulbright Association 61

Gabriel, S. P. 4
Galloway, F., and Jenkins, J. 240
gao kao (entrance exam) 38
Gao, X., and Tao, J. 105–121
Gardner, R. 162; and Lambert, W. 162
Ge, W. 33
gender 8, 141–142, 146, 148–149,
152–155; background 141–142, 148;
and culture 145; differences 144–145,
152; effect of 151; factorial invariance
across groups 148–149; issues 143–144;
stereotyping 143, 152–154
Generation Z 60
global language system 228
globalism, cosmopolitan 259

globalization 100, 137, 250, 255
glocalization 5–6, 255; of educational experiences 250–252
goals: achievement goals 141–142, 143, 144–147, 150, 152–153, 155; mastery 143–145, 147, 149–151, 153; motivational 8, 141–159; performance 143, 145, 147, 149–153
Gomez, E., and Benton, G. 3, 178
Goyette, K., and Xie, Y. 125
Gramling, D. 254
grammatical understanding 193
grapheme–morpheme correspondence 214
Group Areas Act (South Africa, 1950) 69

Hail, H. C. 95
Hakka 164, 166–167, 170, 172
Halliday, M. A., and Matthiessen, C. M. 194, 205
Hamre, B. K. 193, 206
Han, F., and Yeung, A. 141–159
Hannon, P. 49, 54
Harré, R., and van Langenhove, L. 16
Hashimoto, K. 41
Hendryx, J., and Tsai, Y.-H. 227–245
Henze, J., and Zhu, J. 88
heritage language (HL) 13, 15–16, 26–27
heterogeneity 71, 81, 255; of SABC identities 78
hidden curriculum 7–8, 85–101, 258
higher education institutions (HEIs) 31–34, 42, 44
Hokuto Global University (HGU) 34–39, 41–43
Holmes, P. 97
Hong Kong: academic socialization 106–108; local-born CHL learners 13–29; Mainland undergraduates 105–121
Hoon, C.-Y. 50
Hornberger, N. 15
host country 3–6, 8–9, 34, 43, 69, 88, 95, 252, 258
host language 3–6, 8, 68
Hsu, A., Lai, P.-H. and Lin, Y.-N. 240
Hu, J. 191–208
Huang, J. 227
Huang, L. H. 240
Human Research Ethics Committee (Macquarie University) 195
Hungarian-Chinese Bilingual School 184

Hungary: children in 177–188; Ministry of Education 184
hypercentral language 228, 253

identity 1–10, 73, 128, 249–256; ethnic 52, 69, 74–78, 172, 253, 255; factors influencing 74–78; markers 78–80; and positioning 13–29; role of language in fluidity 79–80; SABC 78, 79–80, 81n2; social identity theory 68, 95, 250, see also cultural identity
ideological barriers 110–114, 114–117
immigrant experience 74; and language–identity nexus 68–69, see also migrant experience
immigrants 67, 70–71, 75–78, 123–124, 129–130, 133–134, 141
immobility 228
indefiniteness 41
independent thinking 98–99
individual trajectories, and migrant experience 257–258
individualization, party-state-managed 100
Indonesia, multilingual youths in 47–65
innate ability 153
insiders 209, 211
instruction 214–218; morphological 218, 220–223
instrumental motivation 162–163, 165, 172, 174
integration 124, 130, 132
integrative motivation 162–163, 165, 172, 174
interaction effect 151–152
interactional accomplishments 19
intercontinental life 184
intergenerational literacy practices 7, 49, 52–55
International Baccalaureate (IB) 14
International College (IC, Kasuga University) 34–39, 41–43
international education 38, 41, 43, 180, 182–183, 185, 254; and transnationalism 258–259
international schooling 13–14, 16–17, 19, 24, 26–27, 180–181, 183–185, 254, 258–259; continua of bilingual spaces 20–23
International Student Plan (Japan) 31
international students: in English-medium programs (Japan) 31–46; fee-paying 87, 89; hidden curriculum impact (New Zealand) 85–101

268 Index

internationalization 7, 31, 34–35, 107, 258
interpersonal functions (SFL theory) 191, 193–195, 198
intrinsic orientation scale 147
investment 48–49, 55–56, 58–61
ISIS (Islamic State of Iraq and Syria) 249

Jackson, P.W. 90
Japan: Englishization in 40–41; experiences in 38–41; International Student Plan 31; international students in English-medium programs 31–46; Project for Establishing University Network for Internationalization (2009) 31
Japanese: as competitive edge 36–37; significance 39–40
Japanese Visual Novels games 57
Jaspal, R., and Coyle, A. 79
Jenkins, J., and Galloway, F. 240
Jöreskog, K., and Sörbom, D. 148

K-12 1, 5, 13, 17, 22, 26–28, 253
K-20 5–6
Kim, S. Y., and Chao, R. K. 77
kitchen Chinese 72
Klassen, R. M., and Chiu, M. M. 145
Kuhn, P. A. 227
Kuntjara, E. 47

Lai, F. 145
Lai, P.-H., Lin, Y.-N. and Hsu, A. 240
Lambert, W., and Gardner, R. 162
Langenhove, L. van, and Harré, R. 16
language 1–10; abilities 67, 71, 73, 74, 77, 80, 229–232, 235; denigration of 79; environment challenges 55–58; factors influencing 74–78; foul 114–115; global system 228; heritage 13, 15–16, 26–27; host 3–6, 8, 68; hypercentral 228, 253; learning 211–214; level 162; morphographic 214; neutral 224; peripheral 228; role in fluidity of identities 79–80; supercentral 228; teachers in Taiwan 227–245; working 209, 224
language experiences, in Australian early childhood centers 191–208
language instruction, in Singapore 209–226
Language, Society and Identity (Edwards) 77

language–identity nexus 7–8, 70, 81, 259; and immigrant experience 68–69
laoban (bosses) 178
learner level 15–16, 27–28, 162
learners: local-born CHL 7, 13–29, 251–253, 255; non-heritage 163, 166–171, 173–174
learning 218–220; centripetal 228; language 211–214; situation level 162
learning Chinese, multilingual youths in Indonesia 47–65
learning experience 9, 26, 105, 209, 239–240; satisfaction 88
Lefstein, A., and Feniger, Y. 192
letter-to-phoneme correspondence 214
level: L1 15–16, 27–28; L2 15–16; language 162
Li, D., and Duff, P. 50
Li, G.: and Lu, X. 162–163, 173; and Ma, W. 1–10, 229, 249–256
Li, J. 144
Li, M., and Campbell, J. 88
Li, W. 3; and Zhu, H. 25
Li, X., Su, Y. and Xu, Y. 239
Li, Z. 13–29
Lie, A. 4, 47–65, 252
life: intercontinental 184; strategies and experiences 31–46
Lin, A. M. Y. 257–260
Lin, Y.-N., Hsu, A. and Lai, P.-H. 240
linguistic barriers 110–114; strategic responses to overcome 114–117
linguistic challenges 55–58, 61, 106, 110
literacy 49, 52, 54–55, 58–59; intergenerational practices 7, 49, 52–55
Liu, S. 237
Liu-Farrer, G. 33
lived educational experiences 1–10
local-born CHL learners 7, 251–253, 255; in Hong Kong 13–29
logical thinking 193
long dialogue 203
look-and-say approach 217
Louie, A. 251
low-income countries, migrant entrepreneurs in 177–179
Lu, X., and Li, G. 162–163, 173
Lüdtke, O., and Trautwein, U. 144
Luke, A. 1
luxury concerns 77

Ma, L. 250; and Cartier, C. 2
Ma, W., and Li, G. 1–10, 229, 249–256

Mainland undergraduates: in Hong Kong 105–121; social networks for academic socialization 106–108
mainstream educational policies, discriminatory 129–130
Mak, A., and Chan, H. 141
Mancila, I. 123–139
Mandarin 252
marginal communities 238–239
marginalization 3, 34, 167, 169, 173–174, 180, 204, 258–259
Marsden, A. 3–4
Marsh, H. W. 142, 146; *et al.* 147
mastery goals 143–145, 147, 149–151, 153
mathematics, achievements in 141–159
Matthiessen, C. M., and Halliday, M. A. 194, 205
MBA (Masters of Business Administration) 43
mealtime 197, *199*, 200, *201–202*, 203–204, 206
media 15
memory, collective 3
methodology, educational 100
middleman minorities 178, 251
Midgley, C., *et al.* 144
migrant entrepreneurs 2, 7–8, 180, 183, 187; in low-income countries 177–179
migrant experience 259; and individual trajectories 257–258, *see also* immigrant experience
mindset 119
mobility 228, 239; socioeconomic 33, 76–77, 258; upward 3, 77, 125, 183
monolingualism, cosmopolitan 254–255
morphographic language 214
morphological awareness 217–218
morphological instruction 218, 220–223
mother tongues (MTs) 32, 42, 68, 209–210, 219–220, 232, 254, 259; Cantonese 164, 166; English 164; Hakka 164, 166; Mandarin 252
motivational goals 8, 141–159
motivations: and challenges 161–176; integrative 162–163, 165, 172, 174; for pursuing a degree in Chinese 164–166; situational 163
Mu, G.M. 50
multi-scalar scapes 252
multiculturalism 48, 141, 154–156, 255, 260

multilingualism 1, 3–4, 7, 15, 19, 27, 41, 154, 185, 209, 239, 250, 253, 259–260; limitations and possibilities of 254–255; youths in Indonesia 47–65
multiple abilities 235, 237
multiple-indicator-multiple-indicator-cause (MIMIC) 145, 148–153, 155

narrative analysis 27, 126
National Institute of Education (NIE) 218
National Party (South Africa) 69
nationalism 249
Native Land Act (South Africa, 1913) 69
native speakers 42, 164–166, 171, 230
needs: emotional 5, 7, 49, 51, 57–58; family 77–78; psychological 5, 7, 57–58; socioeconomic advancement 76–77; special educational (SEN) 129, 179
neglect 167, 169, 173–174
Nettelbeck, T., and Dandy, J. 191–192
neutral language 224
New Zealand: impact of hidden curriculum on international students 85–101; studying abroad in 86–90
non-governmental organization (NGO) 116, 131
non-heritage learners 163, 166–171, 173–174
Norton, B. 49; and Toohey, K. 27
nurture 154
Nyíri, P. 4, 177–188

OECD (Organization for Economic Co-operation and Development) 4–5
Oetomo, D. 47
offer (SFL theory) 194–195, 198, *199*, 200–201, *202*, 203–206
Oh, S., and Cooc, N. 125
open questions 195
opportunities, and challenges 123–139
outsiders 4, 251, 258
overseas students, learning to be language teachers in Taiwan 227–245

Pan, C. 4
paradigmatic and analytic approach, to data analysis 109
parallel transnationalism 259
parental efforts 77–78
parental perceptions 128

Park, Y. J. 70, 77–78
party-state-managed individualization 100
pedagogic practices, discriminatory 130–132
pedagogical implications 59–60, 173–174
peers, discriminatory attitudes and behaviors 132–133
People's War of Resistance Against Japanese Aggression (PRC, 1937–1945) 95
performance goals 143, 145, 147, 149–153
peripheral communities 238–239
peripheral language 228
Phinney, J. 69
physical boundaries 108
Pieke, F. 183
PISA (Programme for International Student Assessment) 192
place-based experiences 250, 253
place-nourished experiences 250
play, free 197, 199–203, 206
policy, education 16, 129–130
politics, radical 112
popular culture 165–166, 172, 174
Porche, M. V., and Dickinson, D. K. 193
Portes, A., and Aparicio, R. 124
positioning, and identity 13–29
possibilities 249–256
prejudices 34, 135–136; experiences of 129–133
pressure, greater 167
Pretoria, Chinese community organization 75–76
Pretoria Chinese School (PCS) 71–72, 76, 78
privilege 32, 38, 43; enhancing 36–37
Project for Establishing University Network for Internationalization (Japan, 2009) 31
psychological capital 77
psychological needs 5, 7, 57–58
Putonghua 16–17, 107, 110, 114, 118, 237

Qiandao Ribao 52–53
quality, service 88
question (SFL theory) 194–195, 198–200, *201–202*, 203, 205–206
questionnaires 187n3; Academic Self-Description Questionnaire II 146; School Motivation Questionnaire 146

radical politics 112
re/de-territorializing transnational social field 249–256
real Chinese 78, 251
Reay, D., *et al.* 173
reception, context of 74–75, 80
Recognize First, Write Later principle 210, 217
reliability 146–147; and confirmatory factor analysis (CFA) 148
removals, forced 69
Rensvold, R. B., and Cheung, G. W. 149
repertoire 107, 109, 118
resources 106–107, 113, 115; differentials 109, 111, 118
Richards, R. D. 192, 204
RMSEA (root mean square error of approximation) 148–149
Robertson, P. 250

Safran, W. 3
school, success in 126–128
School Motivation Questionnaire 146
schooling: engagement and disaffiliation towards 133–135; parental perceptions of value 128, *see also* international schooling
school–university transition 23–27
Schwab, J., Westbury, I. and Wilkof, N. 135–136
screening out 179
second-generation 3, 8, 250–253; education in Spain 123–139; emerging trajectories of 185–187
sentiments 106–107, 115, 118, 120
separation, cause for 110
September 11 attacks (2001) 4
service quality 88
Sesotho 71
Shin, S.J. 77
short dialogue 203, 206
Silverstein, L. B., and Auerbach, C. F. 35
Singapore: language instruction in 209–226; Ministry of Education 211
Singapore National Academy (SNA) 52–53
single-track programs 174–175
Sinophobia 4
situational motivation 163
Skeldon, R. 2
Skinner, W. 227

slow-paced classes 179
social constructivism 16, 79
social exclusion 4
social identity theory 68, 95, 250
social networks 8, 76, 109, 113, 118–119, 252; for academic socialization and Mainland undergraduates in Hong Kong 106–108
socialization, academic 105, 106–108, 109–119
socio-educational model 124, 136–137, 162
sociocultural barriers 110–114; strategic responses to overcome 114–117
socioculturalism 1, 3, 5–9, 48–49, 105–106, 108–109, 118, 130, 135, 249, 255, 258
socioeconomic advancement, need for 76–77
socioeconomic mobility 33, 258; need for 76–77
socioeconomic status (SES) 2, 36, 38, 44, 77, 141
sociolinguistics *18*, 27, 107, 119, 250
Song, R. Y. 239
Sörbom, D., and Jöreskog, K. 148
source countries *87*, *89*
South Africa: apartheid 67, 70, 74–77, 80; Chinese in 69–70; Group Areas Act (1950) 69; National Party 69; Native Land Act (1913) 69, *see also* Pretoria
South African Union (SAU) 69
South African-born Chinese (SABC) 67–83, 81n3; identities 78, 79–80, 81n2
spaces, bilingual 20–23
Spain: Law on the General Education System in Spain (LOGSE, 1990) 129; Organic Law of Education (LOE, 2006) 129; Organic Law on Immigration 2 (2009) 130; Organic Law on Quality of Education (LOCE, 2002) 129; second-generation education in 123–139
speaking Chinese 67–83
Special Administrative Region (SAR) 16
special educational needs (SEN) 129, 179
specificity matching principle 151
speech community 76, 106
state-sponsored experiment, in transnational education 184
statement (SFL theory) 194–195, 198–200, *201–202*, 203, 205–206

status, socioeconomic 2, 36, 38, 44, 77, 141
stereotyping, gender 143, 152–154
strategic adaptations 125
strategic responses: Mainland undergraduates adapting to Hong Kong 105–121; to overcome barriers 114–117
strategies: of Chinese families 180–184; and stratification 252–253
strong-link thesis 68–69, 80–81
structural equation modeling (SEM) 145–146, 148, 155
structured activities 197, *199–200*, 201, *202–203*
student-centered teaching 215
students: good 131, 134–135; non-problematic 131
studying abroad 94–95, 97–98; in New Zealand context 86–90; programs 88
Su, Y., Xu, Y. and Li, X. 239
success: in school 126–128; taken for granted 167–169
Suharto 47–50, 53
Sun, B. 224; and Curdt-Christiansen, X. 209–226
supercentral language 228
Swaan, A. de 228
systemic functional linguistic (SFL) theory 193–195, 198, 207

Taiwan: Department of Applied Chinese Language and Literature 228; overseas students learning to be language teachers 227–245; views on 231–233
Taiwanese 81n3
Tannenbaum, M. 68
Tao, J., and Gao, X. 105–121
teacher-centered teaching 215
teachers, views of 209–226
Teachers Network Learning Circle 211, 218
teaching 220–223; student/teacher-centered 215
temporariness 41
territorialization 250
tertiary education 105, 186
thematic analysis 126, 165
thinking: independent 98–99; logical 193
Thogersen, S. 94
Tiananmen Square protests (1989) 96
Toohey, K., and Norton, B. 27
Torr, J., and Davis, B. 195

272 Index

Torres Santomé, J. 130
training, for transnationalism 177–188
transition time 197, *199–201*, 202–203
transnational education, state-sponsored experiment in 184
transnational social field 177; de/re-territorializing 249–256
transnationalism 2–3, 5, 7–8, 15, 32–34, 40, 43–44, 257, 260; cosmopolitan 259; and international education 258–259; parallel 259; process of 41; training for 177–188
Trautwein, U., and Lüdtke, O. 144
Tsai, Y.-H., and Hendryx, J. 227–245
Tsuboya, M. 33
Tsukada, H. 4, 31–46
Tsuneyoshi, R. 31
Tucker-Lewis Index (TLI) 148–149
turn-taking 197–200, *201–202*, 203–206

undergraduates: Mainland 105–121; in UK 161–176
United States Agency for International Development (USAID) 61
United States Information Service (USIS) 61
University Grants Committee (UGC) 107
University of Hong Kong 106
university-level language learners, challenges of 166–170
unproductive classroom practice 222
upward mobility 183; economic 77; social 3, 125
us-against-them posturing 108

value, parental perceptions of education and schooling 128
Vellutino, F. R., *et al.* 192
Vivier, E., and Yu, K. 67–83
voices, of children 209–226

Wahid, A. 48
Wang, G. 238–239
Wang, J. 161–176
Wang, X. M. 238–239
Wang, Y. 4
Waters, J. L. 43
Wei, L. 228, 237
Westbury, I., Wilkof, N. and Schwab, J. 135–136
Western education 32, 43, 99, 183
Widaman, K. F., and Carlson, J. S. 96
Wide Ranging Achievement Test 4 (WRAT 4) 147
Wikipedia 1
Wilkof, N., Schwab, J. and Westbury, I. 135–136
Wood, B. E. 92
working language 209, 224
worlding practice 257–260
Wu dialect 126, 128

xenophobia 185, 187, 249
Xi Yang Yang (The Happy Sheep) 57
Xie, Y., and Goyette, K. 125
Xin Zhong School 50, 56
Xu, Y., Li, X. and Su, Y. 239

Yen, C.-H. 227–228
Yeung, A., and Han, F. 141–159
Yin, R. K. 207
Yiu, J. 124–125
Youth Chinese Test (YCT) 50
youths, multilingual in Indonesia 47–65
Yu, K., and Vivier, E. 67–83

Zhang, D. 77
Zhang, Q. 162
Zhang, X. 85–101
Zhou, M. 3
Zhu, H., and Li, W. 25
Zhu, J., and Henze, J. 88